Girls on the Stand

Girls on the Stand

How Courts Fail Pregnant Minors

Helena Silverstein

NEW YORK UNIVERSITY PRESS

New York and London

NEW YORK UNIVERSITY PRESS
New York and London
www.nyupress.org

Library of Congress Cataloging-in-Publication Data
Silverstein, Helena.
Girls on the stand : how courts fail pregnant minors /
Helena Silverstein.
p. cm.
Includes bibliographical references and index.
ISBN-13: 978-0-8147-4031-6 (cloth : alk. paper)
ISBN-10: 0-8147-4031-6 (cloth : alk. paper)
1. Abortion—Law and legislation—United States. 2. Pregnant
schoolgirls—Legal status, laws, etc.—United States. 3. Teenage
pregnancy—United States. 4. Judicial discretion—United States.
5. Judicial process—United States. 6. Minors—United States.
I. Title.
KF9315.S55 2007
342.7308'4—dc22   2006100337

New York University Press books are printed on acid-free paper,
and their binding materials are chosen for strength and durability.

Manufactured in the United States of America
10 9 8 7 6 5 4 3 2 1

For my parents,
Lillichka and Zelchka

Contents

Acknowledgments

I have incurred many debts over the course of writing this book and am grateful to those who have lent their support. Because of the nature of this research, I leave unnamed virtually all those who agreed to participate in the interviews that provide the empirical nit and grit of this book. Without their involvement this project would not have been possible.

There are many others I can name. Kathryn Lundwall Alessi worked with me on an earlier version of the material treated in Chapter 6, and this book is all the better for my collaboration with such a sharp mind. I have had the good fortune of working with able research assistants, including Shannon Sullivan, Mark Tronziger, and Ashley White. I am especially grateful for the research assistance provided by Emily Francis and Leanne Speitel. Their contributions and insights helped shape this work, and their enthusiastic participation through various iterations of this project proved motivating.

Lafayette College has been a generous sponsor of my work, providing resources for research assistance, travel, and fellowships. I thank the Academic Research Committee for its review of and support for my research.

I have presented portions of this research in various formal settings and shared my ideas with others in numerous informal contexts. For their attention, feedback, and encouragement, I thank Judith Baer, Scott Barclay, John Brigham, Laura Brunell, Susan Burgess, Rose Corrigan, Sue Davis, John Forren, John Gilliom, Howard Gillman, Mark Graber, Laura Hatcher, Ron Kahn, Ken Kirsch, Susan Koniak, George Lovell, William Lyons, Will McClean, Joshua Miller, George Panichas, Doug Reed, Rachel Roth, Carol Sanger, Austin Sarat, Donald Songer, Janie S. Steckenrider, Robert Van Dyk, Stephen Wasby, Keith Whittington, and Karen Zivi. Two colleagues to whom I will always owe a tremendous and unique debt are Michael McCann and Stuart Scheingold. Their tutelage made a lasting mark on me, and their ongoing encouragement is heartening.

Many other friends and colleagues have seen me through this project. I thank Susan Basow, Howard Bodenhorn, Pam Bodenhorn, Paul Cefalu, Debbey Charych, Linda Cornett, Stephen Dunkel, Neil Englehart, Bianca Falbo, Lori Gruen, Amy King, Kate Leeman, Matt McGlone, Owen Mcleod, Diane Miller, Melissa Miller, Todd Nicholson, Michael Oppenheim, Lee Overton, Robin Rinehart, Carlo Rotella, Steve Snow, Lori Stevens, Amy Sullivan, and Andy Vinchur.

I have benefited from the able editorial guidance of Deborah Gershenowitz at New York University Press. I am also grateful for the insights provided by two reviews of my manuscript, one from Jon Goldberg-Hiller and another from an anonymous reader.

Portions of this book draw on work I have published elsewhere and use here with permission. Part II borrows from "Judicial Waivers of Parental Consent for Abortion: Tennessee's Troubles Putting Policy into Practice," *Law and Policy* 27 (2005): 399–428, with Wayne Fishman, Emily Francis, and Leanne Speitel (© Blackwell Publishing and The Baldy Center for Law and Social Policy); " 'Honey, I Have No Idea': Court Readiness to Handle Petitions to Waive Parental Consent for Abortion," *Iowa Law Review* 88 (2002): 75–120, with Leanne Speitel (© Helena Silverstein and Leanne Speitel); and "Road Closed: Evaluating the Judicial Bypass Provision of the Pennsylvania Abortion Control Act," *Law and Social Inquiry* 24 (1999): 73–96 (© American Bar Foundation). Chapters 6 and 8 include parts of "Religious Establishment in Hearings to Waive Parental Consent for Abortion," *University of Pennsylvania Journal of Constitutional Law* 7 (2004): 473–532, with Kathryn Lundwall Alessi (© Helena Silverstein and Kathryn Lundwall Alessi). Chapters 7 and 8 incorporate portions of "In the Matter of Anonymous, A Minor: Fetal Protection in Hearings to Waive Parental Consent for Abortion," *Cornell Journal of Law and Public Policy* 11 (2001): 69–111 (© Helena Silverstein). Chapter 9 draws on "The Symbolic Life of Law: The Instrumental and the Constitutive in Scheingold's *The Politics of Rights*," *International Journal for the Semiotics of Law* 16 (2003): 407–423 (© Kluwer Academic Publishers).

I was raised in a family that placed a high value on education and by parents who overcame extreme hardship and endured considerable sacrifices so that their children would succeed where they, through no fault of their own, could not. My parents deserve much credit and my mother, especially, for not only her praise of my work but also for taking the time to read and understand it. My brother Dubi and sister-in-law Ellen Weiman have also been enthusiastic supporters, reading portions of my work and offering their insights. I have been fortunate as well to have married into a supportive family, and I thank Roberta and Andy Raff and Stuart and Debra Fishman for their kindness.

This book would neither be nor be what it is without Wayne Fishman. Wayne shared this project with me from its inception, generous beyond words and reason in giving his time, energy, and support. He read every word many times over, carefully considering each claim and each turn of the screw. His editorial skills added finesse to my prose. His intellectual insights sharpened my arguments. He is my foremost fan and harshest critic—and I would not want it otherwise.

The life of the law has not been logic: it has been experience. The felt necessities of the time, the prevalent moral and political theories, intuitions of public policy, avowed or unconscious, even the prejudices which judges share with their fellowmen, have had a good deal more to do than the syllogism in determining the rules by which men should be governed.

—Oliver Wendell Holmes Jr.

And so castles made of sand fall in the sea, eventually.

—Jimi Hendrix

PART I

Parental Involvement Mandates

1

A Balancing Act

Rachel Ely was a seventeen year old unmarried high school student when she learned that she was pregnant. Her high school counselor recommended that she have an abortion, arranged for State funding for the abortion, and recommended a particular abortion clinic. No other alternatives were discussed. Rachel was afraid to tell her parents that she had become pregnant. Because Rachel was not aware of any alternatives, she consented to the abortion. Had Rachel's parents known their daughter was pregnant, they would have provided her with the alternatives of keeping her child or placing the child for adoption.

After her abortion, Rachel received no discharge instructions from her physician. Several days later she developed some flu-like symptoms in her chest, which she did not associate with her abortion because she believed that any symptoms she might have as a result of a complication from an abortion would be in her pelvic area. She went to her family doctor when these symptoms became worse. She did not tell the doctor about the abortion because she did not think the symptoms were related.

Sometime later, Rachel became very sick, and her father took her to a local hospital because of her persistent flu-like symptoms. The next morning Rachel was found in her hospital bed in a comatose condition. Subsequently, it was discovered that she had developed bacterial endocarditis—a condition directly attributable to a post-abortion surgical infection. The bacterial endocarditis had caused blood clots to develop and become lodged in the vascular system of her brain, causing a stroke. When Rachel recovered from her coma, she was left a permanently wheelchair-bound hemiplegic.

Had Rachel's parents been notified of the abortion, they would have questioned the possible relationship between the abortion and Rachel's symptoms. With simple antibiotic therapy, her devastating life-long disabilities would not have occurred.

—Focus on the Family and Family Research Council,
Friend of the Court Brief[1]

The tragic consequences of Rachel Ely's furtive abortion illustrate a primary justification for requiring parental involvement when minors seek to terminate their pregnancies. The argument is simple enough. Most, if not all, medical procedures carry the risk of complications. Abortion, a medical procedure, carries such risk. Adults are in a much better position than minors to assess and deal with post-procedural complications. So minors who have abortions in the absence of parental guidance are in greater danger than those who involve their parents.

Protecting physical health is not the only justification for requiring parental involvement when minors seek abortions. Abortion, it is said, is not analogous to other medical procedures such as tonsillectomy or the extraction of wisdom teeth. Because abortion involves the termination of a human life, it is thought to have emotional consequences not typical of most other medical procedures. Loving and caring parents, the argument goes, can help their daughter through the psychological trauma she may experience as the result of her decision to have an abortion.

In addition to its benefits for young women, mandating parental involvement advances the legitimate interests of parents. Rachel Ely was not the only one harmed by the physical complications of her abortion. Her parents suffered as well. While responsible for the upbringing and care of their daughter, Rachel's parents were not consulted at a crucial juncture in her life and were thereby rendered helpless. Moreover, separate from any issues involving physical or psychological well-being, parents are entitled to oversee the decision-making of their minor children. Parents are generally responsible for their children, and this responsibility affords parents certain rights.

The grounds for mandating parental involvement in the abortion decisions of pregnant minors are substantive and commonsensical, and thus even though research indicates that the majority of minors voluntarily turn to parents when facing an unplanned pregnancy, it is not particularly surprising that parental involvement laws have become commonplace.[2] Thirty-four states currently have laws in effect that condition a minor's access to abortion on parental involvement.[3] Among these, twenty-two require physicians to obtain the consent of one or both parents before performing an abortion on a minor.[4] Twelve require the prior notification of one or both parents, usually specifying a twenty-four-hour or forty-eight-hour waiting period between the time of notice and the time the abortion is performed.[5]

As might be expected, parental involvement laws are trumpeted by those sympathetic to the pro-life position. But such laws also receive support from those who generally favor a woman's right to choose abortion, for parental involvement laws do not regulate the abortion decisions of adult women, who are presumably capable of making mature and informed choices.[6] Rather, these laws are a potentially appropriate effort to address the circumstance of a possibly immature girl facing an unplanned pregnancy.

No argument against mandated parental involvement that rejects the import of these considerations stands a chance of being persuasive. Any argument that is going to prevail must do so while absorbing the full force of these considerations and showing why, despite them, mandated parental involvement is misguided public policy. This book aims to make such a case. In this chapter, I flesh out the points in favor of parental involvement laws and outline the case I will make against them.

In Defense of Mandated Parental Involvement

Protecting Minors

It is clear that "[t]here is something disturbing in the image of a young child struggling with the realization that she is pregnant and seeking out an abortionist alone or with equally young friends; there is something appalling about a society that permits this to happen."[7] Indeed, however committed one might be to a woman's right to choose abortion, it is plainly undeniable that minors having abortions is a special case. The circumstance of a pregnant teenager attempting to navigate the difficult and consequential abortion decision on her own cannot be seen as analogous to that of an adult woman facing an unplanned pregnancy. As a report by the American Medical Association (AMA) points out, "minors may not make considered choices about abortion because of immaturity, inexperience, or poor judgment."[8] These deficiencies can lead minors to jeopardize their physical and emotional well-being.

PHYSICAL HEALTH AND SAFETY

The abortion procedure can have serious side effects. The physical risks associated with abortion include, from most to least common, hemorrhage, infection, incomplete abortion, perforation of the uterus, sterility, hysterectomy, injury to the bowel and/or bladder, abdominal surgery to correct an injury, and death.[9]

It is true that the physical risks associated with abortion, especially those performed in the first trimester, are low. It is also true that these risks are substantially lower than those associated with carrying a pregnancy to term. According to the Centers for Disease Control and Prevention, the overall mortality rate for legal abortions in the United States is 0.3 per 100,000.[10] By comparison, the overall pregnancy-related mortality rate is 9.2 per 100,000 live births.[11] In addition, according to the American Academy of Pediatrics (AAP), "Mortality risks seem to be five times greater for teenagers who continue their pregnancies than they are for teens who terminate them. Morbidity rates and medical complications from continuing a pregnancy are more adverse than those from abortion at all stages of gestation."[12]

The fact that abortion in the first trimester poses a low health risk and a lower risk than continuing with pregnancy does not obviate arguments favoring mandated parental guidance in a young woman's abortion decision, for the issue is not the absolute or relative magnitude of the risk but whether the oversight of parents reduces the risk. A minor seeking to conceal an abortion may try to hide post-abortion complications and thereby fail to obtain treatment should complications emerge. Parents who know their daughter has had an abortion can lend a watchful eye to identify physical complications and ensure that their daughter receives treatment when necessary.

If the Rachel Ely case tells us anything, it is that serious and life-altering complications are more likely when parents are kept in the dark about their daughter's decision to terminate her pregnancy. And Rachel Ely's story, while an atypical one, is not unique. The Texas House State Affairs Committee heard similar stories during its consideration of a parental notification statute, including the following one:

> Amy obtained an abortion on Friday, suffered terrible complications, and subsequently died on Sunday. Because her parents did not know, they delayed taking her to hospital until she was unconscious. Her parents were originally told [their daughter] died of septic shock syndrome, but a friend who knew of the abortion told them after [Amy's] death. They then confirmed [her death] was due to a botched abortion, but they were misled because of [Amy's] right to privacy.[13]

A more fortunate girl benefited from her parent's knowledge of her abortion, according to a physician who also testified before the Texas House committee:

> I know from my own personal experience—I have dealt with septic abortion. And it was a young lady that I cared for. She chose to go to one of the local reproductive clinics here in town, obtain their services, and if it were not for her parents knowing about what happened and caring for her, she probably would have died, because by the time I was notified about her, she already had an elevated temperature of 104, she was obtunded, didn't know where she was . . . and if not for the concern of her parents who were able to bring her to the emergency room for treatment and subsequent surgery, there is a strong possibility that she would have died.[14]

Even before the performance of an abortion, parental involvement can benefit minors. Not all abortion providers are equally qualified or experienced, and parents can render valuable assistance in selecting a capable provider. As the U.S. Supreme Court has found, minors "are less likely than adults to know or be able to recognize ethical, qualified physicians, or to have the means to engage such professionals. Many minors who bypass their parents probably will resort to an abortion clinic, without being able to distinguish the competent and ethical from those that are incompetent or unethical."[15] Even if a minor locates a capable provider on her own, she may not be well positioned to present that provider with an accurate medical history, especially when she seeks to hide the fact of her abortion from her parents. Parents are better positioned to ensure that the provider has access to the minor's complete medical history, information that could help medical personnel avoid complications or aid their handling of complications that might develop.[16]

Some have also argued that mandated parental involvement may help shield minors from statutory rape or sexual assault by providing parents with an avenue for discovering abusive relationships. Teresa Stanton Collett, for example, makes this point in her examination of a Texas notification statute:

> National studies reveal that almost two thirds of adolescent mothers have partners older than 20 years of age. In a study of over 46,000 pregnancies by school-age girls in California, researchers found that

71%, or over 33,000, were fathered by adult post-high-school men whose mean age was 22.6 years, an average of 5 years older than the mothers. . . . Even among junior high school mothers aged 15 and younger, most births are fathered by adult men 6–7 years their senior. Men aged 25 and older father more births among California school-age girls than do boys under age 18. Other studies confirm that many teen-age pregnancies are the result of sexual exploitation of minors by men who are substantially older.[17]

While acknowledging that physicians and other professionals are re-quired to report sexual assault to the proper authorities, Collett argues that parents are more likely than others to put an end to the relation-ships that victimize their daughters.[18]

EMOTIONAL HEALTH AND WELL-BEING

Those who favor mandated parental involvement maintain that abor-tion is not simply a medical procedure with attendant physical risks; a minor's mental well-being is also at stake. Several studies have found that abortion carries with it the risk of potentially serious emotional and psychological side effects, including such things as nervous and sleep disorders, guilt, depression, and suicidal tendencies. One study, for example, concludes that at least 19 percent of post-abortion women ex-perience post-traumatic stress disorder.[19] Another finds that 60 percent of women who suffer from emotional complications after abortion re-port considering suicide, and 28 percent of these attempt suicide.[20] And a review of the literature on emotional responses to abortion conducted by Jo Ann Rosenfeld reports that while most women experience a sense of relief after abortion, "the next most common emotional response is guilt."[21]

Among the factors that may predict negative emotional responses to abortion is a woman's age, and several studies indicate that adolescents may suffer more adverse psychological effects from abortion than their adult counterparts.[22] In a 1992 study conducted by Wanda Franz and David Reardon, the authors conclude that adolescents who choose abortion are more likely to be dissatisfied with that choice than adults.[23] And Rosenfeld, citing a 1972 study that finds an increased rate of ad-verse reactions in teens who conceal their abortions from their parents, speculates that "[t]he lack of parental support in younger women may be the cause of the increased frequency of unfavorable responses in [this] population."[24]

Whether abortion poses serious psychological risks is the subject of debate, and some research findings raise questions about the degree to which women in general and minors in particular experience negative post-abortive emotional responses. Rosenfeld's review of abortion research notes that women facing unwanted pregnancies "who obtain a legal abortion during the first-trimester typically report positive emotional effects," and "fewer than 10 percent of such women have long-term psychiatric or emotional reactions, such as sexual dysfunction, severe neuroses or suicide attempts."[25] A more recent review of abortion research explains that

> [w]ell-designed studies of psychological responses following abortion have consistently shown that risk of psychological harm is also low. Some women experience psychological dysfunction following an abortion, but postabortion rates of distress and dysfunction are lower than preabortion rates. Moreover, the percentage of women who experience clinically relevant distress is small and appears to be no greater than in general samples of women of reproductive age.[26]

And as to whether minors are especially prone to psychological harm from abortion, the AAP says in its 1996 review of abortion among minors that "[e]xtensive reviews conclude that there are not documented negative psychological or medical sequelae to elective, legal, first-trimester abortion among teenaged women. No significant psychological sequelae have been substantiated, despite extensive searches of the scientific literature."[27]

Debate over the extent of post-abortive emotional responses in women is bound to continue. Nevertheless, in the face of conflicting research findings, prudence suggests erring on the side of caution—that is, on the side of assuming that abortion will result in negative emotional consequences for a significant number of women.

It is reasonable to think that supportive parents can help mitigate the negative emotional consequences their daughter might suffer as the result of having an abortion. In fact, some studies have concluded that adolescents often underestimate the understanding of their parents and overestimate parental anger.[28] If these results are correct, minors who involve a parent in their abortion decision will often find sympathy and support.

Furthermore, just as parents are better positioned to provide physicians with their child's complete medical history, so are they better positioned to offer an accurate psychological profile. A minor who has a history of psychological problems might, out of fear or embarrassment, conceal that fact from a physician. This is less likely to occur with parental oversight.

The Supreme Court has accepted the claim that adverse psychological responses to abortion are heightened in young women, saying that "[t]he emotional and psychological effects of the pregnancy and abortion experience are markedly more severe in girls under 18 than in adults."[29] States, too, have bought this line. For example, part of the state of Florida's justification for enacting a parental notice law appeals to the idea that post-abortion psychological reactions are more intense among minors than they are among adults: "The medical, emotional, and psychological consequences of an abortion are serious and can be lasting; this is particularly so when the patient is immature."[30]

ADDITIONAL BENEFITS

When facing an unplanned pregnancy, a minor has several choices. Besides choosing abortion, a minor might carry the pregnancy to term in order to raise the child herself or to place the child for adoption. It is not unreasonable to think that parents can help their children select among these options. Supportive parents can provide the monetary and informational resources necessary to pursue alternatives to abortion. In the absence of this support, a minor might wrongly believe that her only feasible option is to terminate her pregnancy. A young woman might conclude, for example, that she could not continue her education if she opts to keep her child. But consultation with supportive parents—parents who might be willing to help raise the child—might lead her to conclude otherwise. Additionally, a minor who does not consult her parents may face pressure to have an abortion from the man who impregnated her. Parental involvement may serve to bolster a minor against this pressure.

Protecting Parental Rights and the Family Unit

If the state's sole interest lay in protecting minors against the detrimental effects of their own immaturity, that interest could, for the most part, be achieved through means other than a parental involvement mandate. States could require counseling before and after abortions with a medical or psychological professional, or both. They could also require that minors involve some adult relative, not necessarily a parent, in their abortion decision. But the state's asserted interest in parental involvement typically includes more than shielding minors from harm. Consider the preamble of the Alabama Parental Consent Statute, which states that in addition to protecting minors the legislature aims to advance the important and compelling state interests of "fostering the family structure and preserving it as a viable social unit" and "protecting the rights of parents to rear children who are members of their household."[31] Alabama's asserted interests in the family unit and parental rights stand apart from the state's interest in safeguarding minors and are used to justify the specific call for parental consultation in the abortion decision.

These interests are clearly significant, and it is not surprising that the Supreme Court has accepted them as a legitimate basis for mandated parental involvement. As Katherine Katz explains, deference to the autonomy of the family unit and parental authority "has been a persistent hallmark of the Court's jurisprudence on the family from 1923 to the present. . . . The Supreme Court's understanding of the family is that the protection of liberty under the Due Process Clause includes parental authority to raise their children as they see fit."[32] According to the Court,

> Our jurisprudence historically has reflected Western civilization concepts of the family as a unit with broad parental authority over minor children. Our cases have consistently followed that course; our constitutional system long ago rejected any notion that a child is the mere creature of the State and, on the contrary, asserted that parents generally have the right, coupled with the high duty, to recognize and prepare [their children] for additional obligations. Surely, these include a "high duty" to recognize the symptoms of illness and to seek and follow medical advice.[33]

This interpretation of the family, including the authoritative role of parents within the family, supports not only parental involvement regulations in general but also specific aspects of those regulations. Statutes that require the involvement of both parents do so not primarily out of concern for the minor—a concern that would be sufficiently allayed by the participation of one parent—but in order to advance parental rights.[34] In addition, statutes that require parental consent give greater weight to the interests of advancing parental rights than do notification statutes. But whether a two-parent consent requirement or a one-parent notification regulation, mandated parental involvement in abortion "is promoted on the basis of its theoretical benefits on strengthening family responsibility and communication."[35]

Risks of Mandated Parental Involvement

There is little doubt that the interests outlined above are legitimate. In fact, the interests are so commonsensical that, as stated above, even defenders of reproductive rights often concede the reasonableness of parental involvement mandates. However, there are also legitimate and commonsensical considerations that speak against mandated parental involvement, against allowing parents wholesale oversight of their daughter's pregnancy.

Concern about indiscriminate parental involvement in the reproductive choices of minors stems from the recognition that the reality of family relations is not always ideal. In an ideal world, teens and their parents would communicate openly and constructively about sexuality and its consequences. Teens facing unwanted pregnancies would feel comfortable approaching their parents for guidance and support, and parents, offering their assistance, would act in their daughters' best interests. Parents and daughters would together and with mutual concern face the challenge of an unplanned pregnancy.

This ideal of constructive and beneficial family interaction exists for many. "For some children, however," reports the AMA, "the home falls far short of this ideal and may be a place of physical abuse and neglect and psychological maltreatment."[36] If Rachel Ely's story symbolizes why states should mandate parental involvement, then the story of a thirteen-year-old Idaho girl impregnated by her father and later killed by him when he learned of her intention to secure an abortion is emblematic of the cruel realities of family dysfunction and the risks associated with universal involvement mandates.[37] So, too, is the less extreme but still grim story of the teen who anticipates being thrown out of the house if her parents discover her pregnancy: "My older sister got pregnant when she was seventeen. My mother pushed her against the wall, slapped her across the face and then grabbed her by the hair, pulled her through the living room out the front door and threw her off the porch. We don't know where she is now."[38]

Citing the realities that families and minors confront, the AMA has concluded that some minors would experience serious physical and emotional injury under a blanket parental involvement provision:

> On the basis of reports to child protection agencies, the federal government has estimated that there are approximately 1.5 million cases a year of physical abuse and neglect of children. Although no study has specifically dealt with violence as a reaction to minors informing parents about pregnancy, it is reasonable to believe that some minors justifiably fear that they would be treated violently by one or both parents if they had to disclose their pregnancy to their parents. Research on abusive and dysfunctional families has shown that family violence is at its worst during a family member's pregnancy, immediately following childbirth, and during the adolescence of the family's children. Studies of family violence have found that 4% to 17% of women are physically abused during their pregnancy. . . . Parental notification often precipitates a family crisis, characterized by severe parental anger and rejection of the minor.[39]

The AAP has arrived at the same conclusion in its analysis of a minor's right to confidential care in decisions to terminate pregnancy. Acknowledging its commitment to strong family relationships and its view that parents generally act to serve the best interest of their children,[40] the AAP nevertheless cautions against involuntary parental involvement when minors seek abortions: "Although parental involvement in minors' abortion decisions may be helpful in many cases, in others it may be punitive, coercive, or abusive."[41] Furthermore, "[t]he risks of violence, abuse, coercion, unresolved conflict, and rejection are significant in nonsupportive or dysfunctional families when parents are informed of a pregnancy against the adolescent's considered judgment."[42]

Even where families are free of abuse and dysfunction, the ideal of open communication between parents and their children often goes unrealized.[43] In some cases, like the following one reported by a pregnant minor in Texas, reluctance to approach a parent with news of pregnancy may stem from a disinclination to burden the parent: "My mother is in the hospital with my older brother. He's dying of cancer. She'd support my decision, but I can't tell her about this right now. She's already gone through so much. . . . Dad left us a long time ago and I have no idea where he is."[44] In other cases, minors simply worry about disappointing their parents.[45] Still others are concerned with protecting their privacy.[46] As the AMA reports, "minors have a profound need for privacy in matters of their health care. . . . Adolescence is a critical period for minors to develop their independent sense of self; the ability to maintain spheres of privacy from parents in areas of personal intimacy is an essential part of that development."[47] For those who do not want to disappoint or create problems for their parents, or for those primarily concerned with retaining their privacy, a blanket parental involvement requirement has potentially serious ramifications. According to the AMA,

> Because the need for privacy may be compelling, minors may be driven to desperate measures to maintain the confidentiality of their pregnancies. They may run away from home, obtain a "back-alley" abortion, or resort to self-induced abortion. The desire to maintain secrecy has been one of the leading reasons for illegal abortion deaths since the US Supreme Court decided the existence of a constitutional right to abortion in 1973.[48]

Finally, we ought not forget that not all minors live with or have easy access to their parents or legal guardians. Sometimes pregnant minors live with a grandparent, an aunt, or an older sibling. "Our parents are somewhere in Mexico, but I don't know if I can find them," reported a woman who was trying to help her younger sister obtain an abortion after being raped.[49] Others can find their parents but may have to look for them in a jail, a mental health facility, or a crack house.[50]

Compromise: The Judicial Bypass Option

There are, then, powerful considerations on both sides of the mandated parental involvement debate. Given the realities of family function and dysfunction, a requirement that minors involve parents in their reproductive choices sometimes serves the interests of protecting the physical and emotional well-being of minors and enhancing the family unit, and sometimes it does not.

These conflicting considerations, though, need not result in a stalemate, for there seems to be a way to satisfy all concerns. Consider a requirement that encourages parental involvement without assigning parents actual or effective veto power over their daughter's decision to terminate her pregnancy. Under this type of requirement, states could mandate parental involvement but provide minors the opportunity to seek third-party authorization to bypass the requirement. Such a compromise balances the case for parental involvement with what in some instances may be the minor's legitimate interest in avoiding that involvement.

The Supreme Court has accepted this compromise position, holding in a line of cases that parental involvement statutes do not impermissibly intrude on the privacy rights of minors when those statutes include a bypass alternative. The Court has ruled that parental involvement mandates accompanied by a bypass procedure establish a sensible and fair middle ground that balances competing interests.[51] In an effort to comply with these rulings, virtually all states that mandate parental involvement authorize judges to be the arbiters of the bypass process, the highlight of which is a promised hearing before a judge, where a minor pleads her case.[52] As detailed in Chapter 2, the bypass option requires waiver of parental involvement if a minor can show either that she is mature and well-enough informed to make the abortion decision on her own or that the abortion is in her best interest.

The mandated parental involvement statutes that are currently in effect are not blanket mandates. Rather, they are a compromise between legitimate and conflicting interests in the abortion debate. On the one hand, the mandated participation of parents in their daughter's abortion decisions serves to protect the physical and mental well-being of potentially immature minors and ensures that parents remain in a position to shape the upbringing of their children. On the other hand, whatever dissatisfaction there may be concerning the potential imposition of a parental veto is assuaged by the availability of a bypass process. It is against this seemingly reasonable position that the argument of this book is addressed.

Making the Case against Compromise

There are those so opposed to abortion that the idea of relaxing any barrier to the procedure is unthinkable. Similarly, some who favor a woman's right to choose will not concede the legitimacy of any regulation that tends to burden that choice. Between these extremes stands the compromiser who believes that an avenue providing judicial authorization for a waiver of parental involvement alleviates the problems of a blanket mandate. This book aims to convince the compromiser that her position leads to consequences she will find unsatisfactory.

Our acceptance of any law is premised on a belief that implementation will occur, that actors will act appropriately when putting law into effect. This is so with parental involvement requirements and the compromise on which they are built. The commonsense appeal of the compromise turns on the supposed effectiveness of the bypass option. In the absence of an accessible and fair bypass process, statutes mandating parental involvement in the abortion decisions of pregnant teens amount in practice to blanket mandates with all their attendant problems.

In reaction to an unwelcome Supreme Court ruling and referring to the then chief justice, President Andrew Jackson famously quipped, "John Marshall has made his decision, now let him enforce it."[53] Jackson's outburst is witness to the fact that laws are not self-implementing.[54] Despite this fact, we live and act under the expectation that laws will be put into effect in a reasonable way by those responsible for implementation. The rule of law demands this expectation.

However, this faith in the law—dubbed "the myth of rights" by Stuart A. Scheingold[55]—is grounded in the naïve view that the legal system is separate from politics and generates a misguided confidence that the articulation of a right is tantamount to its effectuation. As it applies to the case of parental involvement laws, the myth of rights encourages us to believe that the bypass compromise can easily be and is in fact realized in practice. In particular, the myth encourages us to gloss over the fact that bypass processes are neither self-implementing nor insulated from the political battle over abortion. The compromiser, I maintain, subscribes to this myth, assuming that courts will be aware of their obligation to handle bypass petitions and capable of satisfying that obligation in an apolitical fashion.

In the chapters that follow, I seek to demystify the judicial bypass process and dislodge the uncritical acceptance that has served as the foundation for the compromise. I illustrate that in many cases court personnel charged with implementing the bypass option are simply unaware that it exists. Occasionally they are not merely unaware of their responsibility to handle bypass requests but convinced that they have no such responsibility. Even where courts are aware of their responsibility, administrative difficulties often get in the way of implementation. Knowledgeable parties are often unreachable for hours, days, and sometimes even weeks. Political and religious views also breed implementation peculiarities, with some judges refusing to hear bypass petitions, others candidly stating that they will deny such petitions, and still others engaging in practices during hearings that aggressively aim to persuade young women to forgo abortions.

Comparing our expectations about how laws governing parental involvement mandates will be implemented with how they actually are implemented requires a grasp of relevant legal precedent and the details of state involvement regulations. These matters are discussed in Chapter 2. In Chapters 3 through 5, I present the results of survey data collected from those charged with implementing the bypass procedure in order to determine how courts and their gatekeepers handle inquiries into the process. By focusing on the initial stage of gaining access to the requisite information for filing a bypass petition, I question whether those responsible for implementing the bypass are sufficiently informed, available, and willing to point a minor in a direction that will provide her with meaningful access to a hearing. This analysis focuses on three states: Alabama, Pennsylvania, and Tennessee. As discussed in Chapter 2, the specifics of these state laws and the particularities of each state's implementation context create appropriate landscapes for testing the propriety of parental involvement.

In Chapters 6 and 7, I expose some of the discretionary practices judges adopt when they preside over hearings. One of these practices, discussed in Chapter 6, is a judicial mandate that minors receive pro-life counseling from an evangelical Christian ministry in order to obtain a bypass. In Chapter 7, I describe the judicial appointment of attorneys to represent the interests of the unborn at bypass hearings. These stories are not intended as demonstrations of what judges typically do when presiding over bypass requests. Rather, my goal is to expose what is possible given the flexibility and authority judges have in applying and interpreting bypass provisions.

In Chapter 8, I examine what constitutional infirmity, if any, results from the exposed implementation realities. In Chapter 9, I explore the interlocking nexus of mythologies that sustain misplaced confidence in parental involvement mandates. I argue that one's decision about whether to support a particular public policy should depend not only on the sense it might make on paper but also and crucially on the context in which it will be implemented.

2

The Legal Landscape

Since the Supreme Court's 1973 declaration in *Roe v. Wade*[1] that the Constitution extends to women a fundamental right to abortion, states have tested the reach and limits of this right. Several states almost immediately resolved to prohibit or severely restrict abortion were *Roe* to be reversed.[2] Others kept antiabortion statutes on the books.[3] In more pragmatic efforts to limit access to abortion, states enacted regulations that, among other things, prohibited the advertisement of abortion services, restricted the use of public funds for elective abortions, required hospitalization for abortion, and mandated testing to determine the viability of the fetus. Many states approved bills that required spousal consent or notification before the performance of an abortion. Several also imposed informed consent requirements that included waiting periods between the time a woman received information about the abortion procedure and the time the procedure could be performed.[4] Prodded by pro-life activists, this legislative response to *Roe* has persisted, proving that the Court decision "only marked the end of one engagement in a prolonged national conflict."[5]

Legislation mandating parental involvement in the abortion decisions of pregnant minors emerged soon after *Roe*. In 1974, Missouri enacted a far-reaching abortion statute that included a parental consent requirement for minors under the age of eighteen.[6] Massachusetts passed a two-parent consent statute within two years of *Roe*.[7] Some thirty years after *Roe*, only Connecticut, Hawaii, New York, Oregon, Vermont, Washington, and the District of Columbia have failed to pass parental involvement measures.[8]

While courts have overturned many efforts to regulate abortion, parental involvement requirements are among those that have ultimately withstood constitutional scrutiny. In this chapter I trace the line of Court precedent that establishes the blueprint for state involvement statutes. I also provide the details of the Alabama, Pennsylvania, and Tennessee consent provisions.

Supreme Court Precedent

Although parental involvement mandates were among "the primary ways that pro-life groups sought to limit the availability of abortion immediately after Roe,"[9] the initial crafting of these regulations failed to pass constitutional muster. In a series of rulings between 1976 and 1983, the Court overturned several state mandates that required physicians to obtain parental approval before performing abortions on minors.[10] At the same time, however, the Court outlined the parameters for making such requirements constitutionally sound. The Court has yet to establish definitive parameters for statutes that require physicians to notify parents of their minor daughter's decision to have an abortion. Nevertheless, state legislatures have mostly incorporated the guidelines set for consent requirements when adopting notification laws.

Bypass Blueprint

The Court handed down its first ruling on mandated parental involvement in a 1976 case challenging a Missouri one-parent consent requirement that did not include a bypass provision. In *Planned Parenthood of Central Missouri v. Danforth,* a majority of the Court agreed that the Constitution confers on minors a right to abortion:[11] "Constitutional rights do not mature and come into being magically only when one attains the state-defined age of maturity. Minors, as well as adults, are protected by the Constitution and possess constitutional rights."[12] However, acknowledging the state's broader authority to control the activities of minors, the Court asked "whether there is any significant state interest in conditioning an abortion on the consent of a parent or person in loco parentis that is not present in the case of an adult."[13] Finding no significant interest in giving parents the absolute power to control a minor's abortion decision, the Court overturned the Missouri regulation. According to Justice Harry Blackmun's oft-cited holding,

> the State may not impose a blanket provision . . . requiring the consent of a parent . . . as a condition for abortion of an unmarried minor during the first 12 weeks of her pregnancy. Just as with the requirement of consent from the spouse, so here, the State does not have the constitutional authority to give a third party an absolute, and possibly arbitrary,

veto over the decision of the physician and his patient to terminate the patient's pregnancy.[14]

In *Bellotti v. Baird (Bellotti I)*, handed down on the same day as *Danforth*, the Court remanded for further consideration a Massachusetts two-parent consent statute that included the following stipulation: "If one or both of the mother's parents refuse such consent, consent may be obtained by order of a judge of the superior court for good cause shown, after such hearing as he deems necessary."[15] While sidestepping the merits of the challenged statute,[16] the justices signaled how a state might construct a constitutionally sound consent requirement:

> [A] statute that prefers parental consultation and consent, but that permits a mature minor capable of giving informed consent to obtain, without undue burden, an order permitting the abortion without parental consultation, and, further, permits even a minor incapable of giving informed consent to obtain an order without parental consultation where there is a showing that the abortion would be in her best interests . . . would be fundamentally different from a statute that creates a "parental veto."[17]

The signal proffered by the Court in *Bellotti I* was reasserted and detailed three years later in *Bellotti v. Baird (Bellotti II)*.[18] Upon reexamining the Massachusetts consent provision and accepting that the statute, as construed by the Supreme Judicial Court of Massachusetts, permitted minors to seek judicial permission for an abortion only after parental consent had already been denied, the Court overturned the statute.[19] "[I]f the State decides to require a pregnant minor to obtain one or both parents' consent to an abortion," the Court explained, "it also must provide an alternative procedure whereby authorization for the abortion can be obtained."[20] Moreover, "every minor must have the opportunity—if she so desires—to go directly to a court without first consulting or notifying her parents."[21]

The Court in *Bellotti II* went on to outline the basic constituents of a sound bypass proceeding:

> A pregnant minor is entitled in such a proceeding to show either: (1) that she is mature enough and well enough informed to make her abortion decision, in consultation with her physician, independently of her

parents' wishes; or (2) that even if she is not able to make this decision independently, the desired abortion would be in her best interests. The proceeding in which this showing is made must assure that a resolution of the issue, and any appeals that may follow, will be completed with anonymity and sufficient expedition to provide an effective opportunity for an abortion to be obtained. In sum, the procedure must ensure that the provision requiring parental consent does not in fact amount to the "absolute, and possibly arbitrary, veto" that was found impermissible in *Danforth*.[22]

The Court affirmed the framework elaborated in *Bellotti II* in several rulings in the 1980s and 1990s. For example, in two 1983 decisions— one upholding a parental consent requirement that incorporated a judicial bypass provision and the other overturning a consent law that did not[23]—the Court asserted that "the relevant legal standards are not in dispute"[24] and cited *Bellotti II* as the source of those standards. In the 1992 decision *Planned Parenthood of Southeastern Pennsylvania v. Casey,*[25] the Court again adhered to *Bellotti II* in upholding Pennsylvania's one-parent consent requirement and accompanying bypass option: "We have been over most of this ground before. Our cases establish, and we reaffirm today, that a State may require a minor seeking an abortion to obtain the consent of a parent or guardian, provided that there is an adequate judicial bypass procedure."[26] As a result of these and other rulings, the criteria articulated in *Bellotti II* continue to provide the model for legislative construction of parental involvement statutes and their accompanying bypass provisions.

Logic

As articulated in its parental consent decisions, the Court's rationale for the bypass compromise seeks to strike a balance. On one side stands a minor's constitutional right: "A child, merely on account of his minority, is not beyond the protection of the Constitution."[27] Applying this general principle to the right to seek abortion, the *Bellotti II* Court holds that

[t]he abortion decision differs in important ways from other decisions that may be made during minority. The need to preserve the constitutional right and the unique nature of the abortion decision, especially

when made by a minor, require a State to act with particular sensitivity when it legislates to foster parental involvement in this matter. . . . Moreover, the potentially severe detriment facing a pregnant woman is not mitigated by her minority. Indeed, considering her probable education, employment skills, financial resources, and emotional maturity, unwanted motherhood may be exceptionally burdensome for a minor. . . . In sum, there are few situations in which denying a minor the right to make an important decision will have consequences so grave and indelible.[28]

Weighing against the minor's right to abortion is the state's legitimate interest in protecting minors and advancing the rights of parents: "[T]he Court repeatedly has recognized that, in view of the unique status of children under the law, the States have a 'significant' interest in certain abortion regulations aimed at protecting children 'that is not present in the case of an adult.' "[29] According to *Bellotti II,* three reasons justify "the conclusion that the constitutional rights of children cannot be equated with those of adults: the peculiar vulnerability of children; their inability to make critical decisions in an informed, mature manner; and the importance of the parental role in child rearing."[30]

With respect to a child's vulnerability, the *Bellotti II* decision cites prior rulings that have extended to minors certain constitutional guarantees, including, for example, the right to counsel in criminal proceedings. But as the Court cautions, these rulings

have not been made on the uncritical assumption that the constitutional rights of children are indistinguishable from those of adults. . . . Viewed together, our cases show that although children generally are protected by the same constitutional guarantees against government deprivations as are adults, the State is entitled to adjust its legal system to account for children's vulnerability and their needs for "concern, . . . sympathy, and . . . paternal attention."[31]

Concerning the limits of a minor's ability to make informed and mature decisions, *Bellotti II* continues to highlight the distinction between children and adults:

[T]he Court has held that the States may limit the freedom of children to choose for themselves in the making of important, affirmative choices with potentially serious consequences. These rulings have been grounded in the recognition that, during the formative years of childhood and adolescence, minors often lack the experience, perspective, and judgment to recognize and avoid choices that could be detrimental to them.[32]

Finally, *Bellotti II* allows that states have an interest not only in avoiding measures that intrude on parental authority over children but also in instituting laws that foster parental responsibility. Appealing to our nation's history and tradition, the Court notes

> the belief that the parental role implies a substantial measure of authority over one's children. Indeed, "constitutional interpretation has consistently recognized that the parents' claim to authority in their own household to direct the rearing of their children is basic in the structure of our society." . . . Under the Constitution, the State can "properly conclude that parents and others, teachers for example, who have [the] primary responsibility for children's well-being are entitled to the support of laws designed to aid discharge of that responsibility."[33]

In sum, "[t]here can be little doubt that the State furthers a constitutionally permissible end by encouraging an unmarried pregnant minor to seek the help and advice of her parents in making the very important decision whether or not to bear a child."[34] But, according to the Court, while encouraging parental involvement is permissible, a parental veto remains out of bounds.

Salient Issues Unresolved by Precedent

The Court has held firmly to the above principles as they pertain to parental consent mandates. The Court also ruled, in *Hodgson v. Minnesota*, that states must provide a bypass alternative when they demand that both parents receive prior notification of their daughter's decision to abort.[35] The Court has not, however, resolved whether a one-parent notification requirement must be accompanied by a bypass option.

In *Ohio v. Akron Center for Reproductive Health (Akron II)*, the Court upheld Ohio's one-parent notification requirement—a requirement containing a *Bellotti II*–style judicial bypass option—but openly sidestepped the question of whether such an option must accompany parental notice statutes.[36] The Court explained that "it is a corollary to the greater intrusiveness of consent statutes that a bypass procedure that will suffice for a consent statute will suffice also for a notice statute."[37] But providing a possible rationale for dissimilar treatment of mandated notice and consent, the Court commented that notification statutes "are not equivalent to consent statutes because they do not give anyone a veto power over a minor's abortion decision."[38]

This latter statement echoed the Court's earlier holding in *H. L. v. Matheson*, a case that treated Utah's one-parent notification requirement that lacked a bypass procedure.[39] In *Matheson*, the Court upheld the Utah law, but only as it applied in the case of an immature minor. In arriving at this narrow holding, the Court evaded the broader question of whether such a statute would be sustainable in the case of a mature minor. But the Court commented that while mandated consent demands parental approval and could amount to a veto, under a "mere requirement of parental notice," a minor could still obtain her abortion even without parental approval.[40]

The discussions in *Akron II* and *Matheson* suggest that a one-parent notice requirement not accompanied by a bypass option might pass constitutional muster. However, these points have yet to be reconciled with the earlier cited remarks from *Bellotti II*: "[E]very minor must have the opportunity—if she so desires—to go directly to a court without first consulting or *notifying* her parents."[41] This ambiguity notwithstanding, all states that currently impose parental notification, with the exception of Utah, include a bypass alternative that mirrors *Bellotti II*.[42]

Also largely unsettled are the standards for determining when a minor is mature and sufficiently informed to make the abortion decision on her own and when the abortion would be in her best interest. The Court did resolve a specific aspect of the "best-interest" standard in *Lambert v. Wicklund*.[43] There the Court took up a Montana law that obliged judges to waive a parental notice requirement upon a showing that "the notification of a parent or guardian is not in the best interests" of the minor.[44] The District Court and the Ninth Circuit Court of Appeals ruled the Montana bypass unconstitutional, finding a substantive difference between the *Bellotti II* requirement that judges waive parental involvement when the *abortion* is in the minor's best interest and the Montana requirement that judges grant waivers when *notification* would not be in the minor's best interest. The Supreme Court rejected this distinction and reversed the lower court holdings, accepting, at least under a facial challenge, the "assumption that a judicial bypass procedure requiring a minor to show that *parental notification is not* in her best interests is equivalent to a judicial bypass procedure requiring a minor to show that *abortion without notification is* in her best interests."[45]

Aside from the *Lambert* ruling, the Court has offered little guidance on when an abortion serves a minor's best interest. *Bellotti II* states that "[i]n a given case, alternatives to abortion, such as marriage to the father of the child, arranging for its adoption, or assuming the responsibilities of motherhood with the assured support of family, may be feasible and relevant to the minor's best interests."[46] But the Court has also acknowledged that the "circumstances in which the [abortion] issue arises will vary widely."[47] Recognizing similar variation regarding the determination of maturity and informedness, the Court has commented that the "peculiar nature of the abortion decision requires the opportunity for case-by-case evaluations of the maturity of pregnant minors."[48]

It is no doubt true that a case-by-case analysis is necessary to determine whether a minor is sufficiently mature and informed to choose abortion on her own or whether an abortion is in her best interest. But the Court's virtual silence on how these determinations are to be made leaves trial court judges with substantial discretion when deciding whether and under what conditions to grant a bypass request.[49]

There are other aspects of parental involvement mandates that remain unsettled. For example, the Court has not established whether states must include the right to court-appointed counsel in judicial bypass proceedings. In fact, most involvement statutes do include explicit provisions for court-appointed counsel, and some lower courts have determined that parental involvement mandates must include such a provision. The U.S. Court of Appeals for the Seventh Circuit enjoined an Indiana parental notice law in part for its failure to provide counsel for minors seeking to waive notification. As the appellate court explained,

> A minor, completely untrained in the law, needs legal advice to help her understand how to prepare her case, what papers to file, and how to appeal if necessary. Requiring an indigent minor to handle her case all alone is to risk deterring many minors from pursuing their rights because they are unable to understand how to navigate the complicated court system on their own or because they are too intimidated by the seeming complexity to try.[50]

Providing for the appointment of counsel, the appeals court concluded, "is necessary to ensure that the waiver hearing becomes an effective opportunity for the minor to obtain an abortion upon the proper showing."[51]

Similarly, the Florida Supreme Court rejected its state's parental consent requirement for, among other things, not including court-appointed counsel as part of the judicial bypass mechanism. According to that decision, "In proceedings wherein a minor can be wholly deprived of authority to exercise her fundamental right to privacy, counsel is required under our state constitution."[52]

Overview of State Parental Involvement Regulations

The parental involvement legislation currently in effect in thirty-four states takes one of two forms: parental consent or parental notification. In most states, this legislation applies to those under eighteen, though Delaware and South Carolina draw the line at a younger age.[53] Three states direct the involvement of both parents; the rest require the participation of only one. Virtually all statutes specify that a legal guardian may fulfill the role of the parent.[54] Six states permit grandparents or adult relatives to participate in the minor's decision in lieu of parental involvement.[55]

Parental involvement statutes specify a variety of exceptions. Many states explicitly exempt emancipated minors from parental involvement.[56] Medical emergencies provide another common exemption, though statutes differ in their definitions of these situations.[57] Minnesota's statute, for instance, waives its notification provision when "[t]he attending physician certifies in the pregnant woman's medical record that the abortion is necessary to prevent the woman's death and there is insufficient time to provide the required notice."[58] Other statutes include a broader emergency exemption, allowing situations somewhat less threatening than imminent demise to count as emergencies. For example, the Colorado notification statute defines medical emergency as "a condition that, on the basis of the physician's good-faith clinical judgment, so complicates the medical condition of a pregnant minor as to necessitate a medical procedure necessary to prevent the pregnant minor's death or for which a delay will create a serious risk of substantial and irreversible impairment of a major bodily function."[59] Several states

TABLE 1
Parental Involvement Statutes[a]

Parental consent required	Parental notification required	Parental involvement law passed but not enforced	No requirement
Alabama	Colorado	Alaska	Connecticut
Arizona	Delaware	California	Hawaii
Arkansas	Florida	Idaho	Maine[b]
Indiana	Georgia	Illinois	New York
Kentucky	Iowa	Montana	Oregon
Louisiana	Kansas	Nevada	Vermont
Massachusetts	Maryland	New Hampshire	Washington
Michigan	Minnesota[c]	New Jersey	
Mississippi[c]	Nebraska	New Mexico	
Missouri	Oklahoma		
North Carolina	South Dakota		
North Dakota[c]	West Virginia		
Ohio			
Pennsylvania			
Rhode Island			
South Carolina			
Tennessee			
Texas			
Utah[d]			
Virginia			
Wisconsin			
Wyoming			
22	12	9	7

[a] Alan Guttmacher Institute, "Parental Involvement in Minors' Abortions," in *State Policies in Brief*, June 1, 2006, http://www.guttmacher.org/statecenter/spibs/spib_PIMA.pdf (accessed June 8, 2006).
[b] *Me. Rev. Stat. Ann. tit.* 22, § 1597-A (2004) encourages parental consent but allows minors to bypass that consent by receiving counseling.
[c] Involvement of both parents is required.
[d] Requires parental notification in some cases that are exempt from the consent requirement.

incorporate explicit exceptions in cases of child abuse or neglect.[60] In states where statutes provide for the participation of both parents, exceptions typically allow for single-parent involvement under certain circumstances.[61]

In virtually all involvement statutes, the incorporated bypass procedure vests judges with the authority to decide on bypass petitions. However, a handful of states authorize other third parties to make such decisions. In Maryland, physicians determine whether conditions warrant a waiver of parental involvement.[62] West Virginia has a judicial bypass option but also allows physicians to be the arbiters of bypass requests in some circumstances.[63]

The statutes that include a judicial bypass route routinely provide the minor a right to court-appointed counsel and often advise the court of its obligation to notify the minor of this right.[64] A handful of statutes condition the right to counsel on the minor's inability to pay.[65] Some specify that the court may designate a separate guardian to represent the minor's interests.[66] Most statutes specify that resort to the bypass process is free.[67]

Concerning court jurisdiction for handling bypass requests, several statutes specify that a minor may petition a judge either in her home county or in the county where the abortion will be performed.[68] A few limit the venue to the minor's home county.[69] Still others allow the minor to file the petition with a court in any county.[70]

Statutory requirements generally mirror the maturity and best-interest language of *Bellotti II* in specifying the grounds judges must apply when ruling on bypass requests.[71] Also echoing *Bellotti II*, statutes include stipulations for confidentiality, the expedited handling of hearings, and an appeals process.[72] The details of these stipulations vary. For instance, some statutes require courts to hold hearings within forty-eight hours of the time a minor files a petition,[73] while others provide a seventy-two-hour window.[74]

Most statutes do not indicate the degree of proof required for a court to find that a minor has satisfied the conditions of maturity and best interest. In fact, only a handful of statutes specify the standard of proof, and, in most cases, silence on this matter implies that preponderance of the evidence is the standard. Some statutes include a higher standard of proof, however. Ohio's consent statute requires courts to waive consent only on the basis of "clear and convincing evidence."[75] While Supreme Court precedent does not suggest a minimum or maximum level of proof for bypass proceedings, the Court has accepted the "clear and convincing evidence" standard. In *Akron II*, the Court rejected the claim that Ohio's inclusion of a heightened standard of proof imposes an undue burden on a minor's right to secure an abortion. Explaining that precedent does not mandate a lower standard of proof in bypass hearings, the Court also noted that a heightened standard of proof is acceptable "when, as here, the bypass procedure contemplates an *ex parte* proceeding at which no one opposes the minor's testimony."[76]

States continue to direct their energy toward parental involvement laws. In the past six years, Colorado, Florida, Oklahoma, Texas, and Virginia have joined the ranks of states that enforce parental involvement statutes. Florida's entry into these ranks required not only legislative action and gubernatorial approval but also a state constitutional amendment to overturn a court decision rejecting mandated involvement.[77] Similar efforts to alter California's constitution to permit parental notification failed in both 2005 and 2006.[78] Other states that have succeeded in instituting parental involvement requirements have taken steps to bolster their existing mandates.[79] The popularity of parental involvement measures thus persists as states act within, and sometimes test the boundaries of, Supreme Court precedent.

Parental Consent Mandates in Alabama, Pennsylvania, and Tennessee

The Alabama Parental Consent statute, in effect since 1987,[80] sets out a one-parent consent requirement that applies, except in cases of medical emergency, to unemancipated minors under eighteen years of age.[81] A minor who does not wish to or fails to obtain parental consent for an abortion may petition the juvenile court or a court of equal standing for a bypass of that consent.[82] The minor may file that petition in the county in which she resides or the county in which the abortion is to be performed.[83]

Following *Bellotti II*, the Alabama law specifies that consent "shall be waived if the court finds either: (a) That the minor is mature and well-informed enough to make the abortion decision on her own; or (b) That the performance of the abortion would be in the best interest of the minor."[84] Waiver proceedings "shall be confidential and anonymous. In all pleadings or court documents, the minor shall be identified by initials only"[85] and "[n]otice by the court to the minor's parents, parent or legal guardian shall not be required or permitted."[86] In addition, "[c]ourt proceedings shall be given such precedence over other pending matters as is necessary to insure that the court may reach a decision promptly, but in no case, except as provided herein, shall the court fail to rule within 72 hours of the time the petition is filed, Saturdays, Sundays, and legal holidays excluded."[87] The court conducting waiver proceedings "shall issue written and specific factual findings and legal conclusions supporting its decision and shall order that a confidential record of the evidence be maintained for at least four years."[88] In those instances where a court denies a petition to waive consent, an "expedited confidential and anonymous appeal shall be available . . . [and] the record of appeal shall be completed and the appeal shall be perfected within five days from the filing of the notice of appeal."[89]

The Alabama statute further stipulates that no court fees shall be charged to a minor who makes use of the bypass process,[90] and the court conducting proceedings "shall insure that the minor is given assistance in preparing and filing the petition."[91] In addition, "[t]he court shall advise her that she has a right to be represented by an attorney and that if she is unable to pay for the services of an attorney one will be appointed for her."[92]

The Pennsylvania Abortion Control Act, originally passed in 1982 but later amended, contains, among other things, a one-parent consent mandate.[93] That mandate, in effect since 1994,[94] fulfills the requirements of *Bellotti II* and echoes most of the regulations contained in the Alabama statute. The Pennsylvania law prohibits physicians from performing an abortion on an unemancipated woman under the age of eighteen, except in cases of medical emergency, unless the physician first obtains the informed consent of the pregnant minor and one of her parents or, if both parents are unavailable, her guardian.[95] However, if the minor does not wish to or cannot obtain the consent of either parent:

> the court of common pleas of the judicial district in which the applicant resides or in which the abortion is sought shall, upon petition or motion, after an appropriate hearing, authorize a physician to perform the abortion if the court determines that the pregnant woman is mature and capable of giving informed consent to the proposed abortion, and has, in fact, given such consent.[96]

Furthermore:

> If the court determines that the pregnant woman is not mature and capable of giving informed consent or if the pregnant woman does not claim to be mature and capable of giving informed consent, the court shall determine whether the performance of an abortion upon her would be in her best interests. If the court determines that the performance of an abortion would be in the best interests of the woman, it shall authorize a physician to perform the abortion.[97]

Like the Alabama consent requirement, the Pennsylvania statute demands confidentiality and expeditiousness in the handling of bypass petitions. Court proceedings must be confidential, and the record, including the court's findings and conclusions, must be sealed.[98] To ensure confidentiality, the statute requires that the "name of the pregnant woman shall not be entered on any docket which is subject to public inspection. All persons shall be excluded from hearings under this section except the applicant and such other persons whose presence is specifically requested by the applicant or her guardian."[99] To ensure that bypass petitions are handled swiftly, the proceedings "shall be given such precedence over other pending matters as will ensure that the court may reach a decision promptly and without delay in order to serve the best interests of the pregnant woman. In no case shall the court of common pleas fail to rule within three business days of the date of application."[100] The minor also has the right of appeal to the superior court in the event that the common pleas court denies her bypass request.[101]

The Pennsylvania statute states that the minor may participate in proceedings in the court on her own behalf and the court may appoint a guardian ad litem to assist her:[102] "The court shall, however, advise her that she has a right to court appointed counsel, and shall provide her with such counsel unless she wishes to appear with private counsel or has knowingly and intelligently waived representation by counsel."[103]

Neither the Alabama nor the Pennsylvania statute indicates the degree of proof required for a court to waive consent. Unlike Alabama, though, Pennsylvania specifies certain criteria to guide aspects of the court's determinations. The Pennsylvania law explains that to determine maturity,

> the court shall hear evidence relating to the emotional development, maturity, intellect and understanding of the pregnant woman, the fact and duration of her pregnancy, the nature, possible consequences and alternatives to the abortion and any other evidence that the court may find useful in determining whether the pregnant woman should be granted full capacity for the purpose of consenting to the abortion or whether the abortion is in the best interest of the pregnant woman.[104]

The Parental Consent for Abortion by Minors Act, passed by the Tennessee legislature in 1996 and in effect since February 2000,[105] resembles the laws established in Alabama and Pennsylvania, at least in terms of its conformity with the demands of legal precedent. Excepting cases of medical emergencies or if the criminal charge of incest is pending against the minor's parent, the statute imposes a one-parent consent requirement for unemancipated minors under eighteen.[106] Under conditions consistent with *Bellotti II,* the consent requirement shall be waived upon a minor's petition to a juvenile court, "if the court finds either that: (1) The minor is mature and well-informed enough to make the abortion decision on the minor's own; or (2) The performance of the abortion would be in the minor's best interests."[107] The statute does not specify the standard of proof to be employed.

Court proceedings, under the Tennessee statute, are free to the minor[108] and "shall be given such precedence over other pending matters as is necessary to ensure that the court may reach a decision promptly, but in no case shall the court fail to rule within forty-eight (48) hours of the time of application."[109] In addition, "[t]he court shall ensure that the minor's identity is kept anonymous. The minor shall be allowed to proceed under a pseudonym and shall be allowed to sign all documents, including the petition, by that pseudonym."[110] The statute provides that "[a]n expedited, anonymous appeal shall be available to any minor."[111] It further stipulates that "[t]he court shall advise the minor that the minor has a right to court-appointed counsel and shall provide the minor with such counsel upon the minor's request."[112]

While similar in the above respects to most parental consent statutes, the Tennessee law goes beyond the provisions of most states and the requisites of precedent in affording additional avenues to ensure the implementation of the bypass process. Among these avenues is the assistance of a trained court-appointed advocate. According to the Tennessee statute,

> The department of children's services shall assign from existing staff at least one (1) court advocate in each judicial district to provide minors with information regarding requirements and procedures [of the bypass process], to assist in coordination of the activities of court-appointed counsel, to attend legal proceedings with the minor or the minor's next friend, and to make available written material concerning the provisions and applications of [the bypass process]. The advocate shall be trained in the juvenile court procedures, in the procedures established by [the bypass process], and in counseling minors.[113]

The statute also mandates that the Department of Children's Services maintain

> a toll-free telephone number for minors to use in order to obtain the telephone number and address of a court advocate. The department shall further provide and distribute a written brochure or information sheet which summarizes the provisions and applications of [the parental consent mandate and judicial waiver option] and which contains the toll-free telephone number as well as the names, addresses, and telephone numbers of the court advocates in each judicial district.[114]

A final notable element of the Tennessee bypass option is its liberal venue provision, which allows a minor seeking to waive parental consent to file her petition in any juvenile court in the state.[115]

Conclusion

In the chapters that follow I examine the real-world functioning of the bypass in Alabama, Pennsylvania, and Tennessee, states where it is fair to expect successful implementation of the bypass route. These states provide a just playing field on which to evaluate the wisdom of parental involvement mandates.

Alabama's parental consent law took effect fourteen years before I began collecting data on the law. This is ample time for local courts to become acquainted with their statutory obligations. Moreover, over the years, the parental consent statute generated several high-profile cases, including a 1998 case in which a juvenile court judge took the unusual step of appointing an attorney to represent the fetus during a bypass hearing.[116] This case, discussed in greater detail in Chapter 7, garnered significant media coverage,[117] affording additional opportunity and motivation for courts to become informed about their role.

Pennsylvania's law had been in effect more than three years when I began my study. This, too, seems ample time for courts to get their acts together. Moreover, Pennsylvania was home base for the landmark case *Planned Parenthood of Southeastern Pennsylvania v. Casey*, which, among other things, upheld Pennsylvania's parental consent mandate. Media coverage of this case was blanket. Further, and perhaps owing to *Casey*, Pennsylvania had a substantial and well established pro-choice advocacy community. This community, in the aftermath of the *Casey* defeat, devoted significant effort toward paving the bypass route, working with attorneys and courts to craft procedures to facilitate the bypass mechanism.[118]

Tennessee's law was basically brand new when I began my study, having been in effect for just over a year. However, there is absolutely no doubt that Tennessee courts were made aware of their responsibility to serve as the venue for bypass hearings. Pursuant to a U.S. District Court injunction, the Tennessee statute's starting date was conditioned on a requirement that the State Attorney General's Office notify juvenile courts of the law. The statute took effect only after court officials in ninety-one of the state's ninety-five counties acknowledged receipt of this notice.[119] In addition to the U.S. District Court's mandated heads-up to Tennessee's juvenile courts, Tennessee's combination of court advocates and liberal venue provision arguably establishes the most robust set of protections presently on the books for securing access to a judicial bypass.[120]

PART II

Gaining Access to the Bypass Process

3

Satisfaction

Our support for or opposition to a law is based at least in part on our expectations about how the law will play out when put into practice. For example, opposition to the death penalty has been growing, with the American Bar Association calling for the suspension of capital punishment and some governors having imposed a moratorium on death sentences.[1] This growing opposition is not based on a rejection of the idea that murderers deserve to die for their crimes. Rather, it is based on recognition of the systemic flaws that obstruct the equitable administration of criminal justice—on the disquiet generated by dashed expectations about the proper functioning of law.

As with the death penalty, an assessment of parental involvement laws should consider whether our expectations about the functioning of such laws are fulfilled. When the disparity between our expectations about how the law will function and how it actually functions becomes too great, the law ceases to be a tolerable mechanism of governance. To evaluate whether the discrepancy between the expected and the actual is tolerable in the case of the judicial bypass process, I examine in this and the following chapters in Part II a critical juncture in the process: namely, the point of entry. I ask whether a minor who approaches a court seeking a bypass hearing would succeed in finding her way to one.

Surveying Courts and Court Advocates

To find out how judges and judicial gatekeepers deal with inquiries into the bypass process, my research assistants and I contacted by phone each of the county courts in Alabama, Pennsylvania, and Tennessee responsible for handling bypass hearings.[2] In Tennessee, we also contacted personnel in the Department of Children's Services (DCS) who are designated under state law to guide minors through the process.[3]

Because these contacts aimed to gauge how court personnel and DCS employees would react when approached by pregnant minors, we designed the calls to simulate such instances. Thus we did not explain the research-oriented purpose of our inquiry. Instead, we always began with the following statement: "I am calling to find out how a girl who's not eighteen who wants an abortion can get a judge's permission to avoid telling her parents." In addition, the caller did not disclose her detailed knowledge of the law, since we do not imagine that a minor making an initial inquiry would be well-versed about the bypass mechanism.[4]

While we generally aimed to approximate how a minor would contact the court or DCS, the caller did not represent herself as being a pregnant minor, though respondents often assumed she was. In those instances when the respondent asked whether the caller was pregnant, the caller said no and explained that she was only calling to gather information about the process. In addition, even though a pregnant minor might not persist in her effort to discover information when faced with an uninformed or reluctant respondent, we typically pressed respondents for more information. For example, when a juvenile court employee expressed doubt that a judge had the authority to bypass parental consent for abortion, the caller asked if someone else might have more information. We employed this tactic to give courts and Tennessee's DCS every opportunity to prove their readiness to handle bypass inquiries.

Contact began with the main courthouse number for each county or with the juvenile court, when such courts were separately designated.[5] In Tennessee, we contacted designated DCS personnel after completing our contacts with courts. Respondents often referred us to other departments within the court or agencies and individuals independent of the court. We pursued the trail of these recommendations—contacting court administrators, judges' chambers, legal services, abortion providers, the health department, crisis pregnancy centers, and the like—to see whether and with what amount of effort a minor would find her way to a bypass hearing. The only time we did not follow through on a referral was when we were counseled in a nonspecific manner to contact a private attorney.

In Pennsylvania, calls were placed between July and October of 1997. Contacts in Alabama occurred in the fall of 2001. In Tennessee, contacts began in April 2002 and were completed in the early fall of that year.

The three chapters in Part II are organized according to the types of responses given by court personnel. These responses were very often incongruous with what might be considered a well-functioning system. In this chapter, though, I review cases where the actual functioning of the bypass option fits or approximates our expectations. This information serves as a backdrop against which to compare the other types of responses reported in Chapters 4 and 5.

What's Expected

Courts

On August 13, 1997, my research assistant called a county court in Pennsylvania. Here is what happened:

Researcher (R): I'm calling to find out how a girl who's not eighteen who wants an abortion can get a judge's permission to avoid telling her parents.

Court Employee (CE): Yes, you can file to get permission from the court. You have to file an application. It's all confidential. After you file, the court would have a hearing right away, and the court would have to rule within three business days. I have exactly the type of form you need to fill out in the library. . . . It's in here that you've been informed of the risks and consequences. That's something you'd have to do before the permission.

R: What would she have to prove to get permission?

CE: Sound mind and mature and capable of giving informed consent. That you understand risks, other alternatives. It's all confidential. We'd appoint an attorney if you want. You do have to list your parents' names, but they wouldn't be notified. And after the judge rules, the file would be sealed. If she's into her second trimester, that's something the judge would look at. The county would pay for the attorney.[6]

This exchange depicts a virtually perfect response to a bypass inquiry. The court employee made plain the key provisions of bypass proceedings. She noted, in particular, the availability of court-appointed counsel as well as the confidential, expeditious, and cost-free features of the process. She conveyed one of the grounds for securing a bypass, namely the demonstration of maturity. The respondent presented this information with little prompting and without judgment.

Here is another example of a nearly perfect response, given by an administrator in a Pennsylvania judge's chambers:

> CE: What I will need to do is obtain the minor's name, address, and phone number, and we'll get an attorney for her. We have to hire an attorney, and then he would file a petition, and then there would be a hearing before the judge, and it will be kept confidential. [It will be a] closed hearing, only a stenographer, attorney, and herself. Then there would be an order if it was determined that the abortion should be performed. . . .
>
> R: What would she have to prove?
>
> CE: That would be something she would have to talk to her attorney about. But let me see what I have here. Basically the law says that there shall be evidence of emotional development, maturity, intellect, and understanding, and any other evidence useful for the purposes of consenting to the abortion, and if she can't consent, then it has to be decided if the abortion is in her best interest. . . . The court has to appoint an attorney for her. It would be kept extremely confidential. She could work through me if she wants, and it would be confidential. The documents would only have [her] initials. But only the judge, the lawyer, and I would have her name.[7]

Some court employees managed to convey sufficient and appropriate information with an economy of words. Consider an employee of Alabama's juvenile court system who answered our query as follows: "You need to come in person to room 200 [in the] county court. We'll assign you a judge, we'll appoint you an attorney, you'll meet with an attorney. They'll draw a petition for a waiver and hold a hearing within seventy-two hours. . . . Everything is confidential. We don't use names. Just use initials."[8] This response presents most of the key components of the bypass route, however briefly. While we might be concerned that some information is omitted, at the initial point of contact—a point at which a minor arguably needs only enough information to have confidence that the process will be quick, confidential, cost-free, and aided by legal counsel—brevity has its merits.

In Tennessee, several court employees offered brief responses by way of referral to a court advocate known to handle bypass cases. Though these respondents did not themselves communicate procedural details, they acknowledged the existence of the bypass route, expressed confidence that someone knowledgeable would be in a position to assist, and provided contact information for that person. As one court employee said, "I can give you a phone number of the contact person who will work with her on this. She knows about the process and what to do. And she will let that person know what their options are. So the first thing they need to do is call this person."[9] Another said, "You need to go to or contact the Department of Children's Services. . . . The person who used to do this in [our] county is out on sick leave now, so I'll give you the number of someone else. . . . And if she doesn't know, I'm sure she'll be able to tell you the person who can help."[10] These respondents went on to name the designated DCS court advocate and provided her phone number.

Gatekeepers of the courts have, of course, many more tasks to accomplish besides handling bypass inquiries. Moreover, in smaller counties, minors rarely make use of this option. Consequently, we found many court employees unable to fluently and from memory converse about the administration of bypass hearings. To make up for this lack of fluency, court employees sometimes relied on written material.

In Tennessee, where DCS distributes a written brochure that summarizes the provisions of the parental consent mandate and its bypass option, several court employees read from the brochure:

Okay, that's kind of new, we haven't done one. Hold on and let me go get the brochure, okay? . . . We have a contact person. . . . She'll talk to you about your choices, to continue with your pregnancy or give the baby up for adoption, or to go through this new code they have. They say if you try to have an abortion, state law requires that you have the written consent of one of your parents. If your parents refuse to give consent or you do not want to ask for consent, you can ask a juvenile court judge to drop this requirement. You'll have a court advocate. To be excused from parental consent, you have to file a petition—that means you'll fill out a form, I have those—you can file that in any county. Hearings will be confidential, not open to public, use your initials, your name will be on only one copy. . . . You don't have any fees, and you have to be able to tell the court how many weeks pregnant you are. . . . Like I said, we have not had anyone come in, so it's kind of new to me too. Let's see, you can have a court-appointed attorney. Once you come in, we have to conduct a hearing no later than the next day. If the judge doesn't excuse you from parental consent, you can appeal.[11]

In Alabama and Pennsylvania, court employees do not have at the ready such a brochure. Nevertheless, some court employees found guidance in state statutes or in the petitions used to file for a bypass. One Pennsylvania court employee read the entire petition over the phone, starting with "The form is headed as 'Petition for Judicial Authorization for Abortion,'" and adding such details as "you have to swear that all of the statements in this petition are true and correct; any false statements are punishable by law."[12] While reading the petition, this employee interjected, "I'm sorry to be so dumb about this, but this hasn't come up very often."[13]

On the one hand, accurate responses that make essential use of written material can be less assuring than those that do not. Where respondents relied heavily on written material, they often communicated inexperience. This communication was sometimes explicit, as in the cases cited above. In other instances, respondents conveyed their inexperience in more subtle ways, through tone of voice or hesitation. Whether explicitly or implicitly conveyed, inexperience might be off-putting to a nervous minor trying to figure out how to get an abortion without telling her parents.

On the other hand, reliance on written material allowed those inexperienced with the bypass process to communicate information accurately. This was especially true of those who relied on the DCS brochure, like the youth services officer who, when answering the question of how long the bypass process takes, was able to say, "Let me see, I don't recall, I've had training over this but it's been a year. It [the brochure] says, 'How long will it take? Once you file the petition, the court must conduct a hearing no later than the next business day.'"[14] Here, as in the other examples, the benefits of relying on the available written material offset whatever confidence might have been undermined by the court employee's failure of recall.

Eliciting information about the bypass process typically required considerable prompting, as exemplified by the following exchange with a court employee in Tennessee:

CE: What you have to do is you come into our office, and we have you meet with a lady from the Department of Children's Services, and she goes over some things with you, then you're appointed an attorney and a paper is filed, and you have a hearing before the judge.

R: Does it take a long time?

CE: No.

R: Does it cost anything?

CE: No, Ma'am.

R: Does it go on her permanent record?

CE: All the records are sealed. Most people won't even know her real name, only like two or three would even know her name.[15]

The trouble to which a minor must go to obtain information is of concern, and, as we shall see in a later chapter, the effort required to obtain information is often well beyond what is reasonably expected, especially when we consider that minors tend to be less comfortable making demands on authority than adults. That said, it is not too much to ask that a minor pose some questions over the phone in an effort to gather specifics about filing a bypass petition. The fact that a court employee does not produce all the particulars after one question is not troubling.

In each of the cases recounted so far, court employees presented information accurately, although in some cases information was omitted. For example, most respondents failed to mention the availability of an appeals process should a judge deny a waiver petition. But while the Supreme Court has conditioned the constitutionality of parental consent statutes in part on the availability of an appeal, learning about the appellate option during the initial inquiry would not likely make a difference to minors.

In other instances, we encountered responses that contained both accurate and inaccurate information. Some respondents who offered otherwise correct information were vague about the timing of bypass proceedings or the standards for determining when a bypass will be granted.

During one exchange with a Tennessee court employee, we received this in response to a question asking how long the process would take: "I wish I could tell you that it would take a week or two weeks. But I'm not sure."[16] Some respondents sought to explain their uncertainty about timing. One court employee in Alabama offered this upon being asked how long the process would take:

CE: I'm not, I sure don't know, we've not, I don't know.

R: Is there a way of finding that out?

> CE: Well, what you have to do is file your petition, you would come and request to file a petition. Once that's filed, we'd set a court date, that would depend on how soon the petition is filed and when the next available court date is, and it would be hard for me to say when that would be.[17]

In the following otherwise accurate reply, the respondent—an Alabama employee—faltered only with regard to the description of the standards for judging bypass petitions:

> CE: You need to come to the juvenile court, second floor of the courthouse. We will file a petition on your behalf, we'll appoint you an attorney, called a guardian ad litem, and within seventy-two hours we'll set up a hearing. The attorney will explain to you your rights. The hearing is a very closed hearing; the only people are the attorney, the judge, and the court reporter. As soon as the hearing is over, the judge will either grant or deny you the petition. No cost to you.
>
> R: Is it likely she would get it?
>
> CE: My experience has been that if she is mature enough to make the decision and has a reason for the abortion, he will grant it. You come here, make up a name. We won't even want your name, just initials. There's a possibility that we may, may be able to have it while you're here at that time. Otherwise it will be within seventy-two hours.[18]

This respondent noted that judges take maturity into consideration in deciding whether to grant a waiver of consent. However, the respondent offered a description of the grounds for securing a waiver that is, technically speaking, inconsistent with the parental consent statute and legal precedent. Stating that a judge usually grants bypass requests when minors are mature *and* have a reason for the abortion suggests that proving maturity and informedness would not provide adequate grounds for securing a bypass.

In a perfect world, imprecision like that contained in the previous three exchanges would not exist. Indeed, the need to implement bypass proceedings in a timely fashion and under appropriate legal standards is undeniable. Nevertheless, the variety of imprecision present in these examples does not materially damage the propriety of the responses, for a minor hearing such responses is not likely to be dissuaded from filing a petition. To see these respondents' missteps as grounds for doubting the plausibility of the bypass procedure is to demand from people more than they can routinely deliver and would amount to making the argument of this book rest on holding the world to an impossible ideal.

There are, obviously, some errors concerning timing and the grounds for granting a waiver that would render a response unacceptable. However accurate a response might otherwise be, most minors would be dissuaded from filing a petition were they told that a bypass hearing could not be scheduled for a month or that the judge would only grant a bypass in cases of rape. The same cannot be said of those instances when respondents were vague about timing, mentioned only one standard, failed to mention standards at all, or admitted that they did not know the standards. The danger at this stage of the game comes not from ambiguity about timing or the grounds for granting a waiver. The danger is that mention of formidable obstacles, conjured though they may be, could have deleterious consequences for the minor.

Court Advocates

In Tennessee, where the DCS court advocate system aims to provide a gateway into the bypass process, most advocates communicated detailed and correct information. The following exchange illustrates how advocates typically described the features of the judicial bypass.

> *Researcher (R):* I'm calling to find out how a girl who's not eighteen who wants an abortion can get a judge's permission to avoid telling her parents.
>
> *Court Advocate (CA):* What you have to do is go to court and file for a judicial bypass and, when you go to court ask them to appoint an attorney, and they will. And you have to show the judge that it's in your best interest to do that and that you're mature enough to make the decision.
>
> *R:* Does it cost anything?
>
> *CA:* No.
>
> *R:* Does it take long?
>
> *CA:* Oh, it doesn't take long, because there are time limits on everything. From the time you file, they have forty-eight hours. And if they deny it, then if you appeal it to the circuit court and they have to decide in seventy-two hours, which is three days. . . .
>
> *R:* Does it go on her permanent record?
>
> *CA:* No. What they do is you can use an alias. Your name, it's sealed, first

of all, and then on all the documents it's just your initials. No, there's no access to it. So nobody could go back later and look at it.[19]

This advocate conveyed the fundamental components of the process, including a minor's right to a confidential and expedited hearing at no cost and with the assistance of a court-appointed attorney. She also referenced the standards used for judging a bypass petition. Though technically incorrect in her suggestion that a minor must prove both maturity and best interest, this mistake, as I have said, is not troubling.

In serving as the purveyors of information, many advocates also acknowledged their role as guides:

> I do have a pamphlet if they want to meet with me, I can go over it with them. . . . Partly my responsibility would be to go with the girl to court, and make sure she gets representation from an attorney, because she has to have that, and then you go through the process of filing a petition, it's a petition of judicial authorization for an abortion without parental consent.[20]

According to another advocate, "we are responsible for giving everybody their rights. . . . To make sure it goes smoothly, we sort of walk the person through it, is kind of what we do."[21] A third advocate made a similar comment: "[M]y job is to walk with you through the process; if you want to meet with me we can talk about the process."[22]

Advocates sometimes made a point of ending the conversation with an invitation to call back or come to the DCS office for further information. One advocate generously, and humorously, remarked, "If we need to go any further, you've got my name and number, and I'll meet with you any time and any place—well, almost any place."[23] Yet another volunteered this information: "Now, let me tell you, I am the one that handles that, but I will be going out of town for about a week or ten days. Let me give you my back-up person."[24] Even some of the DCS employees who do not serve as court advocates were solicitous. One woman who answered the phone for a court advocate who was out of the office for the afternoon said, "Can you call her back? She's very good and she wants to talk to people who have this problem. You can call back at 8:30 tomorrow morning. If that's not a good time for you, I can have her call you if you want to give me a number."[25]

Several advocates were especially in tune with minors' interest in navigating the bypass covertly. After offering details on virtually all aspects of the process, one advocate indicated her practical appreciation of confidentiality: "I have a brochure here with more information. If you'd like to come down and get it we can arrange that. I hate to send it out in the mail."[26] Another displayed concern for confidentiality in this way: "[I]f she would like to, she can give me a call, I'm usually here, and if I'm not here, she can leave a message. I'll give her a call back. I never leave my name."[27]

Sensitivity to matters of availability and confidentiality show not just a procedural understanding but also an appreciation of the obstacles minors must overcome to file a petition. These types of remarks help to paint a portrait of how reality can come close to matching an ideal.

Some court advocates who conveyed otherwise accurate information exhibited uncertainty about certain aspects of the law. One advocate said, contrary to the law, that the petition must be filed in the minor's home county. In this case, the advocate's error was one of commission rather than omission. Still, this error falls among those that in most cases would not deter a minor from further pursuit of the bypass route.

Other remarks by advocates revealed additional moments of uncertainty.

> *CA:* She'll have to go before the judge, and is she just not wanting to tell her parents or are they saying no?
> *R:* Does it matter?
> *CA:* Yes, it definitely matters. If she's just not wanting to tell her parents that's one thing, if they're saying no, that's something else.
> *R:* So if she just doesn't want to tell her parents can she still get permission?
> *CA:* I don't know.[28]

This response, as it stands, is unacceptable. However, the advocate later made plain when the bypass procedure is available to a minor: "If she's unable to obtain consent—that means the parents refuse or can't give consent—or if she doesn't want to speak with her parent, then she can petition the juvenile court in the county where she lives for a judge's permission to drop that requirement."[29]

In similar fashion, another advocate vacillated while attempting to explain whether the minor must first consult with her parents before filing a petition:

CA: The person, in order to file, they have to be under eighteen years of age, pregnant, and they have to have discussed it with the parents. I think so, they may not have to, uh, uh, if you decide to have an abortion, state law requires that you have the written consent of one of your parents or your legal guardian before an abortion can be performed. If your parents refuse to give consent or you do not want to ask for their help, you can ask a juvenile court judge to drop this requirement. A court advocate will be appointed to assist you in preparing the petition and getting it before the court. The person you're calling for, they need to go to health department or a doctor to get verification that they're pregnant. Any other questions?

R: So they have to talk to their parents?

CA: No, no they don't.[30]

This advocate, like the previous one, made, but quickly corrected, an error about parental involvement. The initial error was, no doubt, one of consequence, and failure to correct it would have rendered the response unacceptable. But while the advocate's uncertainty might give a minor pause, the important point is that the advocate corrected the error.

Conclusion

Supporters of parental involvement mandates routinely appeal to the availability of the bypass option to bolster their argument and stave off worries. Take *San Francisco Chronicle* columnist Debra Saunders, who wrote this in the weeks before the defeat of a November 2005 California ballot initiative that would have required parental notification:

The pivotal question is: Should California law be based on families in which parents are abusive, or should it address the majority of parents who are responsible and only want what is best for their children? I have to come down on the side of the majority of good parents, especially when the judicial bypass exists for daughters of abusive parents.

Why wouldn't a parent vote for this measure?

Becky Morgan, a former GOP state senator and mother of an obstetrician/gynecologist, told me she will vote "no" because of teens who don't have the type of relationship that makes them feel they can tell their parents. . . .

"I will always remember the teenager who said, 'My father gave my boyfriend a key to the house, and when I got pregnant, he threw me out,'" Morgan noted.

I'm with Morgan on that: I don't want laws that would result in a pregnant teen getting thrown out of the house. That's why the judicial bypass is so important.[31]

Saunders and those who share her view presumably envision a bypass process that is typified by the sorts of responses we have seen in this chapter. While not every response achieved perfection, minor errors are not inconsistent with a well-functioning system. The question of interest here, as noted at the outset, is not whether discord between our expectations and reality exists but whether the level of discord is tolerable. What is important at this stage is not whether implementers dot every "i" and cross every "t" when it comes to providing information. Rather, what is important is that those charged with carrying out the law convey that the system stands ready to function, that those interested in pursuing a bypass can do so. Minors should come away from court contacts thinking, "I can do this." If this is the case, then the system has worked, at least so far.

4

Ignorance

Trial courts may ignore precedents quite often, especially misdemeanor courts where appeals are rare. Indeed, such judges may not even be aware of the relevant precedents.
—Bradley C. Canon and Charles A. Johnson, *Judicial Policies*[1]

Ignorance of the law among judges and judicial gatekeepers stands between minors and their access to bypass hearings. This ignorance is substantially at odds with what one imagines the bypass process will provide. While we found widespread familiarity with the provisions of the bypass route among Department of Children's Services (DCS) court advocates in Tennessee, the same cannot be said of courts. Indeed, respondents in 40 percent of Alabama courts, just over 45 percent of Tennessee courts, and a whopping 73 percent of Pennsylvania courts proved inadequately acquainted with their responsibilities under the law.

We encountered a continuum of ignorance during our contacts with courts and DCS advocates. Some respondents categorically denied the availability of the bypass option. Others expressed a complete lack of knowledge or substantial uncertainty about the possibility of avoiding parental consent through a bypass system. Still others communicated specifics about the process but proved misinformed about certain essential features. In this chapter, I detail these ill-informed responses. I also recount the manifest opposition to abortion and the bypass option that sometimes accompanied them.

Sheer Ignorance

Most of the ignorant responses we encountered came from court employees who doubted the existence of or knew next to nothing about the bypass option.[2] Of the 222 county courts charged with handling by-pass petitions in Alabama, Pennsylvania, and Tennessee, 100 demonstrated substantial or complete ignorance about the bypass system or, worse, expressed considerable doubt about its existence. These include 22 of the 67 county courts in Alabama, 41 of the 60 judicial districts in Pennsylvania, and 37 of the 95 courts in Tennessee. More often than not, these courts answered our inquiries by referring us to third parties absent any knowledge of whether these parties would be helpful. In some instances, respondents simply had nothing to offer.

"You're Going to Have to Call a Lawyer"

As discussed in Chapter 2, the Supreme Court has not explicitly required states to give minors the right to court-appointed counsel in judicial bypass proceedings. But many states, including Alabama, Pennsylvania, and Tennessee, have extended this right and, notably, undertaken an obligation to tell minors about it. Nevertheless, many courts failed to demonstrate awareness of this or any other obligation under their state's consent statute. Contacts with courts frequently yielded no insight into the bypass process but, instead, generated a perhaps well-meaning but in any case uninformed recommendation that a minor secure the services of a private or legal aid attorney. This was the most common piece of advice we received from respondents who proved unfamiliar with the bypass option.

The recommendation to contact an attorney was usually accompanied by candid expressions of ignorance about the law. An Alabama juvenile court officer said in typical fashion, "I have no idea. You'll have to check with an attorney."[3] A Tennessee court employee remarked, "Honey, I have no idea. Have you called an attorney?"[4] "I have no earthly idea," admitted another Tennessee respondent before suggesting consultation with an attorney.[5] In Pennsylvania, an employee in the judge's chambers said, "Woo, I wouldn't know how to tell you that. She would need a lawyer. You can't just go to the judge and have a judge deal with it."[6]

When confronted with these suggestions, we pressed for further information about how to secure an attorney. Respondents often declined to offer guidance, sometimes explaining their legal obligation to avoid attorney referrals. As an employee in an Alabama judge's office stated, "I can't give you an attorney's name, it's unethical; it would look like we were trying to recommend a particular attorney."[7] In other instances, respondents offered no explanation. One Tennessee respondent simply said, "You have to go through an attorney. . . . I'm sorry, I can't recommend any."[8] A Pennsylvania court employee said, before abruptly hanging up, "You would have to call an attorney."[9]

Whereas some respondents were plainly reluctant to provide even the most minimal guidance on how to obtain legal services, others tried to offer some general direction. When pressed for further information about counsel, respondents sometimes recommended to "look in the yellow pages."[10] As an Alabama court employee said, "You'd have to look in the phone book under attorneys and decide which one you would want to ask."[11]

Some uninformed respondents suggested, and sometimes provided phone numbers for, lawyer referral services—agencies that match potential clients with private attorneys. Others directed us to the state bar association. These suggestions came without accompanying comments about the conditions under which court-appointed counsel would be provided or any other information about the bypass process. Following these leads ended with the prospect of hiring a private attorney. One lawyer referral agency mentioned by a Pennsylvania court said, "I can refer you to a family planning attorney, but I don't know who would be able to help you to deal with that. I'd have to take her name and address, or at least her name, and refer her to a lawyer. But I don't know who could help without charging anything."[12] The Pennsylvania Bar Association described their referral service in this way: "We would set up an appointment for you with an attorney that handles cases. There would be a thirty-dollar to seventy-five-dollar fee, payable to the attorney at the time of the appointment. Should there be any other fees, that would be between yourself and the attorney."[13] This respondent also suggested a call to legal aid but cautioned, "They may not deal with that type of matter because they don't take everything."[14]

The Pennsylvania Bar Association was not alone in directing us to legal aid. Several court employees directed us in this way, anticipating that legal aid organizations would provide counsel free of charge. Take the following exchange with an Alabama court employee:

> *Court Employee (CE):* I think that's going to have to be a court case. But I don't know, I've never had one. Hold on just a minute. [pause] You're

going to have to call a lawyer. I called the judge's office. They said you'll need a lawyer.

Researcher (R): Is there anyone you can recommend?

CE: I can't recommend a lawyer. I'm legally bound not to recommend a lawyer. You'll just have to pick one and call one.

R: Would a girl have to pay for that lawyer?

CE: I really honestly don't know. You'll have to call one and ask. We've never had one of these. You might call legal services. . . . Just call your lawyer first and see if it's going to cost anything. And then if it is, call legal services.[15]

Those who recommended calling legal aid often indicated some measure of appreciation for the financial burdens minors might face. Nevertheless, federal law bars legal aid organizations that receive federal funds from handling abortion-related cases. Referrals to legal aid, therefore, turn out to be dead ends, as the following response from Tennessee legal services illustrates: "We do not do that here. I don't know how you would go about doing that; I don't know what the law is. I'm thinking if you're under eighteen, your parents have to authorize that."[16] Likewise, a legal services employee in one Alabama county said sympathetically, "I'm sorry, our office is prohibited by federal regulations from giving advice on abortion. She would have to contact some other attorney on that. I'm real sorry."[17]

Judges were among those who failed to indicate that minors have a right to court-appointed counsel and instead recommended securing a private attorney. A Pennsylvania judge who proved barely knowledgeable about the bypass option said this in response to our inquiry: "Well, the Act was challenged in federal court and I'm not sure where it stands now, it may still be on appeal. . . . You might want to talk to a lawyer. Under that Act you have to file a petition, so you'd need a lawyer."[18] In Tennessee, a judge explained, "I've never done it. I'm going to have to give you another number to call. . . . It's lawyers that will do work without charging."[19] In another Tennessee court, a judge's secretary said,

[The judge] told me to give you a number for legal services. . . . [T]here are attorneys there that can help you. You're going to have something written up for a judge to sign, and I don't know what that is and [the judge] doesn't know what that is, so you're going to have to talk to an attorney. And I said I hated to just send you to an attorney . . . so [the judge] said to give you legal services. They have attorneys who don't cost anything.[20]

Like their counterparts in Tennessee and Pennsylvania, some Alabama judges exhibited their limited acquaintance with the bypass process. One juvenile court judge offered this candid response:

I don't know how to help you. . . . I've been doing this seventeen years and I've never had one of these cases. There are provisions about that and recent court decisions, but I'm not well-versed enough to advise you about it. I could say there are three places you might contact. One is your physician. Two is a lawyer. Three is the Department of Human Resources.[21]

"Maybe if You Look in the Blue Pages"

While the recommendation to speak with an attorney was the most common response given by court personnel who proved ill informed about the bypass process, other third parties were also named as potential sources of assistance as respondents flailed about for answers. Many respondents recommended contacting private organizations that deal with abortion or pregnancy, such as abortion clinics, family planning organizations, crisis pregnancy centers, pregnancy hotlines, adoption agencies, and hospitals. Others suggested that a government social service agency, like the health department or human services, might prove useful.[22]

Court employees who rendered such advice, like those who recommended speaking with an attorney, were typically frank about their lack of familiarity with the bypass option. One Tennessee respondent said, "Ma'am, I really don't know who to refer you to, we don't have any papers here in this office or any authority to do that here. So I don't know who to put you in touch with. The only thing I can suggest is that you call Families in Crisis."[23] In another case in Tennessee, a court contact said, "I have no idea. I don't think anybody in our office knows that kind of thing. I've never had anybody call and ask that question. There might be somebody at the health department you could talk to, but I don't know."[24] In Alabama, a court employee first recommended a call to the health department before saying, "I don't know where this is going to get you . . . but here are some numbers. Planned Parenthood, 539-2746; Family Planning, 539-3711; Pregnancy Hotline, 533-3526. Some of those numbers may help you."[25] Similarly, a Pennsylvania court employee offered this candid response:

> I don't have any knowledge in that area at all. Planned Parenting [*sic*] may have some alternatives to offer you. Or . . . maybe if you look in the blue pages, look for different things. Hang on let me look. . . . Crisis Pregnancy Center, 658-6329. Or you might even call family planning or something. How about the Catholic Charities? They offer confidentiality. Family Planning, 658-6681. There's an Allegheny Reproductive Health Center, 800-221-3988. Other than that I honestly don't know.[26]

Some respondents who made referrals to abortion clinics, the health department, or the like did so while expressing skepticism that such a thing as a bypass option exists. In Alabama, for instance, one respondent said:

> She cannot go before the judge to get that done. . . . Call information, just ask for an abortion clinic in Montgomery, and ask them what age a person has to be and can that happen, but I'm almost positive you're going to have to have someone there who is over eighteen. . . . I'm going to give you the number for Planned Parenthood, 1-800-413-9776. . . . If they say you need parental approval, then you're going to have to have parental approval, because I don't think a judge can order an abortion.[27]

With the exception of abortion clinics and family planning organizations, following up on the many referrals offered by court personnel did not generate accurate information about bypass proceedings. Government health departments and human services agencies (excluding Tennessee's DCS) were of little use in offering guidance, as the following response from one of Alabama's county health departments illustrates: "Ma'am, we don't do that, and we are not authorized to give that information out, about abortion clinics. We're not allowed, because we're not supposed to be for abortion."[28] The crisis pregnancy centers and pregnancy hotlines to which we were referred were similarly unhelpful. Each is a pro-life organization, and most—including such places as Birthright, We Care, Concern, Sav-A-Life, and Action Line for Life—

are Christian ministries. Upon contacting these organizations we encountered responses like these: "We are pro-life, we're pro-life, so we don't have anything to do with abortion"[29] and "That's not in our field at all. We help girls *have* their babies."[30]

Only in the case of referrals to abortion clinics and family planning organizations did we come across useful information. In Pennsylvania, most of the abortion clinics not only exhibit familiarity with bypass proceedings but also stand ready to guide minors through the petition process.[31] In Tennessee and Alabama, most abortion clinics know about the bypass option and make referrals to courts or, in Tennessee, court advocates. As one Alabama abortion provider explained, "I give minors the information where they can call and talk to the intake officer in [this county]. And I tell them they may be able to do it in their home counties. Some of the counties will have judges that will give them that service. I encourage them to check it out."[32]

Still, not all abortion clinics and family planning organizations assist minors with the bypass route, as this exchange with a Tennessee abortion provider illustrates:

> *Abortion Provider (AP):* They have to have parental consent, unless they can get a judicial bypass to convince a judge to waive consent.
> *R:* Do you know how to do that?
> *AP:* I don't know, hon, you'd have to call lawyer. . . . Just call a lawyer and tell them you want to find out how to get a judicial bypass for abortion.[33]

Other clinics and family planning organizations asserted that the bypass option does not exist. In Tennessee, one abortion provider said this upon being asked whether an alternative to parental consent exists: "No, not here, not without her parent. Not in Tennessee."[34] A Planned Parenthood affiliate in Tennessee made a similar comment: "Not in this state. You have to go to another state."[35]

"She Can Contact Neighboring States"

In a handful of instances, court employees pointed not to third parties but rather to strategies that would result in circumvention of the parental consent requirement. In each instance, respondents denied that judges have legal authority to waive parental consent.

Two respondents mentioned the possibility of gaining emancipation from parents. "In the state of Alabama," one respondent said, "they're required to have their parent's permission. . . . If she's a minor, a judge couldn't do that. If she's emancipated, that's a different thing."[36] Another Alabama court employee said, "There is no such thing, Ma'am, not through our court system. The only way to do that is to file papers through the court to be declared an adult, and your parents would have to be notified about that. . . . I'm sorry, there's not any such thing."[37]

In Pennsylvania, one respondent suggested securing an abortion out of state. "She can contact neighboring states to see if they don't have parental consent laws. New Jersey doesn't, New York doesn't."[38] Pressed about the possibility of going before a judge in Pennsylvania, this employee replied, "Well that would mean you'll have to go before a judge, your parents will have to be notified. Since you're still considered a minor, you'll have to be represented, so your parents will have to be there."[39]

"I Think Someone Has Misled You on That One"

While the large majority of respondents who proved uninformed about the bypass process rendered some advice about how to proceed, some offered nothing more than doubt about its existence. Several such respondents unequivocally rejected the existence of the bypass option. "I talked with our juvenile court judge," an Alabama respondent said, "and he said that was no longer a law, and that they could no longer do that."[40] Several Tennessee court employees expressed similar assurance in denying that judges may authorize a waiver of consent, saying things like, "I talked to the judge and he cannot do that without your parent's consent";[41] "Without your parent's consent, there's no way you could do that";[42] and "You would need to talk with your doctor or with your parents. The judge can't give you permission."[43] No further advice was forthcoming from these respondents.

Other respondents were more equivocal but still left the impression that avoiding parental involvement would be out of the question. For example, a court employee in Alabama said, "I have no idea, Ma'am. I don't know if a judge gives permission like that or not. We've never had a case like that. . . . I don't want to get your hopes up. I don't think the court would give permission."[44] Similarly, a Tennessee respondent remarked, "I doubt that that could happen if you're under eighteen."[45]

Such respondents sometimes endeavored to explain why it would not be possible to avoid parental involvement, as did the following Tennessee court employee:

> I've never heard of our judge doing that, especially to avoid telling her parent. We don't even allow kids to be in court without their parents being with them. So I know we couldn't do that. I think someone has misled you on that one. . . . I don't think anyone anywhere in the state would do that without a parent. I don't think I'd be steering you wrong to tell you that. It would, see, your parent would have to be the one to sign the papers. A judge wouldn't touch that with a ten-foot pole. So I think she'd have to tell her parents.[46]

Material Errors

The responses so far discussed in this chapter came from respondents who seemed to be completely or largely unaware that such a thing as a judicial bypass process exists. On other occasions, respondents showed familiarity with some, but not all, features of the law. As I suggest in Chapter 3, certain types of errors and omissions are tolerable when they would not discourage a minor from continued pursuit of a bypass. However, errors and omissions can materially damage the propriety of an otherwise appropriate response.

Courts

Fourteen courts—four in Alabama, three in Pennsylvania, and seven in Tennessee—communicated specifics about the bypass process but proved misinformed about what I take to be certain essential features. Consider the following exchange with an Alabama court employee:

> R: I'm calling to find out how a girl who's not eighteen who wants an abortion can get a judge's permission to avoid telling her parents.
> CE: I would need to set an appointment up and have her come in.
> R: I'm calling to find out information on how the process works.
> CE: Come in and see me and make an appointment.
> R: Could you tell me what would she have to do? Like does she need a lawyer?

CE: I would tell her all that when she came in. But it would be best for her talk to a lawyer first.

R: Would it go on her permanent record?

CE: It would be in the computer, yes Ma'am.

R: How long would it take?

CE: I have no idea.

R: Does she need to bring anything in?

CE: Some form of I.D. and all.[47]

This employee made the bypass process appear to be something that it is not. Saying that it would be best for a minor to talk to a lawyer before coming to the court for further information implies that the minor, whether indigent or not, would bear responsibility for obtaining and paying for an attorney. Absent any reference or demonstrable sensitivity to confidentiality, saying that a record of the hearing "would be in the computer" and that the minor would have to provide identification suggests that documentation of the hearing would be public information. Finally, this respondent gave no hint of the need to act with haste.

While this respondent made three errors, what matters is not the number of errors but whether the error or combination of errors would likely hinder a minor's pursuit of the bypass option. Misinformation about the availability of court-appointed counsel is an error that, by itself, materially affects a minor's pursuit of a bypass. As the U.S. Court of Appeals for the Seventh Circuit has pointed out, minors are particularly susceptible to intimidation and confusion when confronting the legal system.[48] When respondents fail to acknowledge that in navigating the bypass process the minor is entitled to and will be afforded the guidance of an attorney (or, in Tennessee, a DCS advocate), they portray the bypass as a road the minor must travel alone and risk sacrificing the minor's rights to her own vulnerability.

We encountered this sort of error in several instances when court respondents clearly knew about the bypass option, as the following exchange with an Alabama judge illustrates:

Judge (J): You need to talk to an attorney and have the attorney file the appropriate petition in the court to get permission to not tell the parents.

R: How should she go about getting an attorney?

J: She should walk into an attorney's office and tell them what she wants to get done.

R: So would it cost money?

J: Well some attorneys will take a case like that without a fee, others will require a fee. If you're unable to hire an attorney who is engaged in a private practice, you might consider talking with someone in legal aid, or the Bar Association's volunteer lawyer program. I'll give you a few hints on how to contact the Bar Association. Call information for Montgomery; ask them to give you the number for the Alabama State Bar. They'll give you [the] name or names of attorneys in this general area who have volunteered to represent people who have no money.[49]

Likewise, an Alabama court employee who communicated some awareness of the bypass option could not say whether the court would make counsel available to a minor:

CE: She's going to have to some way or another get an attorney, do a survey, do a petition to the judge. Then if the judge consents, he'll hold a private court session and have to sign the petition to have it done. But she's going to some way or another have to have an attorney. . . . We have an attorney here Tuesday and Thursday.

R: . . . Would the girl have to pay for the attorney?

CE: I don't know. . . . [I]f she does, it might not be that much, but he also might not charge you. You could make an appointment to see him and talk to him; you can give him a call and make an appointment to see him.[50]

In these exchanges, the suggestions put forward by respondents led to the prospect of hiring and paying for a private attorney. Despite the judge's hints, contacting the Alabama Bar Association did not yield access to a volunteer lawyer. The Alabama court employee's recommendation that we speak with a particular attorney proved no more helpful. The attorney did not explain that the court would pay for counsel if the minor could not afford to do so or that she is entitled to file a petition without paying a fee. He said, instead, "You have to file a lawsuit, you do it anonymously, and you ask the judge for a court hearing, and the judge reviews it and makes a determination based on the facts. . . . Court costs are $154, attorney's fees are about $400. So you're talking like $550."[51]

On other occasions, court employees omitted mention of counsel and simply suggested that the minor would bear the burden of initiating proceedings. In one Pennsylvania court, a woman in the judge's chambers explained the process in this way:

> We do have something in our local rules of court. What needs to be done is you need to file a petition with the court, and the local rules outline what needs to be in the petition. We have this in our law library. If you come in and look at it then you would know what the procedure is. We don't have a form to fill out, so you would need to create the petition yourself and put in the information that they have in the local rules. You may need to get additional information once you see what needs to be in the petition.[52]

Asked if anyone would be available to help with the petition, this respondent did not disclose the court's obligation to provide legal representation. She said, referring to those who work in the library, "They can't actually help you with the petition. We can lead you to the local rules and you can make copies, but that's it."[53]

Misinformation about counsel was not the only notable error we encountered among respondents who exhibited knowledge of the bypass alternative. A number of courts were unaware of their responsibility to preside over hearings, even while able to recount details of the process. For example, a juvenile court officer in Alabama elaborated some of the key features of bypass proceedings, including the availability of court-appointed counsel, confidentiality requirements, and the need to move the process along quickly. This officer nevertheless went on to say, "My understanding from one of the larger counties that has in fact done these is that it needs to be done in the county that the [abortion] procedure needs to be done in. . . . It needs to be filed in the county that the clinic is in."[54] A respondent in one Pennsylvania court made a similar comment: "It's been a long time since we've done one of those. I don't know if they can be done in [this] county anymore because we don't have a clinic in [this] county."[55]

These two responses fail to acknowledge the minor's right to petition for a bypass in her home county, a right created by states in order to spare minors some of the burdens of travel. The creation of this right is an implicit recognition that forcing minors to travel, perhaps great distances, for a bypass hearing is tantamount to offering no hearing at all.

Court Advocates

At the time this research was conducted, the brochure distributed by DCS listed contact information for twenty-eight advocates assigned to serve Tennessee's ninety-five counties. Five of these advocates proved to be unavailable, a matter I take up in Chapter 5. Of the remaining twenty-three, none demonstrated the level of ignorance we found among many court employees. Indeed, twenty-two advocates produced acceptable responses of the sort discussed in Chapter 3. One, however, made material errors in conveying information about the bypass process.

This advocate, who serves seven counties, began by noting, correctly, that a minor would have to petition a court in order to obtain a judge's consent for an abortion. She also indicated that the petition process would be cost free and would not take long. However, the advocate said that a minor would have to consult her parents:

> One of the first things she needs to do is she really needs to talk with the parents; sometimes they're much more helpful than she really thinks they're going to be. Then the next thing she has to do is get counseling. Planned Parenthood organization is one of the organizations that can do that. She's got to do that. Then after she does that, then she can file a petition with the court to have the judge give consent.[56]

This advocate mischaracterized the key purpose of the bypass. After all, most of the point of the bypass option is to give minors an alternative to parental consultation. And unlike two similar cases described in Chapter 3, this advocate did not correct the mistake.

This advocate compounded the mistake with two additional errors. First, she failed to point out that the court would supply an attorney to guide the minor through the process. She said, instead, with respect to filing the petition, "An attorney is not required to help her do that; it's fairly simple, and she would have to fill it out by herself." When pressed on whether a lawyer would help, this advocate replied, "No, no. It's something that she can do herself." Second, the advocate did not indicate that she, herself, would be available to assist the minor. Instead, she referred to the 800 number established by DCS. "I think this phone number may also give you some more options for counseling services," the advocate remarked. "It's 800-435-7495. I've not called this number myself, but that number should be able to refer her to counseling."[57] This advocate did not seem to understand that the hotline is designed to link up minors with advocates and that calling the number would result in a referral back to her.

Adding Insult to Injury

Most of the ignorance that surfaced during the above-reported phone contacts seemed innocent and not intentionally hostile or malicious. Many respondents tried to provide guidance, looking up phone numbers of possible leads or asking for additional time to track down information. Several apologized for their lack of experience. In some instances, however, respondents who proved poorly informed about the bypass option indicated hostility to abortion or opposition to the prospect of avoiding parental involvement.[58]

One juvenile court employee in Tennessee followed up her guess that an attorney would have to be consulted by asking whether the minor had "prayed about this." "She might ought to," this respondent continued. "She may live to regret it."[59]

Some respondents focused on the physical risks associated with abortion and the attendant need to involve parents, as did this Tennessee court employee: "We've never done that. . . . The judge isn't in this afternoon, and I don't know whether he would, like, if something, who's going to be responsible? You see that? . . . The court's not going to take responsibility if something happened. That's the only thing, so I don't know what you'd do with that."[60] Similarly, an Alabama court employee said:

> That's going to be kind of tough to do. I think you probably need to talk to an attorney, and he can bring it to the court's attention about what the girl wants to do. . . . But I would say abortion is something that a parent needs to know about. What if the abortion goes wrong? That parent needs to be—I think it's best to talk it over with the parent. Regardless, the girl will have to live with that situation from this point forward. If something happens to the child that they don't know about, and death is the result, how would that be?[61]

From another Alabama court employee we heard this:

> Honey, I have no idea, I just have no idea. I feel like I don't believe a
> judge or even a lawyer actually would do that. . . . [I]t would be best
> for you to talk to your parents. Because if this court does something—
> this is just my opinion and . . . how I would feel—I would not sign pa-
> pers without parents knowing about it, because if something happened
> to that minor, and the parents would then know and they could sue the
> court or the state of Alabama. So I don't feel a judge or lawyer would
> do that for a minor. I can't say whether they do that somewhere else or
> not, but I don't believe it would be in the best interest for a judge or a
> lawyer to make consent like that without the minor's parents knowing
> about it. What if the doctor cut her somewhere and she bled to death,
> and then they could sue? So, baby, I just don't know what to tell you.
> . . . I really have no idea. That I wouldn't want to be in the middle of.[62]

Others offered even more personal and passionate lectures on the
need for parental or adult guidance, as did this Pennsylvania court administrator:

> Any person will want to know why the person will not tell her parents.
> I think this person should tell her parents. . . . And you think that she
> will do this without her parents finding out? I don't see how that can
> happen. . . . I would strongly suggest that you talk to this person and
> tell this person to tell her parents. This is not something that a person
> should be doing as a juvenile without consulting someone who knows.
> Adoption agencies. If it was a mistake, it was a mistake, it wouldn't
> help having a person make two mistakes. There are some numbers: Ac-
> tion Line for Life (800-848-5683), Birthright, family planning clinic,
> family service agency (622-2515), Concern (800-562-1457). . . . I
> would strongly counsel this person into finding an out before resorting
> to that. As a father, I'm telling you. There's a lot of people that can help
> before that decision is made. The person better know everything.[63]

While some court employees shared their own opinions about abortion or avoiding parental involvement, others spoke on behalf of judges.
One Tennessee court employee said, "I don't know that that is even
possible. I know it would not be possible with our judge. He wouldn't

even sign for a juvenile to get married, even with parental permission. So I don't think he would sign for that."[64]

The one court advocate in Tennessee who made notable errors in conveying details about the bypass process also made discouraging comments about the prospects of securing a waiver of consent from some judges: "Some of the smaller counties, some of the judges in the smaller counties sometimes do not want to do that. I'm not saying they won't do it, but they don't like to do it, so it might be easier to get the judge in some of the larger cities where the abortion is going to be performed to do it."[65]

Some judges themselves affirmed the above-cited speculation about judicial attitudes. In one case, a woman in a Tennessee judge's office attempted to get information about the bypass process from the judge but did not succeed. She explained that she gave the judge a note asking him for information, "but he hasn't answered it yet. I think that's something hard for him to do."[66] After we called back several times and still failed to get an answer, the woman ultimately put the judge on the line, at which time her speculations about his reluctance were borne out. Taking a notably severe and insistent tone, the judge demanded the name and location of the caller, saying, "You're going to answer my questions, Ma'am. . . . There's going to be a whole lot of personal information requested if you're asking for an abortion."[67] The conversation then proceeded in this fashion:

R: I'm just trying to find out information.

J:. . . . I'm not going to sit here and tell you all about that information on the phone. I'm just not. You can go to juvenile court and request the documents that are required. I'm not going to talk to you and tell you the whole scoop on the phone. You need to talk to a lawyer.

R: So this whole process, would it take a long time?

J: I didn't say that. It wouldn't necessarily take a long time. You need to come to the clerk's office to request those documents, and they'll give them to you.

R: You mentioned needing a lawyer?

J: Well the forms we have from the state have a place for a lawyer to sign.

R: So a girl, would she have to pay for that?

J: See, you're asking a whole bunch of questions that you're asking on the phone, and I'm not going to get into the whole scoop on the phone.

That's not what I do. If she wants to do this she has to come down here.[68]

Another notable exchange emerged after an initially responsive woman, this time in a judge's chambers in Pennsylvania, sought to learn about the bypass process. "I've never been asked that question. I'd like to ask one of the judges about that. . . . Why don't you call back," she said.[69] When we did, she reported that she had talked to the judge. "[H]e gave me a statement which I'm going to read. The statement says, 'This court will respond to an application filed for any matters in accordance with the law and rules of civil procedure.' So as long as the proper paperwork is filed, the judge would at least review it."[70] She proceeded to explain, however, that she did not have the proper paperwork. She was also unsure where the paperwork could be obtained or whether a lawyer would be provided to assist. But she said, "If you can't draw up the paperwork yourself, a lawyer might be able to help. . . . I talked to [the] judge, and he said we've not had this incident. He said that you should try to call Central Pennsylvania Legal Services, 800-932-0356. Tell the secretary there that [the] judge requested that you call [them]."[71] After some additional pressing to obtain further information, the woman put the judge on the phone:

> We need your phone number and name. We really can't handle this without that. I don't intend to handle it. I am going to recuse it. Do you know what that means? I'm not going to handle the case. I'm going to hand it over to the AOPC, the Administrative Office of the Pennsylvania Courts, and they'll find a judge who will handle it. We're going to research it. I know about this law, but I don't know the law specifically. I personally won't handle it. I don't know if [the other judge] will. I'll recuse it. But I have to have some information from you. I'll have to conduct a procedure to see whether we can conduct a proceeding. We'll do what we can. We'll check. But we need to contact you. . . . I don't like doing stuff secretly. That's not the nature of our legal system. Our legal system has rights, and people are supposed to know when their rights are infringed. . . . They want me to authorize this kind of procedure. I took an oath to uphold the law. And I will.[72]

The judge did not clearly identify to whom he was referring when saying "people are supposed to know when their rights are infringed."

However, given his reservations about secrecy, his comments about recusal, and his harsh tone, it is reasonable to conclude that his concern lay not as much with the rights of a pregnant minor as with the rights of the minor's parents.

Conclusion

Some 51 percent of the courts in Alabama, Pennsylvania, and Tennessee proved absolutely or materially ignorant of their responsibilities under their states' judicial bypass provisions. The deficiencies in Alabama and Pennsylvania were present despite the fact that the laws in those states had been in effect for some time when this study was conducted.[73] In Tennessee, the deficiencies existed despite the fact that 96 percent of that state's courts had recently and explicitly acknowledged their responsibility under the law.[74]

Courts should be able to rehearse relevant details of the bypass process when queried. When agents of the court deny the existence of such a process or propose means of skirting the involvement mandate, such as traveling to another state, they transparently violate any reasonable expectation about how the bypass process will function.

The failure of respondents to communicate information about the availability and terms of legal representation is an extremely serious matter. If a minor were to confront court personnel who confess ignorance about the bypass process, she would have every reason to be discouraged about the prospects of continuing pursuit of a bypass. But a minor who knows she is going to get an attorney is very likely to have confidence that her quest to obtain a hearing will be successful, even if court personnel prove otherwise uninformed. Indeed, conveyance of information about court-appointed counsel is by itself enough to overcome most other errors and omissions that might be made by respondents.[75] Failure to convey this information makes it appear that the minor without the wherewithal to find and hire an attorney would have to navigate the bypass route on her own. This is unacceptable. At the very least, a minor is entitled to know that there are circumstances under which she will receive court-appointed counsel and what those circumstances are.

Even if a minor secures the services of a private attorney in the face of misinformation about what she is entitled to receive, this still runs counter to our conception of how the bypass process will work. The state has no less failed in carrying out its obligation simply because it has encountered a minor with means sufficient to overcome that failure.

Court personnel who made referrals to abortion clinics, crisis pregnancy centers, Catholic Charities, the health department, and so forth without knowing whether those referrals would prove useful often did so with good intentions. These intentions notwithstanding, in most cases these recommendations led to dead ends. Even in the fortuitous instance when a blind referral leads to discovery of accurate information about obtaining a bypass, this accident should not engender confidence in the process. Consider that while most abortion clinics in Alabama, Pennsylvania, and Tennessee are familiar with the bypass option, their familiarity is typically limited to the procedures in the counties where they are located.[76] Thus, while a minor may discover useful information when she contacts an abortion provider or family planning organization, she might well be directed to the juvenile court system in a county other than her own, left unaware of her entitlement to file a petition in her home county.

Moreover, even if a minor were to find her way to a bypass hearing in her own county by following the blind recommendation to contact an outside agency, that outcome should not lead us to think that the law is functioning properly. We are entitled to expect that those charged with implementing government regulations will be able to do so.[77] A court that offers a blind recommendation fails to discharge its responsibility and simply shifts its responsibility elsewhere. This failure is not mitigated by the consequent action of the regulated party or the purely voluntary behavior of private citizens and non-state institutions. These cannot be seen as surrogates for a well-functioning government.

Not all information about the bypass process is of equal value in the initial quest to obtain a hearing, and we have seen cases of immaterial errors and omissions. However, it is not enough for courts to merely keep the door to the bypass route unlocked or slightly ajar, allowing entry only if the minor secures her own attorney, travels to another county, or creates a waiver petition by researching the local rules. It is all well and good for courts to acknowledge that the state has crafted an avenue for minors to petition for a bypass of parental involvement. But access to a bypass must be reasonably achievable and unimpeded by the court's miscommunications about the law.

The comments that betray personal or political bias against abortion

or the bypass option were made in the context of otherwise unacceptable responses, but they nonetheless magnify the impropriety of the interaction. It is one thing to be told that there is no such thing as a bypass and another to have this information accompanied by an angry or
hyperbolic lecture from a judge or court administrator. The chances of a
minor overcoming polite ignorance would seem to be greater than those
of overcoming bombastic incompetence. Moreover, these comments
provide a window into the real-life difficulties of implementing policy
with recalcitrant actors.

The judicial bypass is supposed to protect against the acknowledged
ills of the parental veto. But the palatability of the bypass compromise
depends on the nature of the material reality that purports to instantiate
it, and in this chapter we have seen that those charged with implementing the compromise are very often wholly incapable of doing so.

5

Misconduct

A possibility always exists, of course, that the legitimate objectives
of any law or legislative program may be subverted by conscious
design or lax enforcement.
—Chief Justice Warren Burger, *Tilton v. Richardson*[1]

We have seen that ignorance impedes access to the bypass
route. But barriers exist even when officials are largely aware of their
responsibilities. In this chapter I address two such barriers: administrative malfunctions and defiance of the law.

Malfunction

Minors who seek to waive parental involvement face obvious time constraints. The window for obtaining an abortion is narrow. It begins with
knowledge of pregnancy, which often comes weeks after conception,
and, according to the American Academy of Pediatrics, "[t]eenagers are
twice as likely as adults to delay the diagnosis of first-trimester pregnancy."[2] For practical reasons, the window for obtaining an abortion
without parental knowledge may all but close with the onset of the
second trimester. Most obviously, the longer it takes to secure an abortion, the more likely it is that parents will discover their daughter's pregnancy. Furthermore, later-term abortions pose greater health risks, risks
that may prevent a minor from having an abortion or that may influence judicial decision-making concerning whether an abortion serves a
minor's best interest.[3] Additionally, a minor whose pregnancy has advanced beyond the first term may confront the challenge of locating a
clinic that performs second-trimester abortions[4] or may find the abortion to be prohibitively expensive.[5]

Recognizing these time pressures, the Supreme Court has held that bypass proceedings "must assure that a resolution of the issue, and any appeals that may follow, will be completed with . . . sufficient expedition to provide an effective opportunity for an abortion to be obtained."[6] Following this directive, state legislatures have included statutory language that demands expedited handling of bypass petitions. As discussed in Chapter 2, both Alabama and Pennsylvania require trial courts to rule within three business days of the time the petition is filed.[7] Tennessee mandates that the juvenile court reach its decision "within forty-eight (48) hours of the time of application."[8] With only minor linguistic variation, the laws in Alabama, Pennsylvania, and Tennessee stipulate that court proceedings shall be given such precedence over other pending matters as is necessary to ensure that the court may reach a decision promptly.[9]

Though attentive to time pressures once a petition has been filed, these statutes do not address how quickly courts or court advocates must respond to those seeking information to file a petition. But it is clearly not enough that courts handle the hearing itself within a narrow timeframe; it also matters how promptly minors can navigate the bypass process, and that, in turn, depends on how quickly they can obtain information from authorized parties.

It is easy to idealize the functioning of the judicial bureaucracy, to suppose a seamless translation of word into action. So, we might imagine, if the state allows a minor to petition a court for a waiver of parental involvement, the minor will be able to pick up the phone, make one or two calls, and reach someone who will tell her what to do. As we have already seen, this is far from the case. In fact, a minor is fairly likely to reach someone who does not know what to do. And, as we shall see below, access to potentially helpful parties may be impeded by such things as court employees who are in court, out to lunch, or otherwise away from their desks; court advocates who are unavailable due to meetings, vacation, or sick leave; busy signals, voicemail recordings, and so forth. Furthermore, delay is sometimes caused by judicial gatekeepers who may well send minors off in search of wild geese.

The remainder of this section exposes these administrative challenges, beginning with the hurdle of reaching a knowledgeable court employee in a reasonable time period and without repeated phone calls. I then turn to bureaucratic inefficiencies that hamper operation of the Tennessee court advocate system.

Courts

In Chapter 3, I presented court employee responses that coincide with our expectations concerning the provision of information. Specifically, we found court employees in thirty-four of Alabama's sixty-seven counties, sixteen of Pennsylvania's sixty judicial districts, and forty-four of Tennessee's ninety-five counties who seemed prepared to implement the bypass process in an appropriate manner.[10] To ascertain the ease with which a minor would gain access to these employees, we tracked the number of calls placed during our inquiries. We found that access to these officials was often problematic.

It would be easy to artificially inflate the number of phone calls by, for example, calling outside of business hours or redialing the same number immediately after encountering a busy signal. To avoid this, I only count calls placed to the same number if those calls were placed more than thirty minutes apart, unless we were otherwise directed by a respondent to call back at a particular time. In addition, and again unless otherwise directed, I count no more than three calls to the same number in a single day. We only made calls during regular business hours, and the counts presented below do not include any initial calls one might make to directory information. I do, however, count calls made in those instances when we came across a wrong number or a number that was out of service, provided that we obtained the number through official channels.

Here is an example of a case from Tennessee in which it took six calls over a period of two days to get an appropriate response from the court:

Tuesday, May 21, 2002, 2:05 P.M. (CST): *Calling the juvenile court*
Court Employee (CE): Juvenile Clerk.
Researcher (R): I'm calling to find out how a girl who's not eighteen who wants an abortion can get a judge's permission to avoid telling her parents.
CE: Hon, I don't know, you probably need to come in. I don't think the judge would do that, I don't think he would, un un. Let me get your name and number.
R: Can I call back?
CE: Well, uh, is it a juvenile or what?
R: Excuse me?

CE: How old are you? . . .

R: I'm just trying to get information about this.

CE: Let me give you this number, hold on a minute and I'll get a number for you to call upstairs, but hold on I'm going to check first. [pause] Ma'am, you need to come up here and talk to someone. . . . The lady you can talk to is Ms. Burgess.[11]

Tuesday, May 21, 2002, 2:10 P.M. (CST): *Calling Ms. Burgess*
No answer.

Wednesday, May 22, 2002, 1:44 P.M. (CST): *Calling Ms. Burgess*
CE: Juvenile services.

R: May I speak with Ms. Burgess?

CE: She's not in. She'll be back in about twenty minutes.

Wednesday, May 22, 2002, 2:13 P.M. (CST): *Calling Ms. Burgess*
CE: Juvenile services.

R: May I speak with Ms. Burgess?

CE: She hasn't got back yet. Do you want her to call you back?

R: No, that's okay.

CE: Try back in about fifteen more minutes.

R: Okay.

Wednesday, May 22, 2002, 2:50 P.M. (CST): *Calling Ms. Burgess*
CE: Juvenile services.

R: May I speak with Ms. Burgess?

CE: She'll be back in about fifteen more minutes.

Wednesday, May 22, 2002, 3:10 P.M. (CST): *Calling Ms. Burgess*
CE: Juvenile services.

R: May I speak with Ms. Burgess?

CE: This is she.

R: I called yesterday to find out how a girl who's not eighteen who wants an abortion can get a judge's permission to avoid telling her parents.

CE: Hang on one second, I have a brochure on that, okay? Okay. There is a 1-800 number. It's 1-800-435-7495. And they will actually, the court does, the juvenile court judge will hear the case, but it goes through the Department of Children's Services and they facilitate it. There will be an advocate for you.

Were a minor to receive this response, she would still have to make another call to the DCS hotline to get the advocate's number and then place at least one phone call, and possibly many more, to ultimately reach the named advocate. Nevertheless, we had some reason to believe that persistence would pay off as the courthouse was generally helpful during the initial call.

The same cannot be said of the following attempt to reach an Alabama juvenile court, which took ten calls on four separate days:

Wednesday, October 10, 2001, 9:43 A.M. (CST): *Calling the juvenile court*
No answer.

Wednesday, October 10, 2001, 10:42 A.M. (CST): *Calling the juvenile court*
No answer.

Friday, October 12, 2001, 12:25 P.M. (CST): *Calling the juvenile court*
No answer.

Friday, October 12, 2001, 2:03 P.M. (CST): *Calling the juvenile court*
No answer.

Monday, October 15, 2001, 12:13 P.M. (CST): *Calling the juvenile court*
No answer.

After five failed attempts and no voicemail guidance, we located a second phone number for this juvenile court. The following calls were placed to that second number:

Monday, October 15, 2001, 12:15 P.M. (CST): *Calling the juvenile court*
Voicemail: We are not here right now. If you would like to leave a message . . . press two.

Monday, October 15, 2001, 1:30 P.M. (CST): *Calling the juvenile court*
Voicemail: We are not here right now. If you would like to leave a message . . . press two.

Wednesday, October 17, 2001, 9:17 A.M. (CST): *Calling the juvenile court*
Busy signal.

Wednesday, October 17, 2001, 9:58 A.M. (CST): *Calling the juvenile court*
Busy signal.

Wednesday, October 17, 2001, 11:00 A.M. (CST): *Calling the juvenile court*
CE: Juvenile Court.
R: I'm calling to find out how a girl who's not eighteen who wants an abortion can get a judge's permission to avoid telling her parents.
CE: You are asking to be, hold on one second. . . . [pause] The best-case scenario is a petition is filed, a guardian ad litem is appointed, an attorney. At that point you're going to have to do it through the court. This is confidential. That individual would have to come up to the office and we'd have to start the process. . . .

Consider as well another protracted effort to gain information from a court in Alabama. Here it took twelve calls and a substantial runaround before we came full circle back to where we had begun:

Wednesday, October 10, 2001, 10:52 A.M. (CST): *Calling the juvenile court*
Voicemail: You have reached the . . . juvenile courthouse. We're sorry that we cannot answer the phone. To speak to Ms. Rinehart, call xxx-xxxx; to speak to Mr. Vinchur, call xxx-xxxx; to speak to Ms. Falbo, call xxx-xxxx.

Wednesday, October 10, 11:22 A.M. (CST): *Calling the juvenile court*
Voicemail (same as above).

Wednesday, October 10, 2001, 11:23 A.M. (CST): *Calling Ms. Rinehart*
Voicemail.

Wednesday, October 10, 2001, 11:26 A.M. (CST): *Calling Ms. Falbo*
Voicemail.

Wednesday, October 10, 2001, 11:28 A.M. (CST): *Calling Mr. Vinchur*
Voicemail.

Thursday, October 11, 2001, 3:38 P.M. (CST): *Calling the juvenile court*
Voicemail.

Thursday, October 11, 2001, 3:39 P.M. (CST): *Calling Ms. Falbo*
No answer.

Thursday, October 11, 2001, 3:39 P.M. (CST): *Calling Mr. Vinchur*
CE: Juvenile Court.
R: I'm calling to find out how a girl who's not eighteen who wants an abortion can get a judge's permission to avoid telling her parents.
CE: You'd have to talk to a lawyer or somebody in Probate Court.
R: Do you have a number?
CE: Call Judge Basow, xxx-xxxx. Probate Court.

Thursday, October 11, 2001, 3:43 P.M. (CST): *Calling Judge Basow*
Judge: County courthouse.
R: May I speak with Judge Basow?
J: This is she.
R: I'm calling to find out how a girl who's not eighteen who wants an abortion can get a judge's permission to avoid telling her parents.
J: That's through circuit court. Judge Miller.

Thursday, October 11, 2001, 3:46 P.M. (CST): *Calling Judge Miller*
CE: Circuit Court.
R: I'm calling to find out how a girl who's not eighteen who wants an abortion can get a judge's permission to avoid telling her parents.
CE: That actually has to go through the juvenile court, I can give you the number.
R: I already called there, and they said to call Judge Basow, and she said to call you.
CE: Well it doesn't happen that often, but it goes through juvenile court. . . . Let me call them, and why don't you call me back in ten minutes.

Thursday, October 11, 2001, 4:08 P.M. (CST): *Calling Judge Miller*
R: Hi, I called a little while ago.
CE: I talked with the juvenile officer. His name is Mr. Vinchur. I think you already have their number. But it's xxx-xxxx.
R: Thank you.

Thursday, October 11, 2001, 4:12 P.M. (CST): *Calling juvenile court number*
CE: This is Mr. Vinchur.

R: I spoke with you earlier. I'm still trying to find out how a girl who's not eighteen who wants an abortion can get a judge's permission to avoid telling her parents.

CE: That's what I'm reading up on. . . . This is all new to me. I went and talked to the judge, what I'm trying to do right now is read. A minor who elects not to seek or does not or cannot for any reason obtain consent from either of her parents or legal guardian may petition, on her own behalf, the juvenile court, or the court of equal standing, in the county in which the minor resides or in the county in which the abortion is to be performed for a waiver of the consent requirement of this chapter. So first of all she would need a waiver of consent. . . .[12]

The number of phone calls required to reach a court official is a useful but imperfect proxy for measuring the magnitude of the barrier to information. For example, in one of the larger counties in Alabama, it only took three phone calls to elicit accurate information. However, our first contact with the juvenile court indicated that the person who handles bypass inquiries would be unavailable for a week and that no one else could provide information about the process.[13]

Overall, and putting aside the number of days it may have taken to reach a helpful official, it took five calls to reach one of Pennsylvania's willing and able courts, and fewer to reach the remaining fifteen. For Alabama, it took five or more calls to reach nine of thirty-four such courts, and in more than half of these instances it took between seven and twelve calls to reach someone who offered an appropriate response to our query. We also placed at least five calls to reach thirteen of Tennessee's forty-four prepared courts. Indeed, in six of these cases, we placed between eight and seventeen calls.

Court Advocates

As noted previously, Tennessee has specifically made it someone's job to guide minors through the bypass process. There is even an 800 number to reach the escort service and a brochure that lists direct numbers for the escorts themselves. Nevertheless, we repeatedly encountered difficulties in our efforts to reach DCS advocates.

Often, the reasons for delays in reaching advocates mirrored those encountered in attempts to contact court employees (busy signals, voicemails, etc.). Incorrect or outdated information in the DCS brochure or provided by the toll-free hotline also contributed to some of these delays. Additionally, because most advocates serve multiple counties and hence have multiple offices, they could not always be tracked down easily.

The following effort to reach an advocate illustrates a combination of obstacles that can create a considerable delay in accessing information:

Friday, June 14, 2002, 3:16 P.M. (EST): *Calling DCS advocate Linda Cornett*

DCS: Children's Services.

R: May I speak with Linda Cornett?

DCS: Hold on a moment. It doesn't look like she's here. Would you like me to take a message?

R: I'll call back. Do you know when she might be in?

DCS: I don't really know who she is, so I don't know.

Monday, June 17, 2002, 3:11 P.M. (EST): *Calling DCS advocate Linda Cornett*

DCS: Children's Services.

R: May I speak with Linda Cornett?

DCS: I don't believe she's in this office. Hold on. Ma'am, you can try her at xxx-xxxx. She's based in Centerville. She's sometimes in this office, but mostly she's in the Centerville office.

Monday, June 17, 2002, 3:12 P.M. (EST): *Calling DCS advocate Linda Cornett in the Centerville office*

DCS: Children's Services.

R: May I speak with Linda Cornett?

DCS: Linda is in Hampton County today.

R: Do you know when she'll be in?

DCS: She should be in tomorrow.

Tuesday, June 18, 2002, 3:00 P.M. (EST): *Calling DCS advocate Linda Cornett in the Centerville office*

DCS: Children's Services.

R: May I speak with Linda Cornett?

DCS: Hold on. [transfer]

CA: This is Linda.

R: I'm calling to find out how a girl who's not eighteen who wants an abortion can get a judge's permission to avoid telling her parents.

DCS: Okay, well I'm not the person who does that anymore, her name is Pam Bodenhorn. Pam would go over everything. . . . Her number is xxx-xxxx.

Tuesday, June 18, 2002, 3:02 P.M. (EST): *Calling DCS advocate Pam Bodenhorn in the Centerville office*
Voicemail: You've reached the office of Pam Bodenhorn. Please leave a message, and I'll get back to you.

Wednesday, June 19, 2002, 3:07 P.M. (EST): *Calling DCS advocate Pam Bodenhorn in the Centerville office*
Voicemail (same as above).

Wednesday, June 19, 2002, 4:27 P.M. (EST): *Calling DCS advocate Pam Bodenhorn in the Centerville office*
Voicemail (same as above).

Thursday, June 20, 2002, 3:37 P.M. (EST): *Calling DCS advocate Pam Bodenhorn in the Centerville office*
Voicemail (same as above).

Thursday, June 20, 2002, 3:38 P.M. (EST): *Calling the main number for the Centerville office*

DCS: Children's Services.

R: I'm calling for Pam Bodenhorn, but I've called her several times and have only gotten her voicemail. Do you know if she's around?

DCS: She just passed me with her phone, so I don't know what the problem is.

R: So she's there?

DCS: She just went into someone else's office. Do you want me to take a message?

R: No, I'll call back.

Thursday, June 20, 2002, 4:53 P.M. (EST): *Calling DCS advocate Pam Bodenhorn in the Centerville office*
CA: This is Pam . . .

Pam went on, after some initial stumbling and hesitation, to provide the appropriate information on how to pursue the waiver route. But arriving at this information took ten calls placed on five separate days.

Part of the delay in this case—a total of four calls—came as a result of a DCS brochure that had not been updated to reflect the change in the designated advocate. But at least DCS had in fact designated a new advocate to replace the former advocate named on the brochure. We did sometimes find that counties were simply not served by court advocates. In these cases, the brochure and hotline referred us to former DCS employees, current DCS employees who no longer serve as advocates, or advocates who were unavailable. In each of these cases, our efforts to gain adequate assistance from DCS failed.

In one case, upon calling the number for a designated advocate and learning that the advocate was unavailable due to extended sick leave, we posed our standard inquiry to the DCS employee who answered the phone. We received this response: "You've got an underage child wanting to get an abortion? I don't know if you can do that lawfully. Hold on a second, let me ask. . . . Our department is not allowed to advise on abortion. You'll have to call the Health Department."[14]

In a second case, after seven unanswered calls placed to an advocate, we sought information from each of the local DCS offices that operate in the counties served by that advocate. These offices could provide no information about the waiver option or the role of the advocate.

In a third case, after repeatedly failing to reach the court advocate, we were transferred to a DCS attorney. The attorney knew about the bypass option and explained that court advocates assist minors through the process. However, his best advice was to contact another county:

> [B]asically, each county is supposed to have a contact person, and we used to have a contact person in [this] county and she retired. So what we're told is what a person has to do at this point is contact a person in the other county, and they could assist because we're the same department, so someone in another county could help.[15]

We received a similar response in a fourth case from a DCS employee who used to function as an advocate. Despite the fact that this employee was referred to in the brochure and by the hotline, she explained, "I'm kind of out of that right now. I don't think they've assigned anybody to take my place."[16] Lacking information on who might assist a minor in the counties she formerly served, this respondent recommended phoning an advocate assigned in another county.

In a fifth case, we were again referred to an advocate in a neighboring county, having been told that the previously designated advocate no longer worked at DCS and had yet to be replaced.

As was our practice, we took the advice we received in these last three cases and called the advocates to whom we had been referred. In two instances, we reached the recommended advocate, but the advocate indicated that she would only handle waivers in her designated counties. In the third instance, we were referred to the recently retired advocate.

The availability of a court advocate system does not alleviate the challenge of actually getting through to an advocate. The brochure distributed by DCS listed contact information for twenty-eight advocates assigned to serve Tennessee's ninety-five counties, but as we have just seen, in five cases covering fourteen counties, we failed to reach the allegedly designated advocate and found no one willing to provide services in those counties. We succeeded in reaching twenty-three advocates who were designated to serve eighty-one counties. As discussed in previous chapters, all but one of these advocates were able to provide satisfactory information. But in eight cases, we succeeded in reaching informed advocates only after placing between five and thirteen calls, not including any calls we made to court personnel who may have referred us to these advocates and employing the same restrictions on counting discussed above.

Defiance

The administrative inefficiencies described above and the ignorance discussed in Chapter 4 largely account for the gap between what we expect from the bypass process and its actual functioning. Yet there are still other factors. In *Judicial Policies: Implementation and Impact*, Bradley C. Canon and Charles A. Johnson identify nonacceptance as a response to court rulings:[17] "Persons who do not accept a judicial policy are likely to engage in behavior designed to defeat the policy or minimize its impact. They will interpret it narrowly, try to avoid implementing it, and refuse or evade its consumption."[18]

Several courts that demonstrated familiarity with parental consent provisions displayed such nonacceptance. In some instances, nonacceptance was manifest not in terms of refusal to comply with legal mandates but in expressions of opposition to abortion similar to those we saw in Chapter 4 made by ignorant respondents. As Canon and Johnson explain, not every nonacceptor will be "in a position to ignore a decision or to refuse completely to comply with it. . . . People may adjust some of their behavioral responses to meet the decision's requirements while they have other, less visible, behavioral responses that may more truly reflect their unwillingness to accept the decision."[19] Consider the following remark made by a woman in a Pennsylvania court administrator's office who obviously knew what to do when queried about the bypass process: "I know this is business, but I can tell you that it's a very stupid thing to do and you'd have to live with it for the rest of your life. Hold on. [pause] The woman you need to talk to is out of the office right now. She'll be back tomorrow."[20]

In other instances, we found nonacceptors who, while possessing sufficient knowledge to implement bypass requirements, appeared ready to ignore or defy the law. We encountered a total of eight such instances in our contacts with county courts—two in Tennessee and six in Alabama. In each, court employees noted the judicial opposition a minor would confront were she to seek to exercise her right to file a petition.

In Tennessee, two court employees indicated that judicial consideration of waiver requests would almost inevitably result in a denial of those requests. According to one of these employees:

> Usually you have to appear before the judge, but, given the circumstances, it's up to the judge's decision. Usually the judge does not sign for a juvenile to have an abortion. . . . That is just something that he chooses not to do. . . . One of the other judges in the surrounding counties may give her consent. But it would be kind of iffy here for the judge to give consent. . . . [I]t's a hard decision for anyone to make, and it is a difficult decision to make; [the judge is] pro-life, and that makes it more difficult for him to sign a consent form.[21]

In the second Tennessee county, a court employee stated unequivocally that the judge would not sign a minor's request to avoid parental involvement in abortion. Asked why the judge would not sign, this employee simply said, "He does not believe in abortion." He further offered this advice for a pregnant minor: "She needs to think about some alternative other than that. A lot of people want to adopt children. In fact, I have two adopted children. [The judge] has an adopted child. There are plenty of people who want to adopt children. So she needs to think of other alternatives."[22]

Several Alabama respondents made comparable remarks about judicial attitudes against abortion or the bypass option. Among these, two recommended that a minor seek her bypass elsewhere because of judicial opposition. One explained that minors have the legal right to file a confidential petition to waive parental consent but said, "I can 100 percent guarantee you that they will not grant [the petition]. The family court judge does not believe it is an issue that should be decided by the court. The judge will not grant it; it's the judge's decision. He will not grant it." Asked whether all the judges in the county would deny a bypass, this court officer replied: "That is correct. That's what we pay them money for—to judge and rule over cases—and the judges here will not allow that proceeding to take place." He further cautioned that if a judge denied a bypass petition, the minor would not be able to file elsewhere: "[T]hey'll have to file it in the county that the [abortion] procedure is done. My judge is going to say 'I will deny it, I don't grant it, so you can't take it in to the other court.' . . . She'll need to find a county that performs the abortion and contact the juvenile office there, and the clinic there. And they'd set up to do it."[23] The juvenile probation officer in a second Alabama county reacted similarly in both conveying judicial hostility to abortion and advising pursuit of a bypass petition elsewhere:

> She has to petition the court, and she has to come to the court and ask for a petition. But I can promise, unless you have some serious medical condition, it won't be granted. My judge is anti-abortion, and he doesn't believe a child should have this done without her parents. You have the *right* to file, and the right to file in your initials; your name won't even be on the petition. But that doesn't mean he will grant it. We had one [case] one time . . . and her doctor advised her to have an abortion for medical reasons, and [the judge] still would not grant it. . . . [D]o you know that if you are attempting to have the abortion in Jefferson County, you can go to Jefferson County to the judge? I know they grant it there. . . . They're going to say, "Do it in your county." But you can have it done there. The odds are real slim here.[24]

In another four counties in Alabama, respondents made clear that judges would not hear petitions. In one, the respondent said that while a minor could file the petition in the county's juvenile court, the judge would transfer the case to the county where the abortion would be performed. "Usually they get transferred up to Montgomery," this respondent explained. "Our judge here usually recuses himself from those types of hearings. He just requests a transfer of venue because he just doesn't do those types of hearings."[25] The change of venue, this respondent further explained, would require that a minor travel to the new venue for the hearing.

Another Alabama respondent said simply, "We don't do that in this county. You'll have to go to Jefferson County to get that done. . . . Our judge doesn't do it; he doesn't believe in it."[26] Mirroring this reply, yet another said:

> We don't do those in this county. My judge says to do it in the county where you're getting the abortion. . . . Whenever we've had people ask us that, most of the people from here they go to Tuscaloosa, the juvenile court there. We don't file those in this county. It says it can be done in the county she lives or in the county where the abortion is to be performed. My judge won't take the case; he said he's not going to get into that here. . . . He has a problem not notifying the parent of it.[27]

Still another Alabama court employee gave this explanation for judicial avoidance of the bypass process:

> You can have it done in the county that you live or in the county that the [abortion] procedure is going to be performed. The judge wants the person to do it in the county that they're going to have [the abortion] done in. . . . [W]e haven't had it done here, 'cause he doesn't want to do it here. It's a small place, and there's a lot of stuff that can arise from that. He wants her to do it in the place where she's going to get the procedure done. . . . It's just that he doesn't want to do it here. He being the judge, he's not going to order something like that to be done.[28]

Echoing court employees in Alabama and Tennessee, some DCS advocates made reference to judicial unwillingness to handle bypass cases. One advocate who accurately described the details of the bypass process said, "We'd go to a judge and see if he's willing to do it, and if not, shop around. They don't have to do it. It's not compulsory. There are judges who do it, but there are many judges that don't believe in it and don't do it." Asked what happens when a judge doesn't "do it," this advocate replied, "Then you have to shop around in the state of Tennessee and see if you can find one."[29]

The following exchange with another advocate further alluded to judicial opposition to the bypass route:

> *CA:* [I]f you want this and you don't want your parents to know, you file a petition in juvenile court, and you can go to any county. . . . I don't think they will, if you want to know the truth, I don't think they'll do it here, but I've never had one, so I don't know for sure. I can give you a name of a person in [another county] who knows what to do. They file a petition for you, and you go to court. This is called a judicial bypass. If you want a lawyer, they'll appoint a lawyer for you; you don't have to pay anything, but if you don't want a lawyer, that's fine. If you're denied, they can appeal it, and it's a real quick situation. What I do is give them a name and number in [another county] because it's a one-day thing and these people do this all the time. . . .
>
> *R:* Is it likely she would get permission?
>
> *CA:* Oh yeah, they do it all the time over there. But the judges up here feel very differently. . . .
>
> *R:* So you don't think the judges here would do it?
>
> *CA:* No. If it's [in one of the counties I serve], I can tell you the judge won't do it. The judge has said he would not want to do it. I had one from another county, and when he found out there that it can be done in [another county], he said, "Good, I don't want to do it." You know in these small rural counties, they feel very strongly about it.[30]

In the above instances, we see indications of nonacceptance of legal mandates that would amount to deliberate judicial defiance of the legal obligation to afford minors access to authorized venues for bypass hearings.[31] This is not to say that all judges must hear bypass petitions regardless of their views about abortion. Where a conflict of interest exists, judicial recusal is not only permissible but may be required. However, there is debate over whether judges may, consistent with codes of judicial conduct, recuse themselves from an entire class of cases. Blanket recusal, whether in bypass hearings or in cases involving such morally charged issues as the death penalty, euthanasia, divorce, and so forth, may signal not simply a conflict of interest but unwillingness to comply with the law. Such wholesale recusal, some legal ethicists argue, amounts to judicial nullification of the law and is therefore improper.[32]

Whatever the resolution of this debate, courts can at the very least handle recusals in a way that respects a minor's entitlement to have her petition heard in the designated venue. In fact, some respondents illustrate how this can be achieved. Consider the following exchange with an Alabama employee:

> *CE:* I talked with our judge, and the procedure is that she needs an attorney. If she cannot afford an attorney, she needs to come in to the juvenile court to fill out an Affidavit of Hardship. All of the procedures are confidential. The affidavit would be given to the judge to approve. Then a judge will appoint an attorney, and then she will need to talk to the attorney to prepare the paperwork. . . .
>
> *R:* I have a couple of other questions about the procedure.
>
> *CE:* I'm probably not going to be able to answer those questions. I got my information from the judge, but he'll probably recuse himself. . . . My judge won't handle that case. He won't handle it.
>
> *R:* Why? . . .
>
> *CE:* [B]ecause he doesn't feel comfortable. I don't know how to answer that question, but he doesn't feel comfortable. . . .
>
> *R:* But someone else will handle it?
>
> *CE:* Yes. Another judge from another county will handle the case.
>
> *R:* In this county?
>
> *CE:* Yes.
>
> *R:* How long will it take?
>
> *CE:* Well to be honest, if they could go and fill out the forms, I have an out-of-town judge coming, that would be this Wednesday. If they can go ahead and get the affidavit prepared, and we'll have someone here on Wednesday to intake the paperwork. And then I will call this judge and ask him how I need to proceed; he may set it for Wednesday, or he may set a separate date. He has a lot of things scheduled this Wednesday, and it may be hard to keep confidentiality down with all the people here on Wednesday. But this judge has done the procedure here for us before.[33]

This response differs from those in which opposition toward abortion or the bypass process leads to unwillingness to ensure the availability of the authorized venue for the disposition of bypass requests. Here, the respondent made it plain that the recused judge would be replaced by another judge. When courts fail to do this and instead place on the minor the charge of traveling to another county in search of a willing judge, that minor may well succeed in her search and successfully file her petition elsewhere. But this possibility does not remedy the fracture created by judges who have abdicated their duty to afford minors their rights to an impartial judicial hearing in their home counties.

Conclusion

There is little that can be done to trace the actual effect on pregnant minors of the ignorance and misconduct we observed in our efforts to gauge access to the bypass route. We can, though, try to place ourselves in the shoes of the pregnant minor in order to envision the consequences of the implementation failures reported here.

Consider first the pregnant teen who has learned from a sister, a friend, a school nurse, an abortion provider, or news reports that there is supposed to be a method in place for securing a waiver of mandated parental involvement. Were this minor to contact her county court and confront, as we did, uninformed, inaccessible, or defiant court personnel, she might justifiably react in ways that undermine the entire point of the bypass compromise.

Imagine, for example, the minor who, on the advice of the court, contacts a crisis pregnancy organization—organizations that, as we have seen, are useless with regard to obtaining a bypass. Imagine further that this advice is accompanied by such statements as "the parents are ruling over her, so a judge can't rule on that"[34] and "I don't think the judge would talk to you about that; I don't think anyone here would talk to you about that."[35] Or suppose the minor is told that she can come read the local rules and figure out how to write a petition[36] or, more simply, is advised to seek an abortion out of state.[37] In each of these cases, a pregnant minor would have good reason to abandon her efforts to pursue the bypass route, an avenue, let us not forget, that is enshrined in state law and blessed by the Supreme Court.

Consider also the minor told by court personnel that she would need to get an attorney, by legal aid that they could not help, or by a lawyer referral service that she would have to pay for counsel. Again, it is not difficult to imagine that a minor might give up her quest for a bypass.

Even in cases where the courts are potentially ready to offer a hearing, their responses could discourage a minor from further pursuit. In the best of circumstances, a minor would have reason to be apprehensive about the prospect of going to court for a hearing. Indeed, Doctor Jane Hodgson, a plaintiff in the Supreme Court case *Hodgson v. Minnesota,* "testified that when her minor patients returned from the court process, 'some of them are wringing wet with perspiration. They're markedly relieved, many of them. They—they dread the court procedure often more than the actual abortion procedure.' "[38] Given this already heightened anxiety, would a minor be likely to persist after a judicial representative says, "I know this is business, but I can tell you that it's a very stupid thing to do and you'd have to live with it for the rest of your life"?[39] Would a minor actually go to the courthouse to fill out papers when no assistance or even basic information is offered over the phone? In the face of such resistance, it would not be surprising if a minor were dissuaded from pursuing a hearing.

That a minor would abandon her efforts for a bypass in the face of these various scenarios is all the more likely given that misinformation or defiant remarks would be coming from authoritative representatives of the judiciary. Information offered from official court personnel holds authoritative sway. Moreover, a minor is unlikely to have the knowledge required to challenge this information or the gumption to persist in the face of resistance. If a court administrator says, "I have the rules right here, and there's nothing on this,"[40] a minor might believe him or her, even if she has heard otherwise.

Were a minor to altogether give up on the possibility of gaining a judicial hearing, she would be left with few good options. She might travel to a nearby state that does not require parental involvement, if one is within reasonable reach.[41] At present, this option is challenging enough, for the distance a minor must travel to such a state may well be substantial. Alabama, for example, is now surrounded by states that require parental involvement, and a minor would have to travel as far as Illinois to find a state that does not impose this mandate. In the future, this option will likely become all the more challenging as states continue to join the ranks of those that have adopted involvement mandates. In addition, both houses of Congress have passed bills to criminally sanction those who help minors obtain abortions out of state if such aid would constitute circumvention of a parental involvement mandate.[42] If this becomes law, a minor who seeks an out-of-state abortion to avoid parental involvement would be forced to make this venture on her own, or she would put on a friend or relative the risk of going to jail.[43]

Perhaps more likely than out-of-state travel, a minor might break down and tell her possibly unsympathetic parents about her pregnancy, believing that she has no realistic alternative. While the unwelcome involvement of parents might turn out to be advantageous for some minors,[44] others might confront abuse upon disclosing their pregnancies[45] or find themselves compelled to carry an unwanted or risky pregnancy to term.[46]

Worse yet, a minor might resort to a self-induced or illegal abortion. It may seem hyperbolic to raise the specter of such a dire outcome, yet the American Medical Association warns of this eventuality.[47]

Short of resorting to such desperate measures or abandoning her quest for a bypass, the determined minor might find herself trying to travel to another county for a hearing. A minor told to contact an abortion clinic might reach one that is ready to assist her through the bypass process, but she would likely discover, as we did, that assistance would only be available in the county where the abortion is performed. Likewise, a minor given a 100 percent guarantee that the judge would deny her petition would, at best, go to another county.

But even in these instances, a minor's efforts might be thwarted. Courts and attorneys willing to handle bypass requests have been known to encourage minors to persist in their home counties, in part out of frustration about judicial unwillingness to implement the law. One Alabama attorney, who has represented several minors in bypass cases, reports:

> We had one that came in, called actually, about two or three weeks ago. She had gone to [one] county to get a waiver of consent, and they said, "we don't do those here." So she called [one of our attorneys, who said,] "You march your butt back up there and tell them they have to do a waiver hearing, according to the statute." And she gave the girl the information on the statute and she gave her the name of an attorney. And [our attorney] called the attorney, who said, "They'll never grant it here."[48]

What happened to this minor is not known. "We expected her to come down," the attorney reported at the end of the story, "but she never showed."[49]

The minor fortunate enough to find her way to a willing county outside her home county still faces the added burden of travel. At minimum, this burden would include additional time and costs and could interfere with the minor's attendance at school or work. For those who only have to travel to a nearby county, the burden would not necessarily be onerous. But the burden for those who have to travel to a distant county might be too substantial to shoulder. In most instances, a minor already has to make two such trips: one to obtain a pregnancy test and abortion counseling and a second for the abortion itself.[50] It might simply be unfeasible to add what would likely be a third trip for a judicial hearing,[51] especially when we consider that the minor may well be without financial resources and trying to conceal her activities from supervising agents, including her parents. As the Supreme Court of New Jersey said when overturning the parental notification statute enacted by its state legislature:

> Although it is irrefutable that burdens and delays already exist in a minor's pursuit of an abortion, we are concerned only with those burdens that are created by state action. In any case, additional impediments added to existing impediments may well prevent the exercise of a fundamental right altogether.[52]

In the event a minor finds herself in a county where a court employee or the DCS advocate proves knowledgeable and willing to help, she still may face the uphill battle of reaching that person. The amount of time, the number of phone calls, and the extent of the goose chase required to reach someone with accurate information may well discourage minors from following through with a bypass request. Under the best circumstances, maneuvering through a bureaucratic web can be daunting, and a minor attempting to navigate such a web hardly finds herself facing the best circumstances. She would almost certainly endeavor to make phone calls covertly, most likely without the ability to leave messages or request a return call. If the minor is in school or holds a job, the window for making calls during regular business hours would be a narrow one. Given the constraints of other activities and the legitimate fear of being discovered, a minor might not have many opportunities to make such calls.

Placing even a single phone call presents a challenge for some minors. The comments offered by the director of a Tennessee abortion clinic and cited in a district court ruling that granted a preliminary injunction against the state's parental consent requirement attest to this challenge:

> Minors will call us, then whisper suddenly, "my mom's home!," and hang up. They will call back, sometimes that day but often a day or two later. The problems are compounded if the calls are long distance. I have had parents of minors call our number because it showed up on their bill. They ask who we are and who called us. We never reveal the name of the caller, but just knowing that someone from the home called our clinic is enough to give the minor away. Minors frequently call from a pay phone or a friend's house. They also miss appointments without calling until a few days later, telling us they could not get to a phone safely to cancel.[53]

The New Jersey Supreme Court is among those that have given weight to the challenges minors face when making covert phone calls: "In the first instance, a young woman must find a way to place the initial call to the courthouse to begin the waiver process. Next, if she chooses to have an attorney, as provided by the Act, she must find a time when she can take his or her telephone call without the knowledge of her parents or siblings."[54]

If making one call or two poses problems, how would a minor fare after making five, six, or sixteen calls without gaining information? What would she do upon learning that she must wait a week before talking to someone who is familiar with the bypass process? The persistent minor would, we presume, persist, and the cautious and persistent minor would persevere without being discovered by her parents. At best, though, the result would be mounting delay.[55] But this outcome imagines a minor who has the wherewithal to endure. Absent such wherewithal, it is easy to imagine that, faced with the need to repeat phone calls, unanswered inquiries, and the like, a minor might relinquish her efforts to secure a bypass or be discovered along the way.

In Chapter 3, I include some models of appropriate implementation of the bypass process, at least at the stage of gaining access. In Chapters 4 and 5, I seek to undermine the assumption that these earlier discussed cases constitute the norm. They do not. The bypass compromise is not borne out in Platonic instantiation. Rather, it is served up as a Kafkaesque plate of ignorance, with a side of bureaucratic bumbling and a smattering of ideological resistance.

PART III

The Judicial Pulpit

6

Judgment Day

In Chapters 3 to 5 in Part II, I explore the point of entry into the bypass route. In Chapters 6 and 7 in Part III, I examine in detail two distinctive practices that have emerged in some courtrooms. Here I take up the judicial command that minors receive counseling from a pro-life Christian ministry. Then I consider the practice of appointing an attorney to represent the interests of the unborn at bypass hearings. It is not my intention to suggest that these two case studies exemplify widespread judicial practices. Instead, the cases reveal the considerable leeway that judges have in implementing involvement provisions, as well as the consequences minors face when judges take advantage of this latitude.

Judicial Discretion

States that wish to require parental consent for abortion can find in Supreme Court precedent language for constructing a constitutionally sound regulation. As discussed, this language includes two standards for determining when waivers must be granted. Judges must waive the consent requirement when a minor is "mature enough and well enough informed" to make the abortion decision on her own or when the abortion "would be in her best interests."[1]

What states will not find in Court rulings is specific language delineating what counts as "mature enough," "well enough informed," and "best interests." As outlined in Chapter 2, the Court has said little about these matters, except that the nature of the abortion decision requires case-by-case analysis of waiver petitions.[2] This lack of specificity is not unique to the language of parental involvement rulings, of course; it is common of appellate court rulings, which typically leave space for lower court judges to use their own judgment and discretion.[3] And, to be sure, some amount of flexibility and discretion fits with our view of law in general and the bypass process in particular.

Still, some have criticized this lack of specificity and the resulting latitude accorded judges.[4] In a study of the application of Michigan's bypass process, Suellyn Scarnecchia and Julie Kunce Field fault the Court for having "failed to provide any rationale for leaving such a significant decision to the discretion of state trial judges."[5] They further argue that, "[r]egarding a highly emotional, political, and moral decision like abortion, each judge is likely to have established personal beliefs. Broad discretion under the [Michigan parental consent] Act opens the door to the conscious or unconscious expression of those personal beliefs by the judge."[6] This, in turn, creates "the risk that judges will simply substitute their own moral choice for that of the teenager."[7]

Legal scholars are not alone in cautioning against the ramifications of broad judicial discretion in bypass proceedings. Among the cautionary are Supreme Court justices. Justice John Paul Stevens questioned the indeterminacy of the best-interest standard in his concurrence in *Bellotti II,* suggesting that its application by judges would inevitably impose personal and societal values on minors.[8] Building on Stevens's comments, Justice Thurgood Marshall took aim at the ambiguity of bypass standards, arguing in *Hodgson v. Minnesota* against the constitutionality of a Minnesota two-parent notification requirement:

> The constitutional defects in any provision allowing someone to veto a woman's abortion decision are exacerbated by the vagueness of the standards contained in this statute. The statute gives no guidance on how a judge is to determine whether a minor is sufficiently "mature" and "capable" to make the decision on her own. . . . The statute similarly is silent as to how a judge is to determine whether an abortion without parental notification would serve an immature minor's "best interests." . . . Is the judge expected to know more about the woman's medical needs or psychological makeup than her doctor? Should he consider the woman's financial and emotional status to determine the quality of life the woman and her future child would enjoy in this world? Neither the record nor the Court answers such questions. As Justice Stevens wrote in *Bellotti II,* the best interest standard "provides little real guidance to the judge, and his decision must necessarily reflect personal and societal values and mores whose enforcement upon the minor—particularly when contrary to her own informed and reason-

able decision—is fundamentally at odds with privacy interests underlying the constitutional protection afforded to her decision." . . . It is difficult to conceive of any reason, aside from a judge's personal opposition to abortion, that would justify finding that an immature woman's best interests would be served by forcing her to endure pregnancy and childbirth against her will.[9]

Justice David Souter, while serving as a New Hampshire trial court judge, also warned that personal beliefs would come into play in bypass cases. Writing in 1981 on behalf of New Hampshire Superior Court judges and directing his comments to the state legislature, which was in the midst of considering passage of a parental involvement requirement, Souter made a case against legislation that would involve judges in the abortion decisions of pregnant teens. Referring to the criticism of the judiciary that "has characterized judicial activity in the application of constitutional standards as no more than imposition of individual judges' views in the guise of applying constitutional terms of great generality," Souter argued that the bypass process "would force the Superior Court to engage in just such acts of unfettered personal choice."[10] The legislation, Souter asserted,

> would express a decision by society, speaking through the Legislature, to leave it to an individual justice of this court to make fundamental moral decisions about the interests of other people without any standards to guide the individual judge. Judges are professionally qualified to apply rules and stated norms, but the provision in question would enact no rule to be applied and would express no norm. In the place of a rule or a norm there would be left only the individual judge's principles and predilections.[11]

Souter further expressed concern about "the necessarily moral character of such choice and the resulting disparity of responses to requests that judicial discretion be exercised":[12]

> As you would expect, there are some judges who believe abortion under the circumstances contemplated by the bill is morally wrong, who could not in conscience issue an order requiring an abortion to be performed. There are others who believe what may be thought to be in the "best interests" of the pregnant minor is itself just as necessarily a moral as a

social question, upon which a judge may not morally speak for another human being, whatever may be the judge's own personal opinion about the morality of abortion. Judges in each category would be obligated to indicate that they could not exercise their power in favor of authorizing abortions to be performed on immature pregnant minors. The inevitable result would be required shopping for judges who would entertain such cases. In other words, a principled and consistent application of the quoted provision would be impossible.[13]

Justices Stevens, Marshall, and Souter predicted that views on abortion would inevitably shape judicial decisions about whether to hear bypass petitions and whether to grant such requests. They anticipated the challenge of gaining consistency in the application of standards, the challenge of getting judges who would, in good conscience, be able to preside over bypass hearings, and the challenge judges face in setting aside their personal preferences and predilections. What these justices may not have foreseen, or at least did not foretell, are some of the brazen acts of political and ideological will that have occurred in the bypass process, acts in which judges structure bypass proceedings and the evidence presented so that they can communicate and impose their own personal views in a calculated effort to persuade minors to reject abortion.

Pro-Life Christian Counseling

One of these practices has shown up in courthouses in three Alabama counties.[14] Interviews I conducted with seventeen people who have participated in bypass hearings, as well as information I obtained in the course of surveying county courts, indicate that at least four judges who preside over bypass hearings have required minors to obtain pro-life counseling from a religiously inspired crisis pregnancy center called Sav-A-Life.[15] The absence of such counseling, these judges claim, provides grounds for concluding that a minor is insufficiently informed about abortion to warrant a bypass. Knowledgeable testimony about the risks and consequences of abortion and alternatives to the termination of one's pregnancy is not taken to be sufficient to establish informedness; counseling offered by someone who stands against abortion is considered indispensable.[16]

"Did You Go to Sav-A-Life?"

Confirmation that judges have adopted this requirement comes from several sources, most notably the judges themselves. One judge mentioned Sav-A-Life when describing the basis for his bypass decisions:

> There are several factors involved, there are agencies that need to be involved to counsel with and talk with this person. They used to be called Sav-A-Life, maybe it's the same now. She has to talk to them about what her options are. There is a hearing that has to be conducted; the burden is on her to prove that she has considered medical, emotional, psychological issues and a reason that her parents should not be involved in the decision.[17]

Another judge explained why he and a judge serving in the same county mandate pro-life counseling: "[We] will want [the minors] to have been to Sav-A-Life to see what there is to help them make the right decision."[18] Upon being asked whether a minor must receive Sav-A-Life counseling to prove informedness, this judge further said, "I would say yes, but normally rather than simply deny, when that's happened in the past I've said, 'Go to Sav-A-Life,' and the girl did go to Sav-A-Life, and I granted the waiver. But they know we're going to ask that, so they've been to Sav-A-Life before the hearing."[19]

As this judge indicated, the pro-life counseling requirement has become routine in some courthouses. Minors typically learn about the requirement prior to the hearing from intake officers and court-appointed attorneys. Even attorneys who question the legality of compulsory pro-life counseling inform minors of this mandate.[20] As one attorney explained, some juvenile court judges "want to make sure [the minor] has spoken with pro-life agencies. That is a requirement, not an option. . . . Intake will send [the minor] to a pro-life agency, because they know the judges will want it."[21] This attorney suggested that the demand for pro-life counseling might be inconsistent with higher court rulings but explained that the existence of higher court rulings and even the trial judge's familiarity with those rulings "doesn't change the reality that if that girl doesn't go to a pro-life agency before coming to that courtroom, she's not going to get her waiver. If intake doesn't send her, I will."[22]

While judges do not appear to require written documentation of visits to pro-life organizations, testimony about these visits comes out during questioning. Describing the conduct of bypass hearings, one judge indicated how lawyers question minors about pro-life counseling:

> Her lawyer will generally ask her, "What have you done? Did you go to Sav-A-Life? Have you considered the alternatives to abortion? Have you talked with any knowledgeable adults? Have you made your plans about what you'll do if there are complications? Where are you going stay afterwards? What are you going to do if suddenly you have to go the hospital? Did you have any kind of sex education? Have you heard both sides of the story, have you heard the pro-choice side and the pro-life side?" So questions are to show that she's informed.[23]

Judges who have conditioned the grant of a waiver request on the receipt of Sav-A-Life counseling ostensibly rely on the first prong of the bypass standard.[24] They argue that pro-life counseling is essential for accomplishing the goal of exposing minors to a balanced and complete perspective on the abortion debate. On this view, to be well informed a minor must be exposed to both sides of the debate, and that exposure cannot come from a source that stands on only one side. Judges grant that minors can learn the medical aspects of the abortion procedure from an abortion provider. However, counseling from an abortion provider, these judges contend, is likely to understate the potentially harmful aspects of terminating a pregnancy and emphasize abortion over its alternatives. Counseling from a pro-life crisis pregnancy center, by contrast, will likely underscore risks—especially emotional ones—associated with abortion and highlight the various options available to young women who choose to continue with their pregnancies. Only with these different slants on abortion will a minor receive comprehensive and balanced facts that are necessary for making a fully informed decision.

An attorney who represents minors characterized the judicial rationale for mandated pro-life counseling in this way:

> In [the judges'] view it's an informed decision if they go. If she goes to [the abortion clinic], you're still only getting one side of the argument. You're not going go to get the conservative, pro-life truth, a video, "this is what they're going to do to you," "your baby is alive right now." And that is part of a well-informed decision.[25]

An attorney routinely appointed to represent the interests of the fetus at bypass hearings used a similar rationale in explaining his successful effort to gain a continuance at a hearing so that a minor could receive pro-life counseling: "I think it's appropriate that she gets both sides of the issue. If she goes to the abortion clinic, she gets a slant. If she goes to a pro-life clinic, she gets a slant from that side."[26] This attorney further explained that "the judge ordered a continuance for the child to go for pro-life counseling. We then went back, the child informed her attorney, then the judge set another hearing, [it lasted] ten minutes, and [he] granted the waiver."[27]

While judges typically justify their pro-life counseling mandate on informedness grounds, at least one judge tried to use the maturity standard to defend this requirement. In a 1999 denial of a minor's bypass request, this judge ruled that the minor in question failed to demonstrate maturity in part through "her failure to seek counseling from a facility that opposes abortion."[28] The Court of Civil Appeals of Alabama overturned the judge's decision and explained that "[a]lthough our [state] supreme court has stated that a minor who does seek the advice of a pro-choice advocate thereby demonstrates maturity, it has never stated the converse—that a minor who does not seek the advice of a group opposed to abortion thereby demonstrates immaturity."[29]

Despite this reversal, this trial judge continued to require Sav-A-Life counseling, albeit with a new rationale. The shift to the informedness standard suggests that, at least for this judge, the rationale for the counseling requirement did not emerge from any careful consideration of the *Bellotti II* prongs but was constructed after the fact to justify his behavior. However, we need not speculate about this matter, for this same judge admitted that part of the reason he and one of his fellow judges send minors to Sav-A-Life is "hopefully to make them see that abortion is not the right decision, because I believe it is the wrong decision."[30] He further explained his pro-life perspective on presiding over bypass hearings:

> [I]f I say no [to the bypass petition], the child has a chance to live. If I say yes, the likelihood is that the child is going to die. I'm the gatekeeper, and I don't like it. Abortion is wrong; I think it can be justified in the traditional sense of rape or incest, where the woman is forced into it, though even in those cases it's still in my heart the killing of a child.[31]

"To Evangelize the World"

If by mandating pro-life counseling judges hope to promote the view that abortion is the wrong decision, they surely achieve this goal by sending minors to Sav-A-Life. But whether judges strive to make minors see that abortion is not the right decision or aim to ensure that minors are well informed, the Sav-A-Life counseling requirement does more than just expose minors to a particular slant in favor of continuing with pregnancy. Judges who make young women go to Sav-A-Life effectively require these women to undergo religious counseling.

Sav-A-Life Outreach Centers, Inc., was founded as a nonprofit organization in 1980 in Birmingham, Alabama. By 2005 it had grown to become the largest crisis pregnancy organization in the state,[32] boasting thirty-eight affiliate offices.[33] It also had nearly thirty additional offices in Florida, Georgia, Louisiana, Mississippi, and Kentucky.[34]

Sav-A-Life was established as an evangelical Christian ministry, and the services and guidance provided by the organization grew out of its evangelical mission. According to a February 2005 mission statement, Sav-A-Life seeks

> to establish and equip Pregnancy Centers in order that communities will be reached for Christ and that abortion will be made unnecessary and undesirable in their region. Our stated mission is accomplished by helping women in unplanned pregnancies make a choice for life physically and eternally. In other words, Sav-A-Life has a two-fold focus: to preserve physical and spiritual lives. Physically, the sanctity of every human life is a God-given truth found throughout Scripture. The absolute truth as given by our Creator in His Word is our foundation. Without question, God's Word gives value, dignity, and sacred worth to the physical life of each person, born and unborn. God gives sanctity to our physical bodies, yet, it is our spiritual beings that were created for eternity. We have the unique privilege of offering the gift of eternal life to those we encounter through this ministry. While we strive to meet the physical needs of any woman who may come through our door, we realize that we could feed her today, but tomorrow she would be hungry again. It would be pointless to offer her only temporary solutions without offering to her the very answer to life itself. We know that long lasting, eternal hope is only found in the person of Jesus Christ, our redeemer.[35]

In July 2005 Sav-A-Life merged with Care Net, a nonprofit organization that equips and promotes "more than 900 evangelical pregnancy centers in North America."[36] Prior to the merger, Sav-A-Life affiliates operated independently of each other, but each accepted a common *Statement of Faith* and *Guiding Principles,* documents that testified to the organization's evangelical purpose.[37] The *Statement of Faith* put forward twelve doctrinal statements, each beginning with the phrase "We believe."[38] Signers of this document certified their belief in the word of God as contained in the Holy Bible; the eternal existence of the Trinity; Jesus Christ as son of God; original sin; the death of Jesus Christ for the sins of others; the resurrection of Christ and his ascension to heaven; the second coming of Christ; and the bodily resurrection of the just and unjust.[39] Signatories testified to their belief that "for the salvation of lost and sinful man, regeneration by the Holy Spirit is absolutely essential, and that the salvation is received by grace through faith in Jesus Christ as savior and Lord and not as a result of good works."[40] They also expressed agreement with the following statement: "We believe in the great commission which our Lord has given to His church to evangelize the world, and that this evangelization is the great mission of the church. Furthermore, we believe it our Christian duty to witness by word and deed to these truths."[41]

Guiding Principles was a policy-oriented statement. It listed twelve points, including the organization's commitment to never discriminate; to provide clients with education on abortion, prenatal development, and premarital sex; and to meet "the physical, emotional, and spiritual needs of women facing a problem, or untimely pregnancy."[42] The document indicated that Sav-A-Life would not give advice or referrals for abortion, abortifacients, or contraception. In addition to these types of policy declarations, *Guiding Principles* spoke to Sav-A-Life's evangelical commitment and its mission to provide "a Christian alternative to abortion."[43] According to the first guiding principle, "It is our desire to be used by God as a tool in spreading the Gospel, and to combat, reduce, and eliminate the sin of abortion."[44] Furthermore, the document explained Sav-A-Life's commitment "to demonstrating the love, forgiveness, and compassion of Jesus Christ through counsel, education, action and creative services," "to helping fulfill the Great Commission," and "to introduc[ing] its clients to Jesus Christ as Savior and Lord."[45]

Even Sav-A-Life's *Activism Policy,* which affiliates were required to adopt, included reference to the organization's evangelical imperative.

This policy statement proscribed affiliates and volunteers from participating in sidewalk counseling and rescues at abortion clinics, explaining that these activities place the ministry at risk. But, encouraging other pro-life activities "such as lobbying, campaigning, marching," and so forth, the document explained that "God has given Sav-A-Life the responsibility to witness, counsel, and test the women in our community."[46]

Sav-A-Life affiliates and volunteers were required to endorse these statements.[47] Thus, while Sav-A-Life's interdenominational ministry accepted volunteers from different religious backgrounds, being Christian was a requirement for volunteering:[48] "Board members, center directors, and volunteers must have individually received Jesus Christ as Savior."[49] And according to its then website, "Sav-A-Life will strive to foster in all staff, volunteers and clients a primary concern for the spiritual well-being of their own families, and recognizes that establishing and maintaining a Christian home is the greatest contribution we will make throughout our lifetime."[50]

A counselor application form used by at least one Sav-A-Life office demonstrates how the organization found Christian volunteers. This application requested that prospective volunteers provide an account of their "personal testimony" by completing the following statements:

I. Before I received Christ, I lived and thought this way:
II. How I received Christ (Please be specific):
III. After I received Christ, these are the changes that took place in my life:

The form also asked the following questions of would-be volunteers:

In Your Opinion, how does a person become a Christian? (Briefly explain)
What is your attitude toward personal evangelism?
Are you willing to be trained in personal evangelism?
In your words, what is Christian counseling?[51]

Upon merging with Care Net, Sav-A-Life Outreach Centers became Care Net South, a Care Net subsidiary,[52] and Sav-A-Life's president became the regional executive director of Care Net South.[53] Sav-A-Life affiliates, many of which retain their moniker, came under the Care Net umbrella.[54]

Care Net, like Sav-A-Life, is a Christian ministry whose affiliates offer "free pregnancy tests, ultrasounds, peer counseling services, post-abortion support and other practical, emotional and spiritual help to empower women and men facing pregnancy related concerns."[55] Its mission is "assisting and promoting the evangelistic, pro-life work of pregnancy centers in North America,"[56] and "all Care Net pregnancy centers are committed to sharing the Gospel of Jesus Christ."[57]

Care Net affiliates must subscribe to the organization's *Statement of Faith* and *Statement of Principle*,[58] documents that echo their Sav-A-Life counterparts. For example, one paragraph of the Care Net *Statement of Faith* is as follows: "We believe in the deity of our Lord Jesus Christ, in His virgin birth, in His sinless life, in His miracles, in His vicarious and atoning death through His shed blood, in His bodily resurrection, in His ascension to the right hand of the Father, and in His personal return in power and glory."[59] And the Care Net *Statement of Principle* opens with the following:

> The pregnancy center is an outreach ministry of Jesus Christ through His church. Therefore, the pregnancy center, embodied in its volunteers, is committed to presenting the gospel of our Lord to women with crisis pregnancies—both in word and in deed. Commensurate with this purpose, those who labor as pregnancy center board members, directors, and volunteers are expected to know Christ as their Savior and Lord.[60]

Sav-A-Life's stated purpose included a commitment "to making the most of every opportunity to share the good news of Jesus Christ,"[61] and it is clear that Care Net shares this commitment.

"Would You Pray with Me?"

To determine how this commitment translates into practice, I conducted in-person interviews with directors of six Sav-A-Life affiliates.[62] These interviews took place before the merger with Care Net and during the time when my research uncovered that some judges were making Sav-A-Life part of the judicial bypass process. While there is every reason to believe that the character of former Sav-A-Life affiliates has not changed since the merger with Care Net, what is under investigation here is the behavior of judges and, hence, what is of importance is the character of the agents of those judges at the time of their agency.

The interviews reveal the fundamental role religion plays in the counseling offered by Sav-A-Life centers. In fact, while the organization's name might connote an image of preserving the life of the unborn, the goal of saving the spiritual life of the mother proves to be at least of equal importance. As one director put it, the goal of the organization is "saving lives one at a time. And not just the baby. The mother's life is really important."[63] And it is the mother's spiritual life and her relationship with Christ that matters, as another director explained. "Our counsel is more focused on the woman than the baby. I know you can tell women all the reasons why they shouldn't have an abortion. We tell her that God loves her, that he has blessed her if the test is positive, even if it may not look like a blessing."[64]

When a minor abides by the judicial command that she seek counseling from a Sav-A-Life center, she is certain to receive not only a pro-life perspective but also one that is steeped in religious faith. Sav-A-Life counselors advance the goal of saving the spiritual life of their clients by witnessing and sharing the gospel. "We seek to share the gospel with everyone who walks through the door," explained the director of one center. "There are 100,000 ways to do that," she continued. "A lot of times at root I say I'm interested in her as a woman, as a person. But I'm interested in her spiritual well-being. So I simply . . . ask about her relationship with Christ, where she stands in her thinking."[65]

At a second Sav-A-Life I visited, the director made a point of noting that they do not force the gospel on anyone. "God doesn't have to hold anybody down. Jesus is a gentleman. He knocks. I can't change a heart or a life, but I can introduce them to someone who can change a heart or a life." Still, the director made clear that her center is "a Christian ministry and we share the gospel." In particular, this Sav-A-Life uses an approach called "Evangelism Explosion." "It's a method of evangelism," the director explained:

> There are several different methods. In this one we ask, "If you die tonight, will you go to heaven?" . . . And then we say, "God loves them. No man is perfect. Jesus was perfect. God loves them, but He's just and will punish sins." We tell them . . . "Jesus lived a perfect life, and He died on the cross. He paid the debt for our sins. He rose on the third

day." We accept that in faith and what Jesus did on the cross will get us to heaven.[66]

The director of a third Sav-A-Life described the method of evangelism in similar terms, after explaining that they witness "to every client at least once":

> We have gospel tracts we go by. We're all different denominations, so we do different things. But we stick to the basic plan of salvation. There are a lot of differences between what I believe and what a Catholic believes. But we ask them if they believe in heaven or hell and if they die will they go to heaven or hell, and if they've received God. We'll show the Bible and say the only help is a relationship with Jesus Christ, and they can accept that or they can not. If they accept, we give them a Bible, and we try to get them to go to church.[67]

This director further explained that clients are told that admission to heaven entails more than merely being a good person; it requires accepting Jesus Christ as one's savior.

At a fourth Sav-A-Life, counselors who share their testimony rely heavily on the Bible. Minors who visit this center will be asked "about spirituality, whether they believe in Christ, whether they're an unbeliever, whether they've committed their life to Christ." "All of our counsel is from a biblical basis," the director explained. "Our view is that the Bible is true. All our counselors are Christian. All our counsel is based on what He says, that is, what God says. And God for us is Jesus. All our counsel is based on the word of God." In addition to counseling about God and love and heaven and hell, minors might also receive counseling about Satan. According to the director, those who receive counseling are told, "God can turn this around if she lets them. God has allowed the sperm and the egg to unite. . . . Also there's another force and that's Satan, and he's looking to kill and destroy, and Satan is trying to get a foothold in their lives."[68]

Sav-A-Life counselors hope that interactions with clients will lead to a decision to pray and receive Christ. In fact, the organization tracks whether clients have received Christ. In February 2005, Sav-A-Life Outreach Center's website noted that of the 45,000 women ministered to each year, 2,000 "receive Christ."[69] In addition, some of those interviewed referred to their practice of documenting how many women accept Christ. One director said, "Our numbers of receiving Christ are not as high as other Sav-A-Life centers."[70] Another director shared the following data: "Historically, about 10 to 12 percent pray with us or say they've committed their life to Christ. Over twelve years, we've given 8,905 pregnancy tests: 2,744 tested positive; 5,749 were single; 1,014 prayed to receive Christ or commit their life to him."[71]

As the following anecdote shows, providing counseling without talking about religion would go directly against the central mission of Sav-A-Life:

> We had a situation where a boyfriend called, and he complained that we talked to his girlfriend about her relationship with God and church. He said religion is a private thing. I said, "You know, your girlfriend came in and read the intake form and knew that we're a Christian ministry. The reason the church supports us and gives us money is because we're going to talk about God. You telling us not to talk about Jesus Christ is like going to Papa John's and asking for ice cream."[72]

Sav-A-Life's religious message comes overtly into view in the physical décor of their offices. Bibles and other religious literature are usually within reach, especially in counseling rooms. The Lord's Prayer, the Ten Commandments, and Bible verses appear on plaques, in artwork, and on embroidered pillows. Figurines of Jesus Christ and the Virgin Mary stand on display on desks, tables, and bookcases. Crosses grace some of the walls, though depictions of angels may be more ubiquitous. Also common are angelic and innocent portrayals of young children, sometimes kneeling in prayer and other times surrounded by gentle animals of the forest.

Maybe the most palpable evidence that Sav-A-Life seeks to discharge its privilege of offering the gift of eternal life to those encountered in its ministry emerged when some directors tried to present me with this gift. In one case, a director expressed the hope that I would find not only what I was looking for through my research but also something I was not anticipating, namely, God. In a more extensive effort—in fact, one that lasted at least thirty minutes—the director of another center explained that Jesus loves me and is my messiah. She recited a passage from the Bible and read through a pamphlet entitled "Four Spiritual Laws." She remarked that I would live in the physical world maybe seventy or eighty years, and after that I would go either to heaven or hell for eternity. "Wouldn't it be better to go to heaven than hell?" she asked, and further explained that hell would be my eternal destiny if I refused to accept Jesus as my savior. As I set out to leave, I shook her hand and thanked her for taking the time to speak with me; she kept my hand, put her other hand on top of my own, and asked, "Would you pray with me?"[73]

"Hear the Screams"

While prayer and conversion are clearly the primary goals of Sav-A-Life counseling, some who render advice about unplanned pregnancies also talk about abortion in physical and emotional terms. On the physical aspects of abortion, one director said this about her counsel to women:

> I tell them that you need to know that you may miscarry a later wanted child. . . . I also tell them about the link between abortion and breast cancer. . . . We have a book . . . of certified court cases of women hurt, killed, or maimed from abortion. One that sticks in my mind is a girl who was hemorrhaging after an abortion, and they wheeled her out on the sidewalk and she bled to death. I always tell that abortion is a surgical procedure.[74]

At some Sav-A-Life offices, women may be asked to watch a video that depicts the abortion procedure. "It shows the baby after a saline abortion," one director explained.

> It's my favorite video. That's what I recommend, but we tell them what's in it. We ask after that what they thought of the video, and they say, "It was horrible." And we ask, "Was the video horrible?" and they say that abortion is what is horrible, not the video. We want them to know what abortion is about.[75]

This same director explained how, after calculating the date at which a client's pregnancy will reach twelve weeks, she goes on to describe a first-trimester abortion procedure:

> "You have until X date until it will be twelve weeks." We tell them about abortion in the first twelve weeks. We tell them about the suction

machine. The suction machine pulls off the arms and the legs, and separates the bodies. They use another instrument sometimes if they need to
crush the head. We tell them this, and we say, "I want you to do nothing until close to the twelve-week period. And come back in."[76]

Counselors also portray abortion as having potentially severe emotional consequences and emphasize regret and guilt. According to one
director, "We say it is a choice you will regret making. We have a video
that shows women who regret making the decision to abort. . . . Half of
the women who abort experience emotional feelings, have nightmares,
guilt. . . . A lot of girls get depression. There's an increased risk of suicide."[77] Another director explained how she counsels women on the
emotional regret that may accompany abortion:

> We don't ever tell a girl she can't have an abortion, because she can.
> "We would like for you not to have one because you'll regret it." I'll of-
> ten ask a girl if they're going to have children. I'll tell them, "I'm not a
> nurturing person, but most mothers are nurturing. If you think adop-
> tion would be difficult, you don't know how you'll feel because you've
> killed your baby." I don't like to say that. "The decision of whether to
> have a baby is a decision that you'll have to live with."[78]

This director was not alone in linking regret and killing. Another director explained her approach to talking about abortion in this way:

> I use the woman who killed the four children in Texas. "The mother
> who killed her four children, what a monster! But she probably just did
> what she had to do." And I compare what those kids went through
> to what a baby goes through in an abortion. There's a video, *Silent
> Scream*. You can see the baby fighting to get away from it. The heart
> rate triples. The only difference is that the mother in Texas audibly
> heard the screams. We have an abortion recovery ministry. It's a sup-
> port group, a Bible study. But you do hear the screams for the rest of
> your life in your dreams. God makes women that way. We just have to
> face that it's the way God made us up.[79]

Conclusion

Most minors who seek to waive parental involvement for abortion endeavor to demonstrate that they are sufficiently mature to exercise their will without parental supervision. But being mature does not mean being invulnerable, and only the most tenacious minor is likely to emerge unscathed from a bypass process that is coupled with counseling of the type described in this chapter.

Under the pro-life counseling mandate, a pregnant minor confronts an obvious added delay. In a process already pressured by time and laden with secrecy, any extra steps impose fresh burdens, including magnification of the anxiety surrounding possible exposure.

Furthermore, a teenager navigating this specially crafted detour along the bypass route is compelled to do much more than simply hear a fair and balanced account of the pros and cons of terminating her pregnancy. The minor, already dealing with more than is normally attendant to an unwanted pregnancy, is subjected to religious interrogation in a setting where proselytizing is the main order of business. She will face thirty to sixty minutes of counseling not only about alternatives to abortion but also about God, Jesus Christ, and possibly Satan. She will hear Bible scriptures, face the personal testimonials of those who have been saved, and be asked to pray and receive Christ. In some instances, a minor will be asked to contemplate whether her death will land her in heaven or hell for the remainder of eternity.[80]

The context of this type of evangelizing is not comparable to the familiar door-to-door proselytizing carried out by some religious groups. In the latter context, those facing unwelcome spiritual discourse can simply close the door. By contrast, a minor sent to Sav-A-Life by a judge is effectively powerless to rebuff the onslaught of religious testimonials. Would a minor feel free to decline a request to pray, knowing that the chances of securing a bypass of parental consent turn on the visit to Sav-A-Life?

A minor meeting with a Sav-A-Life counselor will also confront nonreligious tactics designed to shock and provoke. These counselors equate abortion with killing and murder, and they exaggerate the negative consequences that can accompany the termination of pregnancy. Recipients of Sav-A-Life counseling have been compelled to watch sometimes graphic videos that depict the abortion procedure and fetal remains. Such tactics would be difficult for an adult to withstand, let alone a teenager.

It is unlikely that when the *Bellotti II* Court carved out the compromise now known as the bypass process they envisioned a practice whereby trial court judges effectively compel young women to receive pro-life religious counseling. But some judges have shown imagination in shaping the language of judicial precedent and transformed the process into a religious exercise. As imaginative as these judges have been, there is little doubt that they have stretched the bypass process beyond the realm of the recognizable.

7

Facing the Fetus

On a Saturday afternoon of the following spring, with a warm mist of rain falling, [Julian] McPhillips pulls his car off the busy Montgomery thoroughfare into the edge of a retail parking lot and lowers his driver-side window. "This is one of two we've done, over the years," he says, pointing to the billboard above. "The message changes from time to time, but the theme is the same."

In stark black-and-white, the sign features a drawing of a fetus inside the uterus, alongside the text, "Before I formed thee in the womb, I knew thee . . . (Jeremiah 1:5)." A telephone number for Sav-A-Life is listed below. (The other billboard reads, "Abortion Stops a Beating Heart: Please consider the Alternatives, Including Adoption." The same telephone number appears).

"The people at Sav-A-Life tell us they've had a very good response, that a number of women have come in because of the billboard and changed their minds and not had an abortion," he says.

—Carroll Dale Short, *The People's Lawyer*[1]

When a minor appears before a judge to petition for a bypass of parental involvement, we expect the setting to be neutral, unadorned by a billboard such as the one described here. Yet some judges have gone one better, appointing attorneys to serve as guardians for the unborn. These judges have placed walking and talking pro-life advertisements in the center of bypass proceedings, claiming the legitimacy of the rule of law for what is nothing more than pro-life propaganda. This chapter tells the story of guardianship appointments in Alabama.[2]

"Providence for the Unborn"

On July 6, 1998, a pregnant minor, three months shy of her eighteenth birthday, sought a waiver of parental consent from the juvenile court in

Montgomery County.[3] The minor's petition was put before Judge W. Mark Anderson, one of three judges responsible for reviewing bypass requests in Montgomery. In accordance with internal courthouse procedures, the court intake officer assigned the minor legal counsel. Reaching beyond ordinary procedures, the judge appointed a guardian ad litem to represent the fetus. Such guardians are officers of the court and are normally appointed to represent parties incapacitated by age or other disability.

Judge Anderson had presided over bypass hearings prior to this case. In fact, Anderson had previously made clear both his opposition to abortion and his willingness to grant waiver requests. In an earlier bypass case, he wrote a lengthy judicial order that expressed his "fixed opinion that abortion is wrong"[4] and his belief that the minor's decision to terminate her pregnancy would compound one mistake with another more terrible one—namely, the death of her unborn child. Still, Anderson waived parental consent upon finding that the minor was sufficiently mature and informed to have the abortion and upon concluding that, given the maturity finding, the law allows the judge no alternative but to grant the bypass. The order noted that the minor would turn eighteen in a month and could wait until then to have the abortion without a judicial bypass. But quoting from Shakespeare and referring to Macbeth's plan to assassinate his own father, Anderson reportedly wrote, "like Macbeth, 'If it were done when 'tis done, then 'twere well It were done quickly.'"[5]

Anderson selected attorney Julian McPhillips, an avid supporter of Sav-A-Life, to serve as guardian for the fetus in the July 1998 case.[6] "Though many people in [Montgomery] were surprised when Judge Anderson appointed an advocate for the anonymous teenager's baby," explains Carroll Dale Short, author of McPhillips's biography, "nobody who knew McPhillips was surprised at the judge's choice of attorney. He's possibly the area's most high-visibility figure in the pro-life arena, with a successful record of defending anti-abortion protesters who are arrested outside city clinics."[7]

When the minor's court-appointed counsel, Beverly Howard, received notice that a guardian would represent "Baby Ashley" at the hearing, she filed a motion to strike the appointment. Anderson denied the motion, basing his authority for the appointment on Rule 17(c) of the Alabama Rules of Civil Procedure. Rule 17(c) states that "when the interest of an infant unborn or unconceived is before the court, the court may appoint a guardian ad litem for such interest."[8] Anderson justified his use of Rule 17(c) by noting the importance of giving the "unborn child" an "opportunity to have a voice, even a vicarious one, in the decision making."[9] He did not appeal to the Alabama Parental Consent Statute, for neither it nor any other involvement statute that is currently in effect includes provisions concerning the appointment of fetal representation.[10]

Howard also filed a motion asking the judge to recuse himself from the case, given his previously declared opposition to abortion. Anderson rejected this motion as well, explaining that his personal views would not interfere with his ability to follow the law. In support of this contention, Anderson pointed to the fact that his attitudes about abortion did not prevent him from approving previous bypass petitions.

Bypass hearings in Alabama and elsewhere ordinarily take less than thirty minutes. In these hearings, it is typical for the lawyer and the judge to question the minor in an effort to elicit testimony that speaks to the two-pronged bypass test. A minor usually answers questions that address her level of education, grades, future plans, career interests, and employment history. Her attorney commonly inquires about the medical aspects and risks of the procedure. A minor can also expect questions about whether she has considered alternatives to abortion, what plans she has made to handle any physical or emotional consequences, why she would choose abortion over other alternatives, and why she would make such a choice without involving her parents.

During this bypass hearing, Howard posed questions along these lines, yielding testimony concerning the minor's level of maturity and her familiarity with abortion and its alternatives. Answering Howard's inquiries, the minor testified that she was a high school honors student with a college scholarship in hand. She managed her own money, investigated the financial assistance available should she have a child, and received counseling from Sav-A-Life about the alternatives to abortion.[11] She explained the risks of abortion and expressed her view that proceeding with childbirth would interfere with her ability to pursue college. The petitioner also expressed fears about her father discovering her pregnancy, saying that he "had been known to point a gun at boys who looked at her provocatively."[12]

In his position as guardian, McPhillips called two witnesses on behalf of the fetus, over the repeated objections of the minor's counsel. These witnesses included a physician who testified about the physical development of the fetus and the executive director of a Sav-A-Life center who testified about alternatives to abortion and her experiences with post-abortive women.

Anderson allowed the guardian considerable latitude not only in calling witnesses but also in questioning the petitioner. During an extensive cross-examination, McPhillips put many questions to the minor about the life and death of the fetus. For example, McPhillips asked the young woman whether she was aware that the "baby" already had a heartbeat. "And you are not concerned after you have had the abortion that some day you may wake up and say my gosh, what have I done to my own baby?"[13] Though the minor acknowledged that she might experience regret, McPhillips persisted: "You are not worried about being haunted by this? Here you have the chance to save the life of your own baby. . . . And still you want to go ahead and snuff out the life of your own baby?"[14]

McPhillips invoked religion in pursuing this line of inquiry. Over protests from Howard, he asked the minor whether she was familiar with Bible scripture in which God says to the prophet Jeremiah: "Before I formed thee in the womb, I knew thee." McPhillips also asked the minor if she had prayed about her decision. After acknowledging that she had and indicating her belief that abortion is a sin, McPhillips asked if she was willing to "pay the price for this sin?"[15] "You say that you are aware that God instructed you not to kill your own baby, but you want to do it anyway? And are you saying here today that notwithstanding everything that you want to interfere with God's plan for your baby?"[16]

Among her many objections, Howard protested the use of the term "kill," to which McPhillips insisted, "Your honor, it's killing. I didn't say 'murder,' although it's murder."[17] This provoked another objection from Howard, who argued that bypass hearings do not extend the right to kill but rather determine whether a minor is in a position to make a decision about abortion without parental consent. In an effort to make the questioning "more palatable," Anderson suggested that the parties refer to the procedure as "cooperating in the termination of the life of the unborn child."[18] McPhillips, though, was undeterred:

> If you sugarcoat it too much, she doesn't understand what she's doing. Killing is what she would be doing. She may choose not to. But if in the

event you choose to have an abortion, I'd like to ask her if she realizes that there's a life there. Does she understand that a beating heart is going to be put to an end?[19]

After a four-hour hearing that generated some 150 pages of transcript, Anderson granted the bypass. Taking the opportunity to voice his own views about abortion and the life of the unborn, the judge offered the minor these reflections:

I know this has not been an easy afternoon. . . . We're dealing with a decision that is going to stop a beating heart. . . . But what we have done here today is not for the purpose of giving you a hard time. . . . I feel that we are dealing with a human life and the end of the human life. . . . Whatever that decision is and whatever you do, I hope God will be with you.[20]

Anderson also expressed his views in his written order granting the bypass. He praised the guardian's performance, stating that McPhillips had done

a yeoman's job of protecting the interests of his ward, to the extent that this unfortunate law allows. What we call life is but a brief passage in eternity. There must be a special providence for the unborn who not only are deprived of the opportunity to live but of having a saving faith in spite of the sin whose commission is the natural inheritance of man.[21]

Despite these comments, Anderson indicated that he felt "confined to issue the waiver of parental consent" pursuant to state law:[22]

From the record made through almost four hours of testimony and arguments of the most acrimonious nature, it is clear to the court that a waiver is not in best interest of this young woman. It certainly is not in the best interest of the unborn child. Those findings are abundantly clear from the efforts and evidence of Mr. McPhillips. But unfortunately those two findings are not determinative of the issue raised by this proceeding. This court is bound to uphold to the law, however distasteful that may be and regardless of whether the law is consistent with this court's fixed opinions. This is the law. Required consent shall be waived if . . . the minor is mature and well informed enough to make the abortion decision on her own. . . . The court hereby grants the minor's petition for waiver of consent.[23]

Silence Is Golden

The provisions enumerated in the Alabama parental consent statute afford minors the right to appeal a judge's denial of a bypass petition.[24] No other party is explicitly given the right to appeal. This fact notwithstanding, McPhillips sought and received a stay of Anderson's order, and appealed the decision to the Court of Civil Appeals.

By challenging Anderson's order, McPhillips provided the Alabama appellate courts an opportunity to rule on the permissibility of guardianship appointments. Both the Court of Civil Appeals and the Alabama Supreme Court, to which the case eventually fell, passed up this opportunity.

Rather than ruling on the broad question of whether guardian appointments are legally appropriate in the context of bypass hearings, the Court of Civil Appeals confined itself to the narrow question of whether a guardian, once appointed, has the right to appeal the grant of a bypass petition. In a one-page per curiam opinion dismissing the appeal, the appellate court explains that the right to an appeal in such cases is "purely statutory."[25] Furthermore,

> [t]he legislature did not provide a right to appeal from the granting of a petition for a waiver of parental consent. The statute specifically states that an appeal may lie for any "minor" to whom the court "denies" the petition. This specific wording does not leave room for judicial interpretation. In this case no minor was denied a waiver. Therefore, there is no right to appeal.[26]

Faced with this dismissal, McPhillips appealed to the Supreme Court of Alabama. In a ruling issued on August 3, 1998, the high court affirmed Anderson's decision to grant the bypass of consent.[27] All the justices concurred in the finding that the minor proved herself to be sufficiently mature and well informed to proceed with the abortion absent parental involvement. Nevertheless, the ruling was sharply divided over the issue of whether a guardian can appeal the grant of a bypass peti-

tion. The court's per curiam ruling, joined by four justices and concurred with by a fifth,[28] states:

> The Legislature, as the Court of Civil Appeals correctly noted, did not
> provide a right to appeal from an order granting a petition for a waiver
> of parental consent. We can conclude only that the Legislature under-
> stood its subordinance to the Supremacy Clause of the United States
> Constitution and that it recognized that, pursuant to the United States
> Supreme Court's decision in *Roe v. Wade* (1973), it could not constitu-
> tionally confer upon a nonviable fetus the right to appeal, through a
> guardian ad litem, an order granting a minor's request to have an abor-
> tion.[29]

The opinion rejects the right of the fetus to appeal through a guardian
but neither rejects nor confirms the trial court's authority to appoint the
guardian ad litem in the first place. Instead, the ruling, like the decision
of the Court of Civil Appeals, is silent on this point.[30]

Diverging from this opinion, four justices expressly addressed the
legitimacy of guardianship appointments and argued in favor of the
guardian's right to appeal. The opinion of these justices supports Anderson's application of Rule 17(c) and cites precedent requiring the appointment of a guardian to represent the interests of an unborn child
during certain types of divorce proceedings:[31]

> If a guardian ad litem is required for an unborn child when its legiti-
> macy is at stake, then, a fortiori, it would appear that the appointment
> of a guardian ad litem, although not specifically provided for in the Pa-
> rental Consent Statute, would at least be authorized, if not required, in
> a case such as this one, involving a minor who is seeking a waiver of
> parental consent to have an abortion.[32]

Having established their position on the legitimacy of guardianship
appointments, the dissenters also argue that "[i]t is well settled that a
guardian ad litem appointed to protect the interests of the unborn has a
right to appeal."[33] Furthermore,

> it seems clear that the Legislature intended, in adopting the Parental
> Consent Statute, to preserve the life of the unborn, and it deliberately

was doing what it could within the constraints of the Federal Constitution, as interpreted by the Supreme Court of the United States, to accomplish that purpose. . . . The general rule of law is that guardians ad litem are desirable in many proceedings to ensure that the proceedings will have the adversariness necessary for the full presentation of the issues, and in the proceedings now here for review such an appointment would be consistent with the purpose and intent of the Legislature in adopting the Parental Consent Statute. . . . [W]e conclude that the Legislature, when it provided the minor a right to appeal, did not intend to prohibit a guardian ad litem appointed to represent the interest of an unborn child from appealing from an adverse order. Stated differently, we do not believe that the Legislature, by failing specifically to provide in the Parental Consent Statute for a guardian ad litem's right to appeal, intended, by omission, to defeat such a right of appeal.[34]

With four justices indicating that a trial court may appoint a guardian ad litem to represent the fetus in bypass hearings, and with another five justices remaining silent on this point, Alabama trial courts retain the discretion to designate an agent to speak on behalf of the unborn. Indeed, as McPhillips explained,

the [Alabama] Supreme Court decision was a victory at least on this point. . . . Four judges were saying I should be a guardian for the unborn, but the others didn't even comment on the issue of whether I should have the right to be a guardian ad litem. I talked to the judge, Judge Anderson, and he deserved an award for being a profile in courage, and we took that as a green light for there being a right to have a guardian, and so he continued to appoint guardians for the unborn.[35]

Ongoing Use of Fetal Representatives

In an effort to explicitly sanction that which the Alabama Supreme Court did not, the Alabama legislature in 1999 considered a bill requiring that an attorney be appointed to represent the state in bypass cases and granting to the trial court the option of designating a guardian to represent the unborn.[36] Drafted by the president of the Alabama Pro-Life Coalition, the bill died in committee but not before being endorsed by then Alabama Attorney General William Pryor.[37] According to one news report, Pryor, one of President George W. Bush's controversial appointments to the federal bench,[38] was reported as saying that an "attorney representing the government should be involved to protect the state's interest in preserving life."[39] In addition, "Pryor said he envisioned attorneys with networks like Alabama Lawyers for Life, of which he used to be a member, agreeing to represent the state for free and 'potentially' taking an adversarial [position] against abortions."[40]

Notwithstanding this legislative failure and given the green light provided by the Alabama Supreme Court, Judge Anderson has made it a routine practice to appoint guardians at bypass hearings. Judge John Cappel, also of Montgomery County, has adopted this practice.[41] As a result, since the 1998 case in which McPhillips served as guardian, at least three different attorneys have represented the unborn in at least seventeen bypass hearings.[42]

Those who have represented the unborn since McPhillips admit that their common objective is to protect the fetus' interest in being born. As one guardian explained, "In a nutshell, my role is to protect the interest of the unborn child, and I believe my role, through the questions, is to see if I can change the child's mind and convince her to carry the child to term."[43] Another explained that "the law is clear: if this girl is mature enough, then they have a right to make that choice. My job is to see if she meets those conditions."[44] But this job, the guardian said, is secondary: "I'm there representing the unborn, my goal primarily is to save that unborn fetus' life. . . . The unborn fetus has no voice other than my voice, and if we don't make sure that the voice is heard, at least to the limit of the law, then that unborn fetus doesn't have a chance."[45]

To give the fetus a chance, guardians try to demonstrate to the minor that there is a living human being growing inside her body, that she may suffer physically and emotionally as a result of aborting the fetus, that some women who have abortions develop psychological problems and may even become suicidal, that there are many families willing to adopt, and that money is available to assist with both prenatal care and the raising of children. They do so through extensive cross-examination.[46]

One guardian explained that the questions presented during cross-examination overlap to some extent with those posed to the minor by her counsel. Among these questions are "Where do they intend to spend the night? What are the risks?"[47] In addition, this guardian also asks: "Have you talked with anybody who had an abortion before? Do you know that people who suffer abortions tend to be more suicidal? . . . [H]ave you watched any videos?"[48]

Similarly, as another guardian explained, "I'll go through preliminary questions, her school activities, what her career plans are, do they have a job, do they have a bank account, what kind of level of maturity they have in general."[49] This guardian continues through a list of some seventy questions to inquire

> [i]f they've seen pictures of the baby, of the fetus; if they've talked to a medical doctor. And then a whole series of questions about how the procedure is performed, what the risks are, what the complications might be, what they will do in the event they confront complications. I discuss psychological and emotional consequences, post-abortion syndrome in men and in mothers as well. Ask if they've talked to any adults, a minister, counselor at school, clinic; if they've seen videos or printed materials about the procedure. And then I ask them about alternatives: raising it themselves, adoption, Catholic Social Services. There are a number of agencies that will take the child. I usually ask if they've been to any pro-life agencies. Do they believe this is in their best interest? I ask if she thinks abortion is wrong. Then a couple of scenarios: if there was a couple in their church, well educated and they couldn't have a child and they really wanted one, would she consider giving the child to them for adoption? I try to get them to think if there are alternatives. . . . Usually we'll ask do they go to church, what church, what's the view of the church regarding abortion, have they thought about whether there are churchgoers who would want to adopt, do they attend regularly.[50]

Owing to the fact that guardians are obligated to advance the interest of the fetus, the questions put to the minor are in many instances designed to compel her to consider the nature of human life, personhood, and killing. A minor will typically be asked whether she believes abortion is wrong and whether choosing abortion runs counter to her religious views. If the minor answers either of these questions affirmatively, she will be expected to resolve the discord between her beliefs and her decision to terminate her pregnancy. Indeed, one guardian went so far as to ask a minor who already had a child whether she could imagine killing that child. When the minor said no, the guardian pressed her to explain how she could justify aborting the fetus she was carrying if she could not conceive of killing her born child.

Guardians sometimes use fear to persuade the minor to forgo her intended course of action. Consider the following report of a guardian's questions, taken from a dissenting opinion in an appeal of a bypass denial:

> The minor testified that she and her boyfriend plan to marry when they are older and that they have discussed having three children. The lawyer the trial judge appointed to represent the fetus asked if the minor, knowing that "one of the risks that you are going to face is the possibility that you will be sterile after this procedure," was "willing to place your future three children at risk." The lawyer then asked, if she died as a result of the abortion, "Would that not take away not only your three children but your boyfriend's future wife and his three children?" The lawyer also asked if the minor had ever heard of post-abortion syndrome in men. He asked if she was aware that men are "very often affected psychologically by their child being taken in abortion" and if she was willing to "place [her boyfriend] at the same risk" she was taking. The lawyer also said to the minor: "If you did have a complication and you had to go to the hospital, your church congregation is going to find out what's happened. How is that going to effect [*sic*] your going to church every Sunday?"[51]

While guardians use cross-examination as the primary method for advocating birth over abortion, some guardians have called witnesses to present evidence on behalf of the fetus.[52] Like McPhillips, two other guardians brought in the director of a Sav-A-Life center to testify about the psychological effects of abortion. These guardians also put on the record the testimony of a woman who had previously undergone an abortion. These "experts" were called "to try and put out information," one guardian explained.[53] "That lady who had had the abortion said once if she said it twenty times, 'if I had known then what I know now, I would never have done what I did.' So information is the tool."[54] With that testimony presented, the guardian asked the minor "whether she knew what she was getting into."[55]

Additional opportunities for appellate review have emerged with the continued use of guardians, but these have yielded little beyond the

1998 decision.[56] In 1999, the Court of Civil Appeals considered a case in which a minor's appeal of a bypass denial was accompanied by a guardian's motion to file a brief in support of the judge's order. Overturning the judge's denial of the bypass request, the Court also rejected the guardian's motion. In a footnote and without explanation or support, the Court of Civil Appeals wrote that "[a] majority of the [Alabama Supreme] court did not address whether the trial court had the authority to appoint a guardian for the fetus. Likewise, in this case, we do not address the propriety of appointing the guardian, and we have denied the guardian's motion to file a brief in support of the trial court's order."[57]

In 2001, a minor appealed a judicial order denying her bypass request and directly raised the question of whether the trial court had violated her constitutional rights by designating an agent for the fetus.[58] The Alabama Supreme Court ruled that the trial judge had erred in denying the bypass and offered the following characterization of the guardian's participation:

> [T]his was not a nonadversarial proceeding. [The minor] was cross-examined by a lawyer appointed to represent the fetus, and she adhered to her testimony and to her position that an abortion was the most appropriate course of action for her, despite being given full exposure, through an extended cross-examination, to opposing viewpoints that strongly emphasized the negative effect of the abortion procedure and that advocated the benefits of having a child.[59]

While explicitly acknowledging that the presence of a guardian generated an adversarial hearing, the court sidestepped the opportunity to address the propriety of designating agents for the fetus. "[I]n light of our holding," the court explained, "we pretermit any discussion of [the minor's] argument concerning the trial court's appointment of a lawyer to represent the fetus."[60]

One Alabama Supreme Court justice has registered criticism of guardian appointments. In a harshly worded dissent challenging both the denial of a bypass request and the appointment of fetal representation, Justice Douglas Inge Johnstone characterized such appointments as gratuitous and claimed the petitioner was "a victim of prejudice against abortion."[61] Quoting from the hearing transcript, the dissent criticized the trial judge's statement to the minor that appointing "a lawyer to represent your unborn child" allows "someone to represent the silent voice in this case."[62] Johnstone argued that "[g]ratuitously appointing a guardian ad litem for the 'silent voice' casts the inquiry as a contest between a baby struggling to save its own life and the mother fighting to kill the baby."[63]

"Judgment Is the Lord and Is Eternal"

Judge Anderson has suggested that guardian assignments help ensure that the minor is asked the right questions at the hearing and free the judge from the position of cross-examining the young woman. Nevertheless, not even Anderson claims that this is the main reason for guardianship appointments, and there is no question that the primary motivation for such appointments in Montgomery, Alabama, is judicial opposition to abortion.

By all accounts, Judges Anderson and Cappel oppose abortion. According to one attorney who has represented minors, "It has been said more than once to Cappel, 'you have got to put your personal opinions aside on this.' He is adamant about abortions."[64] Another suggested that the emergence of guardianship appointment owes to the fact that both "Anderson and Cappel are personally opposed to the concept of abortion, and they want somebody fighting against that."[65] Similarly, Beverly Howard stated in a televised interview after representing the minor in the first case involving a guardian:

> I think this case came about because the judge assigned to hear it is well-known as an opponent of abortion—as is Mr. McPhillips, who is a member of 'Attorneys for Life'—and not necessarily because he believes that's the law. . . . What's happening is that people who oppose abortion are using this as a *forum* to get to people—or to girls—that they normally wouldn't even be able to speak to outside of a clinic. In the courtroom they're able to get within two feet of them, and a girl—in this case a minor girl—is ordered to answer the questions asked. And some of them, I think, are highly inappropriate for a judicial setting.[66]

It is not surprising that some attorneys who represent minors explain the appointment of guardians in terms of the ideological views of the judges. But they are not alone. Designated guardians have similarly pointed to the pro-life views of these two judges as the motivating force behind the appointments. As one guardian asserted, "Judge Anderson doesn't want anybody to get an abortion. . . . He is very religious. And he doesn't want to grant these things."[67] According to another, among the reasons Anderson and Cappel provide fetal representation is "to try to persuade the child to carry the fetus to term."[68]

Consider also the comments of McPhillips who, sharing the television camera with Howard, explained why Anderson chose him to serve as a guardian: "I have a heart for unborn children just as I do for other underdogs and victims I represent in my law practice. In fact, I say there's no greater underdog, or victim, in life . . . and I emphasize the words 'in life' . . . than a baby who's about to be killed in his or her mother's own womb."[69] When McPhillips explained to me how he came to represent the fetus, he said, "Well, the judge who was handling the case was a conservative Republican, very pro-life and he knew I was pro-life."[70]

The widespread and uncontested perception that Anderson and Cappel appoint guardians because of their views about abortion derives from the fact that these judges have not been shy to express their views. During an interview with me, Anderson was forthright in explaining the genesis of guardianship appointments in terms of protecting the innocent life of the unborn:

> It bothered me that the truly innocent party was unrepresented. So I came up with the idea that perhaps a lawyer should be appointed. In June 1998, I was at a lawyer's conference, and they had a question period in a discussion about guardians. So I asked a question, whether if someone were to appoint a guardian ad litem to represent the unborn in waiver hearings, what would happen. And the speaker, a judge, said, "I wouldn't touch that with a ten-foot pole." So I thought I would ask for an attorney general opinion about whether I had the authority to do that. Well, he was a newly appointed Republican with an election coming up, and I didn't want to do that to him before his election. So I ran it by him at another lawyer's conference. I said, "If I had a question for you, could I ask," and he said, "Yes." In the meantime, before I could ask the question, up pops another one of these cases. And I had to have a real soul search. If what I believe is right, then I need to do it regardless of the consequences. Either I believe what I say I believe or not. And I believe it. And consequently, I appointed Julian.[71]

Anderson described his continued use of guardians in similar terms. Reading from an unspecified Alabama ruling that did not deal with parental consent for abortion, Anderson quoted the following passage: "Our supreme court has said 'It is the . . . court's duty to guard and protect the interest of its infant wards with scrupulous care.' "[72] Anderson went on to explain that, in light of this, judges have a heavy burden in bypass cases, and, specifically, a duty to protect children, both born and unborn. He admitted that he believes abortion is the wrong decision and suggested that Cappel shares this view. When asked to reflect on the fact that his appointment of a guardian may turn out to be a precedent-setting move, he offered the following response: "I don't really focus on being the father of something, because I've got plenty more stuff to do. But if it saves a life, it was worth it."[73]

Anderson and Cappel also candidly express their opposition to abortion during bypass proceedings. As discussed, Anderson clearly indicated his position about abortion to the young woman who faced questioning from the first designated guardian. Over the years, he has continued this practice. For example, Anderson explained to a minor in a 2001 bypass hearing:

> What you have asked the Court to allow you to do is something that is extremely serious and fatal to your child. And it has been my practice for three years now when I'm faced with these cases to not only have a lawyer for you but to have a lawyer to represent the interest of the unborn child, and that's why [he] is here. Both of these lawyers have been in many—I would even say too many—of these cases, because even one is too many.[74]

Cappel also plainly expresses his pro-life position to minors. According to the report of one attorney,

> Judge Cappel will usually say, "This is an enormous decision, and I don't want you to make it. I want you to consider the life of this baby; it will stop a beating heart. Your baby right now is perfectly formed, has ten little fingers and ten little toes, and I don't want you to end this baby's life. And if you don't make this decision, in seven months you'll be a mommy and you'll have a perfect little baby."[75]

Even when they grant bypass petitions, Anderson and Cappel convey their pro-life views. It is not uncommon for these judges to forthrightly state that they are constrained by the parameters of the law to grant the petition despite their opposition to abortion, and both judges typically remind the minor in their written orders that such a grant does not require her to have an abortion. As noted earlier, Anderson indicated in one such order his "fixed opinion that abortion is wrong."[76] He did in this case go on to grant the waiver request, though not before offering the following commentary: "Judgment is the Lord and is eternal, yet his forgiveness and mercy are limitless."[77]

Conclusion

What transpires under the searching inquiry of the guardian is an adversarial exercise that pits the minor against an attorney who hopes to convince the young woman to adopt a particular conception of morality and personhood. In a nonadversarial process, a minor might be asked in a reasonable and neutral fashion whether she has considered the potential emotional ramifications of her decision. But when an adversary enters the picture, investigation along these lines can morph into queries about the minor's willingness to snuff out the life of her own baby. Thus, the act of introducing an agent to represent the fetus alters the nature of a bypass hearing. In placing before the minor an adversary who is legally obligated to thwart her quest for an abortion, inquiries are bound to and have in fact become aggressive.

Outside of anecdotal accounts, we do not know whether pregnant minors have been deterred from pursuing bypass requests upon discovering that hearings in front of some judges include questioning by a representative of the fetus. Neither do we know whether minors have traveled to another county or state to avoid judges who impose this measure. And while we can presume that minors feel pressure under the inquiring probes of the fetus's attorney, we do not know whether that pressure has led young women to change their minds about choosing abortion.

What we do know is that some self-described pro-life judges, confronting a conflict between their judicial responsibilities and deeply held personal beliefs, have found a way to embed those beliefs into the fabric of legal proceedings. It is true that some minors have been granted judicial bypasses despite facing fetal representatives. Indeed, in the notorious McPhillips case, Judge Anderson found for the minor. Nevertheless, "all's well that ends well" is not the proper conclusion to draw from these facts. Minors who face this judicial innovation are subject to intimidation and delay, and it is not unreasonable to think that a minor facing these prospects would consider her alternatives and perhaps find that her interest does not lie in exercising her rights. No one should think that it is permissible for judges to use the bench as a platform for rhetorical onslaught against vulnerable minors as long as the judges ultimately relent. Judicial browbeating is not mitigated by a minor's ability to withstand it.

PART IV

Law and Politics

8

The Constitutional Fine Print

In the wake of several Alabama appellate court decisions that sustained lower-court denials of bypass petitions, Justice Douglas Inge Johnstone of the Alabama Supreme Court remarked that the "appellate courts of this state will continue to flout the abortion rights of minors unless and until some minor successfully petitions the United States Supreme Court for certiorari review."[1] As we have seen, the chasm between our expectations about how the bypass process will function and how it actually functions is wide, and from here it may seem a short leap to the conclusion that the application of parental consent mandates in Alabama, Pennsylvania, and Tennessee would be found to violate the abortion rights of pregnant teens.

In this chapter I suggest that what at first might appear to be a no-brainer turns out, at least, to be a brain-teaser and, in some instances, a brain-breaker. That is, it is far from certain that all of the practices described above, from the transparent implementation failures of Part II to the judicial gerrymandering of Part III, would fail constitutional inspection. The Court in *Bellotti II* laid out the basic framework for constitutionally sound consent provisions.[2] But since then, the Court has put forward the undue burden standard as the benchmark for reviewing abortion regulations in general, holding that women have a right to choose abortion free from substantial obstacles imposed by government.[3] What is at stake under the undue burden standard is the meaning of "substantial obstacle," and the history of the Court's application of this predicate raises serious doubts about whether an airing before the Court of the practices taking place in Alabama, Pennsylvania, and Tennessee would result in the ruling Johnstone expects.

The Undue Burden Standard

In the 1992 watershed case *Planned Parenthood of Southeastern Pennsylvania v. Casey,*[4] the Court considered the constitutionality of Pennsylvania's one-parent consent mandate, as well as provisions requiring informed consent, a twenty-four-hour waiting period, and spousal notification. Awaiting this much anticipated decision, Court watchers wondered whether the justices would jettison *Roe*[5] and return unchecked authority to regulate abortion to states. The plurality opinion in *Casey* —authored jointly by Justices Sandra Day O'Connor, Anthony Kennedy, and David Souter—disappointed pro-life advocates by reaffirming *Roe*'s finding of a constitutional right to abortion. The *Casey* plurality sustained what it described as *Roe*'s "essential holding," ruling that the Fourteenth Amendment Due Process Clause includes a right to choose to abort a nonviable fetus without undue interference from the state. At the same time, the plurality disappointed the pro-choice camp by adopting the undue burden test to fashion a constitutional makeover of *Roe*.

Under the standard of review that had been established in *Roe,* state regulations of abortion would survive constitutional scrutiny only if they served a compelling government interest. Applying this high level of scrutiny to the trimesters of pregnancy, the Court in *Roe* held that the state's two asserted interests in regulating abortion—protecting maternal health and protecting prenatal life—do not become compelling until the later stages of pregnancy. The state's interest in maternal health only becomes compelling, the Court ruled, when the first trimester ends.[6] The compelling point for protecting prenatal life comes even later. Only with the onset of the third trimester (then thought to be the point of fetal viability) may the state regulate and even go as far as to forbid abortion for the purpose of protecting potential life, though only when such regulation does not interfere with the life or health of the woman.[7]

In its refashioning of *Roe,* the *Casey* Court rejected both the trimester framework and the requirement that states demonstrate a compelling interest when regulating abortion. Retaining the conclusion that prior to the onset of fetal viability the state may not proscribe abortion to protect fetal life, *Casey* nevertheless endorsed the state's interest in regulating on behalf of potential life from the moment of conception. According to the plurality, "The woman's liberty is not so unlimited, however, that from the outset the State cannot show its concern for the life of the unborn."[8] While deciding that the Constitution protects a woman's right to choose to terminate her pregnancy prior to viability, the Court argued that it does not at all follow that the State is prohibited from taking steps to ensure that this choice is thoughtful and informed. Even in the earliest stages of pregnancy, the State may enact rules and regulations designed to encourage her to know that there are philosophic and social arguments of great weight that can be brought to bear in favor of continuing the pregnancy to full term and that there are procedures and institutions to allow adoption of unwanted children as well as a certain degree of state assistance if the mother chooses to raise the child herself. The Constitution does not forbid a State or city, pursuant to democratic processes, from expressing a preference for normal childbirth. It follows that States are free to enact laws to provide a reasonable framework for a woman to make a decision that has such profound and lasting meaning.[9]

The authors of *Casey* thus concluded that "[t]o promote the State's profound interest in potential life, throughout pregnancy the State may take measures to ensure that the woman's choice is informed, and measures designed to advance this interest will not be invalidated as long as their purpose is to persuade the woman to choose childbirth over abortion."[10] Furthermore, discarding the compelling interest standard, the plurality held that a state may advance such measures as long as they do not impose an "undue burden" on women.[11] A finding of an undue burden, the Court explained,

is a shorthand for the conclusion that a state regulation has the purpose or effect of placing a substantial obstacle in the path of a woman seeking an abortion of a nonviable fetus. A statute with this purpose is invalid because the means chosen by the State to further the interest in potential life must be calculated to inform the woman's free choice, not hinder it. And a statute which, while furthering the interest in potential life or some other valid state interest, has the effect of placing a substantial obstacle in the path of a woman's choice cannot be considered a permissible means of serving its legitimate ends. . . . Understood another way, we answer the question, left open in previous opinions discussing the undue burden formulation, whether a law designed to further the State's interest in fetal life which imposes an undue burden on the woman's decision before fetal viability could be constitutional. The answer is no.[12]

The *Casey* Court's elaboration of the undue burden test and its retention of certain aspects of *Roe* aim to weigh a woman's liberty interest against the state's interest in potential life. *Casey* thus echoed *Roe*'s acknowledgement that individual and state interests over abortion often collide. But compared to *Roe,* the balancing act elaborated under *Casey*'s undue burden standard tips the scales heavily in favor of the state by permitting substantially more regulation of abortion. The *Casey* decision advances this new balance by explicitly sanctioning state use of abortion regulations to declare a preference for childbirth over abortion.[13] The plurality insists that

> [w]hat is at stake is the woman's right to make the ultimate decision, not a right to be insulated from all others in doing so. Regulations which do no more than create a structural mechanism by which the State, or the parent or guardian of a minor, may express profound respect for the life of the unborn are permitted, if they are not a substantial obstacle to the woman's exercise of the right to choose. . . . Unless it has that effect on her right of choice, a state measure designed to persuade her to choose childbirth over abortion will be upheld if reasonably related to that goal. Regulations designed to foster the health of a woman seeking an abortion are valid if they do not constitute an undue burden.[14]

But what counts as a substantial obstacle? If the state has license from the onset of pregnancy to create mechanisms designed to express profound respect for the unborn, to encourage women to forgo abortions, and to instruct women on the philosophic and social arguments in favor of pregnancy and childbirth, how far may the state go without crossing the undue burden threshold?

The Court's application of the undue burden test to specific regulations affords some insight. In *Casey,* the Court sustained two types of provisions that were rejected under the *Roe* framework in earlier cases.[15] Among these was an informed consent requirement mandating the provision of certain information before an abortion may be performed on a woman, minor or adult. The Court ruled that states may require more than the communication of information that pertains to the woman's health. As long as the information provided "is truthful and not misleading," states may insist that doctors inform women of the availability of information relating to the consequences of abortion to the fetus, "even when those consequences have no direct relation to her health":[16]

[W]e permit a State to further its legitimate goal of protecting the life of the unborn by enacting legislation aimed at ensuring a decision that is mature and informed, even when in so doing the State expresses a preference for childbirth over abortion. In short, requiring that the woman be informed of the availability of information relating to fetal development and the assistance available should she decide to carry the pregnancy to full term is a reasonable measure to ensure an informed choice, one which might cause the woman to choose childbirth over abortion. This requirement cannot be considered a substantial obstacle to obtaining an abortion, and, it follows, there is no undue burden.[17]

Casey also sustained a mandated twenty-four-hour waiting period between the provision of consent information and the performance of an abortion. The plurality conceded that the waiting requirement has the effect of creating added costs and delays on the exercise of a woman's right to choose abortion. "The findings of fact by the District Court," the plurality explained, "indicate that because of the distances many women must travel to reach an abortion provider, the practical effect will often be a delay of much more than a day because the waiting period requires that a woman seeking an abortion make at least two visits to the doctor."[18] Furthermore, "the District Court found that for those women who have the fewest financial resources, those who must travel long distances, and those who have difficulty explaining their whereabouts to husbands, employers, or others, the 24-hour waiting period will be particularly burdensome."[19] But whether these added burdens are undue, the Court concluded, is another matter. "[N]ot every law which makes a right more difficult to exercise is, *ipso facto,* an infringement of that right," the Court wrote.[20] "The fact that a law which serves a valid purpose, one not designed to strike at the right itself, has the incidental effect of making it more difficult or more expensive to procure an abortion cannot be enough to invalidate it."[21]

With this principle in mind and notwithstanding the lower court's findings that the waiting period would prove burdensome for many women, the Court upheld the waiting period. The plurality emphasized, in support of this conclusion, that the district court had not rested its rejection of the waiting period on a finding that the burdens imposed a substantial obstacle but, rather, on the finding that the waiting period did not further the state's interest in the woman's health and interfered with the exercise of sound medical judgment. "Hence, on the record before us, and in the context of this facial challenge," the plurality explained, "we are not convinced that the 24-hour waiting period constitutes an undue burden."[22]

In contrast with the sustained provisions, the *Casey* plurality rejected a requirement that spouses receive notification before the performance of an abortion. Spousal notification, the plurality held, is

> likely to prevent a significant number of women from obtaining an abortion. It does not merely make abortions a little more difficult or expensive to obtain; for many women, it will impose a substantial obstacle. We must not blind ourselves to the fact that the significant number of women who fear for their safety and the safety of their children are likely to be deterred from procuring an abortion as surely as if the Commonwealth had outlawed abortion in all cases.[23]

In attempting to demarcate the boundary that separates permissible from impermissible abortion regulations, *Casey* ostensibly draws the line between encouragement of childbirth on the one hand and hindrance of abortion on the other. However, a more plausible, if more troubling, reading of *Casey* suggests that the boundary sits not between encouragement of childbirth and hindrance of abortion but, on the one hand, between encouragement of childbirth and discouragement of abortion and, on the other hand, the likely prevention of safe abortions. In other words, on a reasonable reading of *Casey*'s undue burden standard, for an abortion regulation to amount to a substantial obstacle, it must have the purpose or the likely effect of *stopping* a significant number of women from obtaining abortions, or the effect of creating considerable health risks. That women would confront considerable challenges in the face of an abortion measure is, on this reading, not sufficient to find the measure constitutionally flawed.

Among the reasons to interpret *Casey* this way is that, beyond the inferences that can be drawn from the Court's conclusions about the challenged Pennsylvania regulations, the plurality says little about how far states may go in persuading women to pursue childbirth rather than abortion. Noticeably absent from the joint ruling is treatment of the distinction between persuasion and pressure. Justice Harry Blackmun, writing separately, would have limited what the state may do when encouraging abortion, saying that such "measures must be designed to ensure that a woman's choice is 'mature and informed,' not intimidated, imposed, or impelled."[24] But the joint opinion does not adopt this type of limiting language.

Furthermore, while it is true that the plurality declares that states may not "hinder" abortion,[25] this pronouncement runs counter to virtually everything else established in *Casey* about what states may do with respect to impeding abortion. At least insofar as the encouragement of childbirth constitutes a hindrance to abortion—and surely it does—the joint opinion may be read as permitting states to hinder abortion. As Justice Antonin Scalia observes in commenting on the joint opinion's characterization of undue burden,

> An obstacle is "substantial," we are told, if it is "calculated[,] [not] to inform the woman's free choice, [but to] hinder it." This latter statement cannot possibly mean what it says. *Any* regulation of abortion that is intended to advance what the joint opinion concedes is the State's "substantial" interest in protecting unborn life will be "calculated [to] hinder" a decision to have an abortion.[26]

If the reading I have presented of *Casey* is a fair one, then the refashioning of *Roe* is even more extensive than it might initially appear. The license given to states to regulate abortion under *Casey* is a far cry from *Roe* and renders the so-called fundamental right to abortion much less fundamental than other rights afforded constitutional protection.

The discussion that follows applies my own (and, seemingly, Justice Scalia's) reading of the undue burden standard to the empirical analysis presented earlier in this text. Though *Casey* affirmed Pennsylvania's consent mandate without an explicit application of undue burden—relying, instead, on *Bellotti II*—the undue burden test is applicable to parental involvement regulations. Lower-court application of *Casey* indicates such a reading is derivable from Supreme Court precedent. For example, in *Planned Parenthood v. Miller,* the Eighth Circuit Court of Appeals invalidated a South Dakota parental notification requirement based on the undue burden standard.[27] Such an application of undue burden to parental involvement requirements does not come out of the blue. Just two years shy of *Casey*, the Supreme Court used the language of undue burden when upholding an Ohio parental notification requirement.[28] In addition, Justice O'Connor, co-author of the *Casey* ruling, adopted this language in her concurrence in *Hodgson v. Minnesota*, saying, "It has been my understanding in this area that if the particular regulation does not unduly burden the fundamental right then our evaluation of that regulation is limited to our determination that the regulation rationally relates to a legitimate state purpose."[29] Finally, while *Casey* does not explicitly apply the undue burden test to Pennsylvania's parental consent mandate, neither does it limit application of the test to those regulations of abortion that affect adult women.

While the undue burden test reaches parental involvement regulations, it does not replace the *Bellotti II* standard but stands alongside it, filling in where *Bellotti II* leaves off. *Bellotti II* provides guidelines for constructing involvement statutes, but these guidelines are not exhaustive. For example, they do not specify whether the bypass route must be available free of charge, and they do not provide a standard of review for assessing whether states violate the constitutional right to abortion by charging minors who use the option. The undue burden test supplies the measure for such an assessment, thereby providing the criterion for answering constitutional questions outside the scope of *Bellotti II*.

Guardianship Appointments

I begin with an examination of whether the designation of guardians to represent the interests of the unborn at bypass hearings has the purpose of placing a substantial obstacle in the path of a minor seeking an abortion. In light of the evidence recounted in Chapter 7, it is undeniable that for Judges Anderson and Cappel guardianship appointments grow out of judicial opposition to abortion and a desire to persuade the minor to choose childbirth rather than abortion. By designating guardians to represent the fetus, these judges provide a forum to present the minor with pro-life views, views that seek to dissuade the minor from aborting her fetus.

Is it fair, then, to conclude that Anderson and Cappel intend by appointing guardians to place a substantial obstacle in the minor's path to abortion? We would surely arrive at an affirmative answer to this question were we to appeal to the ordinary sense of the expression "substantial obstacle." However, this expression is a technical one, deriving substance from Supreme Court pronouncements. These pronouncements include the stipulation that states and agents of the state may "create a structural mechanism . . . [to] express profound respect for the life of the unborn."[30] This is precisely what the appointment of a guardian for the fetus is designed to achieve. The designation of a guardian is "aimed at ensuring that a woman's choice contemplates the consequences for the fetus,"[31] and this aim, *Casey* tells us, does "not necessarily interfere with the right recognized in *Roe*."[32]

The appointment of guardians in Alabama has forced minors to confront new and considerable challenges. And we can surmise that these appointments are intended, in part, to make the hearing more difficult. But because we can reasonably cast the judges' primary purpose in terms of encouraging childbirth and discouraging abortion, rather than in terms of preventing abortion, *Casey* makes it possible to conclude that the motivation behind appointing guardians in Alabama is constitutionally permissible. Although the line between encouraging childbirth and preventing abortion is a fine one, that is the line that *Casey* requires be drawn in determining the constitutionality of abortion regulations.

Alternatively, a strong case can be made that Anderson and Cappel have crossed the line—that their behavior is not consistent with an intent to merely encourage childbirth over abortion but to prevent abortion. Even if we conclude that Anderson and Cappel have breached the undue burden threshold, this would only lead to the conclusion that *their* guardianship appointments are unconstitutional. Such a conclusion would not prevent a judge or a state legislature, with the specific and stated intent of encouraging childbirth over abortion, from requiring fetal representation during bypass proceedings. As long as officials assert their interest as protecting potential life, and not as preventing abortion, guardianship appointments would fit into the *Casey* framework of what counts as a constitutionally acceptable purpose for regulating abortion.

If the purpose of fetal representation satisfies constitutional requirements, these appointments may yet prove unduly burdensome based on their effect. As we have seen, for the typical waiver hearing, one that does not include a guardian ad litem for the fetus, the minor has to make arrangements to travel to the courthouse, meet with an attorney, and go before a judge, all the while trying to maintain her anonymity and during what is already a trying time in the young woman's life. When guardians are added to the mix, the minor still has to make the requisite arrangements to go to court, meet with an attorney, and so forth. But the hearings are longer and have been delayed by cooling-off periods[33] and appeals filed by guardians.[34] Additionally, what is in the absence of a guardian essentially a nonadversarial, fact-finding inquiry becomes an adversarial proceeding, with an attendant magnification of anxiety.[35] Minors have confronted testimony from pro-life advocates and faced extensive cross-examination from an attorney whose legal mission it is to see to it that the minor gives birth. Inquiry as to whether the minor is mature and capable of giving informed consent to a medical procedure is expanded to include inquiry concerning whether she comprehends the "philosophic and social arguments of great weight that can be brought to bear in favor of continuing the pregnancy to full term."[36]

Guardianship appointments make what is already a challenging process all the more challenging. But do the added challenges constitute a substantial obstacle? Again, under an ordinary sense of the phrase, the answer is obviously yes. Like the predicament of the proverbial straw-hauling camel, the addition of a guardian places one more obstacle on top of another, making the hurdle the minor confronts more difficult to overcome.

Nevertheless, under the authority of *Casey,* the added challenges do not unduly burden minors. First, the fact that hearings involving fetal representation last longer than the typical hearing is not enough to invalidate the use of guardians. Only a few of the hearings have lasted more than two hours. And even those delays might withstand constitutional scrutiny, given the Court's acceptance of twenty-four-hour waiting periods.[37] With respect to what are now more routine hearings—hearings that usually last less than ninety minutes—the additional time is inconsequential under *Casey.*[38]

Second, while hearings have become increasingly adversarial with the involvement of guardians, this does not necessarily constitute an impermissible barrier to abortion. McPhillips may, indeed, have gone too far in his interrogation. And for the sake of the argument, we can grant that his involvement posed an undue burden on that particular minor. Still, *Casey* does not preclude adversarial bypass proceedings. Because *Casey* permits the state to make women aware that there are strong arguments in favor of childbirth and against abortion, and because guardians work toward this end, their presence and the attendant adversity would appear to be acceptable.

Third, and maybe most important, there is little indication that minors have been prevented from obtaining abortions due to the presence of fetal representation. The appointment of a guardian for the fetus would create a substantial obstacle if a significant number of minors were "deterred from procuring an abortion as surely as if the [state] had outlawed abortion in all cases."[39] But unlike the case of spousal notification, evidence does not demonstrate at this point that minors have been deterred from pursuing bypass requests. In fact, even with the presence of guardians, minors have successfully petitioned for waivers of consent, and there is no reliable evidence to suggest that minors forgo abortions because of guardians.

In response to the above, it might be argued that the orders of Montgomery County judges requiring such things as a cooling-off period are unconstitutional. It might also be argued that the religious overtones of some of these hearings are constitutionally suspect. When direct questioning related to Bible scripture comes into play, so do First Amendment issues. Similarly dubious are questions like the following one posed by a guardian to a minor: "If you did have a complication and you had to go to the hospital, your church congregation is going to find out what's happened. How is that going to effect [*sic*] your going to church every Sunday?"[40]

These constitutional concerns are genuine but beside the point. Such conduct does not demonstrate the constitutional impermissibility of the guardianship appointments themselves. What raises concern are the orders and the religious questions, not the presence of the guardian. Therefore, it cannot be said in light of *Casey* that the mere appointment of a guardian to represent the fetus has the effect of imposing a substantial obstacle on a minor.

Sav-A-Life Counseling

Whereas current precedent may permit fetal representation, the judicial directive that minors receive counseling from a Sav-A-Life crisis pregnancy center fails constitutional inspection. However, rather than failing *Casey*'s undue burden test, the constitutional infirmity of this requirement owes principally to a violation of the First Amendment's Establishment Clause, which provides that "Congress shall make no law respecting an establishment of religion."[41] Given Sav-A-Life's evangelical mission, judges who condition bypass grants on the receipt of counseling from this ministry effectively require religious counseling, thereby violating each of the three legal tests conjured by the Supreme Court to interpret the Establishment Clause—the *Lemon* test, the coercion test, and the endorsement test.[42]

Lemon Test

In the 1971 case *Lemon v. Kurtzman*,[43] the Court advanced what has come to be known as the *Lemon* test to assess alleged breaches of the Establishment Clause. *Lemon* requires, "[f]irst, the statute must have a secular legislative purpose; second, its principal or primary effect must be one that neither advances nor inhibits religion; finally, the statute must not foster 'an excessive government entanglement with religion.'"[44] Failure of any prong of *Lemon* amounts to an Establishment Clause violation.

To satisfy the first prong of the *Lemon* test, mandated Sav-A-Life counseling must be motivated by a secular purpose. As we have seen, there are some grounds for suspecting that religious views inspire the Sav-A-Life mandate, at least for some judges. Furthermore, there is no doubt that the goal of discouraging abortion is behind this mandate. However, judges also contend that pro-life counseling, when offered in conjunction with counseling provided by abortion clinic personnel, ensures balanced information on pregnancy options. It is arguable, then, that the judges' stated goals stand up as secular, whether or not they arise from some deeper religious conviction. Whether judges aim to ensure balanced information or to encourage childbirth, these goals serve a secular purpose and do not obviously fail the first prong of the *Lemon* test.

The mandate does fail the second prong of *Lemon*. Among the ways in which government conduct would impermissibly advance religion is when that conduct supports religious indoctrination. The Court has said:

> Although Establishment Clause jurisprudence is characterized by few absolutes, the Clause does absolutely prohibit government-financed or government-sponsored indoctrination into the beliefs of a particular religious faith. Such indoctrination, if permitted to occur, would have devastating effects on the right of each individual voluntarily to deter-

mine what to believe (and what not to believe) free of any coercive pressures from the State, while at the same time tainting the resulting religious beliefs with a corrosive secularism.[45]

Despite this holding, the Court has been reluctant in recent rulings to presume that religiously affiliated institutions will engage in indoctrination. For instance, the Court held in *Bowen v. Kendrick*[46] that Congress may pass legislation directing funds to religiously affiliated institutions that provide education and counseling services to adolescents. In deciding this facial challenge, the Court rejected the presumption that such funding would inevitably result in religious inculcation. The Court concluded instead that as long as the religiously affiliated grantees prove not to be "pervasively sectarian"—that is, institutions "in which the secular cannot be separated from the sectarian"[47]—the presumption of state-sponsored religious indoctrination can be rejected. But the Court also explained that "a relevant factor in deciding whether a particular statute on its face can be said to have the improper effect of advancing religion is the determination of whether, and to what extent, the statute directs government aid to pervasively sectarian institutions."[48] The *Bowen* Court also left open the possibility that an "as applied" challenge might reveal the constitutional deficiencies of the congressional funding statute if it could be shown that, in practice, the flow of aid reaches pervasively sectarian religious institutions. This piece of Establishment Clause precedent holds, in sum, that government may, as part of an otherwise religiously neutral program, directly sponsor religiously affiliated institutions with the aim of encouraging those institutions to provide education and counseling services to adolescents. But the Establishment Clause is breached when the sponsored institutions are pervasively sectarian.

Application of these tenets to the Sav-A-Life mandate reveals constitutional deficiencies. While precedent holds that religious inspiration or affiliation with a religious institution does not by itself make an organization pervasively sectarian,[49] Sav-A-Life's evangelical imperative makes it impossible to imagine that the sectarian character of the organization is less than pervasive.[50] Recall the group's *Statement of Faith*, which states that all affiliates and volunteers—who are required to sign the statement—"believe that all who receive by faith the Lord Jesus Christ are born of the Holy Spirit and thereby become children of God, and there is no other way of salvation," and "believe in the great commission which our Lord has given His Church to evangelize the world, and that this evangelization is the great mission of the church."[51] Signers thereby embrace their "Christian duty to witness by word and deed to these truths."[52]

Interviews with Sav-A-Life directors also leave no doubt that Christianity guides all of the organization's activities. These directors attested to the central and indispensable role religion has in their organization and were forthright in revealing that the defining characteristic of their organization is sharing the gospel. As one director summed up, "Our mission is to share the Gospel of Lord Jesus Christ with women who are in crisis pregnancy and to do that with services we offer."[53]

Since Sav-A-Life is a pervasively sectarian institution engaged in the practice of religious indoctrination, mandated Sav-A-Life counseling impermissibly advances religion in contravention of the second prong of *Lemon*.

Mandated counseling also breaches *Lemon*'s third prong. A precise definition of "excessive entanglement" is hard to come by in Supreme Court precedent, but considerations surrounding this prong typically attend to the tangible connections between church and state, such as administrative oversight of religious institutions that accompanies funding programs.[54] While the Sav-A-Life mandate does not involve much in the way of administrative oversight and interaction, the entanglement failure comes from the lack of government supervision and from what constitutionally required government supervision would entail. Given that evangelical Christian ministries provide the mandated counseling, "to ensure that religion is not advanced would require extensive and continuous monitoring and direct oversight of every counseling session."[55] But such monitoring and oversight would create excessive entanglement, thereby violating First Amendment prohibitions.[56] In short, when grounds exist for assuming that government-supported religious organizations are pervasively sectarian—as is the case with Sav-A-Life—more intensive monitoring would be required to protect against the risks of indoctrination. This, in turn, would foster excessive entanglement by virtue of the necessary government intrusion into the operations of this religious organization.

Failure under *Lemon* is by itself enough to show a violation of the Establishment Clause. But even while lingering as a primary gauge of permissible government involvement with religion, the *Lemon* test has been much derided, and conservative jurists have attempted to remove it from life support.[57] Therefore, it is worth observing that the constitutional infirmity of mandated Sav-A-Life counseling is not tied to the fate of the *Lemon* test.

Coercion Test

In *Lee v. Weisman*,[58] the Court ruled that an invocation and benediction by a clergy member at a public secondary school graduation ceremony violated the Establishment Clause. The Court rested its finding on the principle that "government may not coerce anyone to support or participate in religion or its exercise, or otherwise act in a way which establishes a [state] religion or religious faith, or tends to do so."[59] In so holding, the Court adopted the coercion test as an independent means for assessing Establishment Clause challenges.

The coercive aspect of the Sav-A-Life counseling mandate is straightforward. The only way to construe mandated Sav-A-Life counseling as noncoercive is to suggest that minors have another option available to avoid participation in such counseling—namely consulting with their parents. But this is unconvincing. A minor who rejects Sav-A-Life counseling cannot be said to freely choose parental involvement. This is especially true when a minor seeks a bypass after her parents refuse to consent, for in that instance a minor is not choosing between involving her parents and receiving counseling. Rather, she is choosing between continuing an unwanted pregnancy and receiving counseling. That choice is surely untenable.

While the coercive aspect of mandated Sav-A-Life counseling proves uncomplicated, this alone does not settle the outcome of the coercion test. It must also be shown that the coerced behavior constitutes participation in a religious activity.[60]

Sav-A-Life counseling may not be a precise analogue of public recitations of prayer that have been deemed unconstitutional in the Court's recent applications of the coercion test.[61] Still, proselytizing by sharing the gospel—a practice employed by each of the Sav-A-Life centers I visited—surely counts as a religious activity. When a counselor asks a young woman "about her relationship with Christ"[62] or says that "the only help is a relationship with Jesus Christ,"[63] she engages in a religious activity. Providing counseling based on "Evangelism Explosion"[64] —for example, asking a young woman, "If you die tonight, will you go to heaven?"[65]—is likewise a type of religious exercise. Showing women the Bible or certain religious tracts, as counselors at Sav-A-Life do,[66] is comparable to leading someone in a prayer. However the gospel is shared, whether through direct prayer, reading of Bible verses, or comments about the benefits of committing one's life to Christ, the evidence demonstrates that Sav-A-Life counseling is a religious activity.[67] Thus, when judges stipulate that minors obtain counseling from Sav-A-Life, they effectively force young women to participate in a religious activity and, in so doing, violate Establishment Clause strictures against coercion.

It does not help matters that judges who require a pregnant minor to receive counseling from Sav-A-Life do so in advance of determining whether that minor is sufficiently mature to proceed with an abortion absent parental consent. In so doing, the judicial policy of mandating counseling runs the following additional risk: a minor later deemed immature will have been required to receive religious counseling. While government may not coerce anyone—whether mature or immature, adult or child—to support or participate in religion or its exercise, the Court has expressed particular apprehension when such coercion affects those of an impressionable age.[68]

Endorsement Test

The endorsement test derives from several concurring opinions authored by Justice O'Connor[69] and holds that "[d]irect government action endorsing religion or a particular religious practice is invalid."[70] The test does not preclude government from acknowledging or taking account of religion.[71] However,

> [i]t does preclude government from conveying or attempting to convey a message that religion or a particular religious belief is favored or preferred. Such an endorsement infringes the religious liberty of the nonadherent, for when the power, prestige and financial support of government is placed behind a particular religious belief, the indirect coercive pressure upon religious minorities to conform to the prevailing officially approved religion is plain.[72]

A judge who requires counseling offered by an evangelical Christian mission impermissibly endorses religion by sending "a message to nonadherents that they are outsiders, not full members of the political community, and an accompanying message to adherents that they are insiders, favored members of the political community."[73] Though not a public communication, the message is arguably stronger because it comes in the context of a coercive practice. Indeed, under enforced participation in Sav-A-Life counseling "an audience gathered by state power is lent . . . to a religious cause."[74]

Secular Pro-Life Counseling

The constitutional flaw of the counseling mandate imposed in Alabama arises from the pervasively sectarian character of Sav-A-Life. Interestingly, however, it does not follow that a pro-life counseling mandate, stripped of sectarian purpose and content, would produce a constitutional violation. A counseling mandate imposed by a judge who did not recommend a specific counseling organization and imposed in a state where minors could obtain pro-life counseling from a secular organization, or even from a religious organization that is not pervasively sectarian, would seem to survive constitutional scrutiny. Such a requirement would be free of Establishment Clause infirmity. Moreover, constructed in this fashion, this requirement would be a mere incremental strengthening of informed consent mandates, which have already withstood the *Casey* undue burden test. To be sure, a nonsectarian pro-life counseling mandate would prove more burdensome than the informed consent mandates already in place, for the former would entail an in-person counseling session and thus added delay. Still, this hypothetical burden is not different in kind or degree from those already allowed under *Casey*.

It is worth pointing out that virtually all crisis pregnancy centers, both in and beyond Alabama, are Christian ministries. So the prospect that a minor could obtain secular pro-life counseling at a crisis pregnancy center is remote.

Gaining Access to Bypass Proceedings

Concerning the surveys of courts conducted in Alabama, Pennsylvania, and Tennessee, the undue burden test asks whether the behavior of those designated to handle the bypass process amounts to the creation of a substantial obstacle in a pregnant minor's path. As we have seen, many courts are incapable of offering basic and accurate information about the bypass procedure in a timely fashion. The progress of a minor toward obtaining a judicial hearing would obviously be impeded by interaction with one of these courts. But the question of whether the state has created a substantial obstacle depends on the state's readiness as a whole to implement the bypass process.

It is hard to deny that the magnitude of ignorance we encountered in Alabama and Pennsylvania adds up to a substantial obstacle. Recall that in Pennsylvania almost three-quarters of the courts proved woefully ignorant of their responsibilities, and in Alabama two-fifths proved similarly ignorant. Even under my interpretation of *Casey* whereby regulations are permitted unless they are likely to prevent a significant number of women from obtaining abortions, Pennsylvania and Alabama would seem to have violated constitutional demands.

The situation in Tennessee is another matter. While we came across considerable ignorance during our contacts with courts, we also found that in over three-quarters of Tennessee counties a minor seeking to gain information on the waiver route would, upon reaching a DCS advocate, receive adequate information. In all, we found only fourteen counties where both courts and DCS advocates proved poorly informed about the bypass process. Whether this magnitude of ignorance amounts to a constitutional violation is unclear, especially given that the venue provision in Tennessee permits minors to petition for a bypass in any county in the state. It is at least arguable that the degree of ignorance revealed in Tennessee—15 percent of the state—is within the margins of acceptability under standing precedent.

But we encountered more than just ignorance in Tennessee. Recall that in thirteen Tennessee counties, it took between five and seventeen calls to reach informed court personnel and an average of nearly five calls to reach a DCS advocate who proved prepared to guide a minor through the process. We also encountered instances in which the delay in obtaining information resulted not from the number of phone calls but from personnel who proved unavailable, sometimes for many days.

For a pregnant teen who seeks a waiver of parental involvement, the obstacle created by having to place numerous phone calls is genuine. Still, precedent can be read as permitting the magnitude of administrative deficiencies we found in Tennessee. Consider *Hodgson v. Minnesota,* where the Court upheld the forty-eight-hour waiting period that accompanied Minnesota's two-parent notice requirement. The Court did so in the context of an "as applied" challenge and despite lower-court findings that the regulation created sometimes notable delays and increased health risks. According to the lower court, the imposed waiting period often transformed into delays of a week or more between parental notice and termination of the pregnancy.[75] This magnitude of delay, the lower court found, increased the medical risk associated with abortion to a statistically significant degree. Conceding the lower court's findings concerning the harm associated with the practical implementation of such a waiting period, the Supreme Court nevertheless concluded that the forty-eight-hour delay imposed only a minimal burden on the right of the minor to decide whether or not to terminate her pregnancy:

> Although the District Court found that scheduling factors, weather, and the minor's school and work commitments may combine, in many cases, to create a delay of a week or longer between the initiation of notification and the abortion, there is no evidence that the 48-hour period itself is unreasonable or longer than appropriate for adequate consultation between parent and child.[76]

Furthermore, both the district court's analysis in *Hodgson* and the Supreme Court's decision acknowledged some delays produced by judges who were unwilling to hear bypass cases, and both courts found such delays unproblematic. Even though the district court judge ruled against Minnesota's consent requirement, he concluded that the bypass process "as presently executed by Minnesota courts and the other offices that participate in bypass proceedings complies with the procedural requirements set forth in *Bellotti II* and approved in [*Planned Parenthood Ass'n v.*] *Ashcroft*." This conclusion is remarkable, given that the district court judge also found that

> [d]espite conscientious efforts to provide an expeditious court bypass option in non-metropolitan areas, a number of counties are not served by a judge who is willing to hear bypass petitions. A minor in one of these counties must travel to another county, most commonly a metropolitan county, to obtain an expeditious hearing of her petition. Although burdensome, this necessity also does not reflect a systemic failure to provide a judicial bypass option in the most expeditious practicable manner.[77]

Precedent thus suggests that a plausible case could be made that minors are only incidentally and not unduly burdened by the magnitude of delay associated with the administrative inefficiencies and judicial recusals seen in Tennessee. After all, it appears that delays of a week or more are permitted, even when the state's own failures contribute to those delays.

The Myth of Roe

While *Roe v. Wade* has attained iconic status in the political and cultural discourse of this country, there is a new sheriff in town and his name is *Casey*. With *Roe's* displacement, states may well find constitutional support when requiring fetal representation to persuade young women to carry their pregnancies to term. Pro-life counseling of the nonreligious variety might also find constitutional sustenance. And while widespread ignorance of the bypass option is constitutionally indefensible, *Casey* may well tolerate involvement mandates wherein minors face the prospect of maneuvering through a maze of bureaucracy.

Casey's permissiveness comes from its failure to intelligibly distinguish between encouraging childbirth and hindering abortion. This unintelligibility empowers states, under the guise of advocating childbirth, to place significant barriers in the path to abortion, precisely what the ruling purports to forbid. *Casey* invites states to devise, for the sake of the fetus, whatever obstacle course they wish women to maneuver through, as long as the obstacles, however high and onerous, are capable of being hurdled and do not impose serious health or safety hazards.

That *Casey* may be read as providing sanction to such obstacles does not mean states should accept the invitation to craft bad public policy. But states (and judges) have accepted this invitation, imposing regulations that advance a particular moral view of personhood, pregnancy, childbirth, and abortion. Because *Casey* permits states to increase the price tag for abortion and inflict mounting delays under the auspices of so-called incidental burdens, minors can be made to bear the weight of the state's moral perspective.

Young women are not the only targets of such added burdens. Several states have fortified the informed consent provisions that apply to all women seeking an abortion. Some have done so by way of requiring in-person counseling instead of phone counseling.[78] Others, like Ohio, now require that the treating physician, rather than a nurse or physicians' assistant, communicate state-mandated information on abortion.[79]

Additional steps to augment informed consent provisions are in the works. Michigan has enacted a provision requiring a doctor who has taken an ultrasound of the fetus to offer the woman the option of viewing that image before an abortion.[80] Following this lead, the Georgia Senate passed legislation that would require all women seeking an abortion to be offered the opportunity to view an ultrasound or sonogram of the fetus.[81]

In light of these ongoing efforts, we should not be surprised to see state legislatures pursue statutes to codify the judicial practices we have seen minors face in the bypass process and extend them to adult women. For example, under *Casey* and given the current political climate, legislation requiring all women to obtain pro-life counseling or to meet with a designated representative of the fetus prior to obtaining an abortion may well be forthcoming.[82] What measures would better serve the goal of "ensuring that a woman's choice contemplates the consequences for the fetus"?[83]

But requiring an adult woman to discuss her abortion decision with a pro-life counselor or a guardian who speaks for the fetus is a chilling prospect, one that should be seen as striking at the heart of liberty. As Justice John Paul Stevens rightly notes,

> Serious questions arise . . . when a State attempts to "persuade the woman to choose childbirth over abortion." Decisional autonomy must limit the State's power to inject into a woman's most personal deliberations its own views of what is best. The State may promote its preferences by funding childbirth, by creating and maintaining alternatives to abortion, and by espousing the virtues of family; but it must respect the individual's freedom to make such judgments.[84]

The popular American consciousness is replete with pious sounding myths—"the separation of church and state," "freedom of speech," "one man, one vote," "separate is not equal." Among these platitudes is *Roe,* so familiar in its rock star status that it goes by one name, like Madonna and Prince. But as is the case with these other ubiquitous aphorisms, what lies behind *Roe* is far less substantial than what is imagined. The fact is that whatever *Roe* may have once been, it is no longer, and whatever confidence it may have instilled is no longer justified. *Casey* is a much different beast whose wrath has not yet been fully felt or digested by the popular imagination.

9

Myth-Guided Policy

> The law is real, but it is also a figment of our imaginations.
> —Stuart Scheingold, *The Politics of Rights*[1]

The argument of this book is directed at those who have made a good-faith compromise on the parental involvement issue. These compromisers, a group to which I once belonged, have in mind a picture of what a world with such mandates will be like. Pregnant minors will be encouraged to seek guidance from parents, and courts will protect those who choose otherwise. We have seen, though, that many courts are not prepared to do their duty, whether due to ignorance, recalcitrance, or incompetence. We have seen judges who are willing to employ hardball tactics to get minors to bend to their will. Whatever the Supreme Court might decide about how much implementation failure is too much or what obstacles too burdensome, it is up to the good-faith compromiser to decide whether the realities of parental involvement mandates sufficiently approximate her picture to warrant continued support. This is a personal decision. To my mind the case is clear. I invite the reader to be her own judge.

Scope of Bypass Irregularities

Evidence suggests that the types of implementation failures we have seen in Alabama, Pennsylvania, and Tennessee are not unique to those states. For example, Melissa Jacobs's study of Texas conducted in 2003 found that only 108 of 254 county courts were prepared to handle the judicial bypass procedure of that state's parental notification law.[2] Jacobs found that unprepared courts were commonly confused about the court's duty to appoint an attorney. . . . A large number said that a minor would either need to obtain an attorney on her own or represent herself. . . . Some explained that a minor would not need an attorney. . . . A significant number of clerks expressly stated that their judges would not appoint an attorney or would not have time to appoint one.[3]

Jane's Due Process, a nonprofit advocacy group that helps Texas teens navigate the bypass route, reports that minors sometimes confront resistance from judges who follow their personal predilections when handling waiver requests. One minor reportedly gave the following account of her hearing: "The judge started crying. He left the room and when he came back, he said that I reminded him of his granddaughter and that he wouldn't sign the order because it wasn't a 'life or death' situation."[4] Another said this of her effort to obtain a hearing in Texas: "I went to the courthouse to file my application [for judicial bypass] and the judge came out of his office and told me that he would give me a hearing but he didn't believe in abortion and that he would never give me the okay to have one."[5] In North Carolina, the *Roanoke Times* reports, court clerks in one county, in blatant disregard of confidentiality requirements, called the parents of a pregnant teen who sought a petition to waive parental involvement.[6]

Maybe the most widespread and longstanding display of resistance to involvement mandates comes in the form of judicial refusal to hear bypass petitions. Several accounts suggest that judges in Indiana, Massachusetts, Minnesota, and South Carolina have opted out of bypass hearings. A 1992 newspaper article reports that minors looking to waive parental involvement in Indiana are often advised to go out of state in part because judges refuse to hold hearings.[7] Recusals in Massachusetts date back to the early 1980s. According to a 1983 article, 8 of 62 Massachusetts judges authorized to hear bypass cases were unwilling to do so, "claiming that they have moral problems with abortion," and another 2 were unwilling to "hear petitions filed by minors who are more than 12 weeks pregnant."[8] Despite reports that Massachusetts has one of the smoothest functioning bypass systems, the recusal trend continued. As a 1992 *New York Times* story indicates, "some [minors] must travel long distances because the judges in their areas will not schedule abortion hearings."[9] Jamie Sabino, an attorney who has helped organize lawyers to represent minors at hearings, said this of Massachusetts recusals: "This is the only area of law where judges recuse themselves just because they don't want to hear a certain kind of case. They don't say, 'I won't hear that case because I don't believe in capital punishment,' but somehow, in this country, abortion is outside the regular rules."[10]

Minnesota has also seen its share of recusals. Patricia Donovan's 1983 analysis of the bypass process states that judicial recusal "is especially acute in Minnesota, where very few judges aside from the three juvenile court judges in Minneapolis, St. Paul and Duluth have assumed their responsibility to implement the law."[11] A similar pattern is evidenced in the findings of fact delivered by U.S. District Judge Donald Alsop in *Hodgson v. Minnesota*. Reviewing the bypass process from 1981 to 1986, Alsop found several Minnesota counties where judges refused to preside over bypass cases.[12]

In South Carolina, the consequences of recusals are illuminated by a story told by Billie Lominick, a woman who helped her grandson's girlfriend, Mary, secure an abortion out of state. In a statement before the U.S. House Judiciary Committee, Lominick explained her failed efforts to find a South Carolina court that would hear a bypass petition.[13] "Mary was in an abusive home," Lominick reported.[14] "So I called around the State to get her an abortion, and no one—no judge would hear me."[15] Lominick explained that after more phone calls,

[we] were only able to find two courts in our whole state that would take judicial bypass cases. The closest judge who would hear a petition was over an hour from our home. . . . Our hopes were dashed, however, when we learned that the judge had announced only a month earlier that the court would only take cases from minors residing within that county.[16]

In the end, Lominick arranged for a bypass hearing in Georgia, three hours from their home in South Carolina.[17]

Because bypass hearings are closed and records are sealed, it is difficult to determine the scope of pro-life judicial activism in this context. Authoritative information about bypass cases is sometimes available from appellate rulings. But not all states publish such rulings, not all such rulings are especially revelatory of judicial practice, and, presumably, not all minors who are denied bypasses appeal. Moreover,

extremely well hidden are those problematic judicial practices that occur in the context of hearings that result in bypass grants. As one lawyer who routinely represents minors in bypass cases in Massachusetts
said,

> The vast majority of judges handle these hearings with some dignity
> and some compassion, but we tell people to avoid 25 percent of the
> judges. . . . Laws are generally implemented through appeals. The
> judges know that as long as they grant a minor's petition, there is noth-
> ing to appeal, and therefore no one will look at how they conducted the
> hearing.[18]

Nevertheless, others have reported judicial antics similar to those I have
described.

The judicial practice of appointing guardians to represent the unborn
that has taken hold in Montgomery County, Alabama, was not invented
there. In 1989 a Florida judge appointed a guardian to represent the
fetus at a bypass hearing. Though the judge found in the minor's favor,
the guardian went on to appeal the ruling to the Florida Supreme
Court, at which time the high court rejected the appointment.[19] A judge
in Louisiana faced similar rejection upon appointing fetal representation
in 1991.[20] And an article in the *Nation* indicates that a judge in Indiana
was also overruled after appointing fetal representation.[21]

Unlike in Alabama, trial judges in Florida, Louisiana, and Indiana
have been rebuffed when appointing guardians for the fetus. But the ra-
tionales put forward in at least two of these reversals do not close the
door to future guardianship appointments. In Florida, the high court
was notably brief when it came to explaining its rejection of the appointment, saying only that "[p]reliminarily, we find that the appointment of a guardian ad litem for the fetus was clearly improper."[22] In
Louisiana, the state Supreme Court granted a motion "to revoke the
lower court's appointment of an attorney," stating simply that the
state's parental consent statute "does not contemplate the appointment
of an attorney for the fetus or an adversarial proceeding."[23] In neither
instance did the high courts reject the appointments on federal constitutional grounds. Nor did the courts provide arguments or referrals to
precedent to bolster the holdings. Additionally, the mere fact that such
appointments have been tried suggests a judicial disposition toward cre-
ativity when it comes to discouraging abortion.

At the very least, the door to guardianship appointments remains open for other states to test, and reports indicate that judges in Texas may be doing so. The survey of Texas courts conducted by Jacobs revealed two courts that "stated that a guardian ad litem would be appointed for the fetus" in bypass cases.[24] Relatedly, there may be a back-door avenue for giving voice to fetal interests in the courtroom. Some guardians appointed for the minor in Texas "have been reported as saying that instead of representing the 'best interests of the minor,' they represent 'the fetus.'"[25] Additionally, as the *Nation* reports, "Judge James Payne in Indianapolis, for example, routinely appointed antiabortion lawyers to represent pregnant girls."[26]

Like guardianship appointments, the judicial practice of mandating pro-life counseling has appeared outside of Alabama. According to the *Nation,* judges in Mississippi "require visits to an antiabortion counseling center before granting a hearing."[27] Lynda Zielinski, an Ohio social worker whose job included interviewing juveniles prior to their hearings, says this in a 2006 account of the functioning of the bypass process:

> In our juvenile court I have observed a number of judges, who fall into several categories. Each is guided by personal beliefs—not about maturity, but about abortion.
>
> One type of judge believes that the agencies we rely on for pregnancy counseling don't give proper emphasis to the "pro-life" viewpoint, and so provides a separate list to the Jane Does. Judges in that category require them to visit one of these places and bring back some literature as proof, then quiz the young women on their errant sexual behavior.[28]

Lending support to the practice of requiring pro-life and even religious counseling as part of the bypass process is Judge Priscilla Owen, formerly of the Texas Supreme Court and now on the bench of the U.S. Court of Appeals for the Fifth Circuit.[29] A controversial Bush appointment to the federal courts and on some people's shortlist for a slot on the Supreme Court,[30] Owen earned some renown for her opinions in bypass appeals. In the Texas Supreme Court's first ruling on that state's parental notification statute, Owen wrote a concurring opinion expressing support for a more stringent counseling requirement:

> The Court properly requires a minor to consult a health-care provider about the general risks of an abortion. But that is insufficient. . . . I

would require a minor to demonstrate that she has sought and obtained meaningful counseling from a qualified source about the emotional and psychological impact she may experience now and later in her life as a result of having an abortion. She should be able to demonstrate to a court that she understands that some women have experienced severe remorse and regret. She should also indicate to the court that she is aware of and has considered that there are philosophic, social, moral, and religious arguments that can be brought to bear when considering abortion. A court cannot, of course, require a minor to adopt or adhere to any particular philosophy or to profess any religious beliefs. But requiring a minor to exhibit an awareness that there are issues, including religious ones, surrounding the abortion decision is not prohibited by the Establishment Clause.[31]

Despite the apparent problems with the bypass process, the minor who finds her way into a bypass hearing has a very good chance of getting her petition granted. For example, of the 3,573 bypass petitions filed in Minnesota between August 1981 and March 1986, some 3,558 were granted.[32] A study of 477 bypass cases heard in Massachusetts between December 1981 and June 1985 revealed only a single bypass denial.[33] And a 2003 "survey of [Ohio's] largest juvenile courts shows that nine times out of 10, a judge approves a teen's request to have an abortion without notifying a parent."[34] My own study confirms that Pennsylvania judges who hear bypass petitions rarely deny them.[35]

Some supporters of involvement mandates have seized on the high rate of bypass grants to suggest that the process is slanted in favor of the minor. For example, "Mary Spaulding Balch, who monitors state legislation for the National Right to Life Committee, said it suggests that judicial bypasses amount to 'little more than a rubber stamp.' "[36] Similarly, according to Pennsylvania lawyer and pro-life activist Joseph Stanton, "The petition is boilerplate, and the hearing has all the earmarks of a rubber stamp."[37]

The high approval rate of bypass petitions does not provide grounds for concluding that the process is functional or lacking in problematic consequences. First, it is likely that the high success rate owes in part to the character of those minors who choose to pursue this route and succeed in finding their way to hearings. Older and more mature minors tend to avail themselves of the bypass option.[38] Furthermore, both judges and lawyers who handle bypass cases often comment that the very fact that a minor has the facility to overcome the hurdles on her way to a courthouse in search of a waiver provides some evidence of maturity.[39] A high rate of success, therefore, may tell us more about the minors who choose the bypass option than about the functionality of that option. As a Minnesota judge testified, "What I have come to believe . . . [is] that really the judicial function is merely a rubber stamp. The decision has already been made before they have gotten to my chambers. The young women I have seen have been very mature and capable of giving the required consent."[40]

Second, that a minor might ultimately make her way to a hearing before a judge who is likely to grant her request says nothing of the effort she makes to get there.[41] Indeed, the high rate of bypass grants owes in part to forum shopping. Abortion providers and court personnel often advise minors to avoid certain judges and to seek relief from others. The same survey of Ohio noted above indicates that when judges show a disposition to deny bypass petitions, "[a]bortion providers steer girls to another county, already knowing what the answer will be."[42] Cincinnati, located in Hamilton County, provides a case in point. "[F]ew teens even ask for permission in conservative Hamilton County, the birthplace of Right to Life," reports Phil Trexler of the *Akron Beacon Journal*.[43] "Despite being the state's third-largest county, the number of requests to Cincinnati judges compares more closely to smaller, rural counties," with only two bypass requests filed between 2001 and 2003.[44] "[T]eens are routinely referred to courts outside the abortion-debate inferno in Hamilton County," and they travel far from Cincinnati "because of a long history of denials and subsequent appeals."[45]

Also contributing to the high rate of bypass grants is the fact that, with many conservative judges refusing to handle bypass requests, the judges willing to hear these petitions often have liberal inclinations. There is every reason to believe that these judges, like their conservative counterparts, approach hearings with a political lens and, unlike their counterparts, are disposed toward granting bypass requests. Take, for instance, an admittedly pro-choice judge who offered the following frank comments about his own liberal outlook when asked to compare himself with a pro-life judge:

All of us come to the bench with biases. The trick is to contain the biases and try to do what you think is right under the law. My own philosophical view causes me to act the way I act in these cases. I don't know that I put my views aside. I'm guilty of that. I'll do it the way I think is right. I'm in a position to advance my views and I'll do that, but I'll follow the law. Where's the threshold for maturity? My threshold may be a lot lower [than a pro-life judge]. I meet these women. I'm impressed with them. I'm satisfied. I don't rubber stamp it. I'm genuinely interested in these women. And for me, if we have an intelligent, rational conversation, then I'll find them to be mature.[46]

This judge also expressed a view that is repeated by many who handle bypass cases: "I'm not sure if she's not mature enough to have the abortion whether she'd be mature enough to go through with the pregnancy."[47] Legal scholar Jamin B. Raskin elaborates this paradox in a similar fashion:

[H]ow can a girl or young woman be too immature to decide whether to have a baby, but mature enough to go through pregnancy, give birth, and make a thousand important decisions regarding how to nurture, raise and educate the child (or children, in the case of twins or other multiples)? . . . [I]t would never be in the best interest of such an immature young person seeking an abortion to be denied one and instead forced to go through the complicated physical, emotional, and personal changes imposed by pregnancy, childbirth, and motherhood.[48]

This perspective may lead judges to conclude that when a minor fails to prove the maturity prong of the *Bellotti II* standard she has, in so doing, shown that a bypass is in order by proving that the abortion would serve her best interest.

Thus, supporters of involvement mandates are correct to observe that judges regularly approve bypass petitions and that this is, in part, indicative of a liberal bias, but these points do not offset or redress the problems associated with getting to a hearing in the first place. Nor do they advance the case for parental involvement mandates—at least not if one accepts the compromise view that blanket mandates are unacceptable. Rather, they provide additional evidence of the political manner in which these petitions are handled and the lack of congruity between what we hope the bypass process will achieve and what it in practice achieves.

Mythologies

If the parental involvement compromiser has a too rosy conception of how the bypass process will work in the world, what accounts for this? Presumably not a failure to recognize that pro-life advocates generally serve as the champions of parental involvement and aim to prevent abortions through such legislation. In fact, pro-life advocates do not shy away from professing that their primary aim in sponsoring involvement legislation is not to secure parental rights but to end abortion.

For example, on Sunday, June 5, 2005, Texas Governor Rick Perry signed legislation mandating parental consent for abortion, replacing a notification bill that had been in place since 1999.[49] Though not a surprising move, what was surprising, or at least extraordinary, was the bill-signing ceremony. In a gesture boldly signifying the political and religious character of the abortion battle, Perry took the ceremonial signing event to the school gymnasium of an evangelical church. The governor's remarks to an audience of about 1,000 were preceded by speeches given by several pastors and followed by a closing benediction.[50] As Associated Press writer Matt Curry described the occasion, "Even for Texas, the scene was remarkable: The governor, flanked by an out-of-state televangelist and religious right leaders, signing legislation in a church school gymnasium amid shouts of 'amen' from backers who just as well could have been attending a revival."[51]

Governor Perry gave a superficial nod to the interests of the pregnant teen, saying, "A nurturing home with a loving mother and loving father is the best way to guide our children down the proper path."[52] But like his decision to sign the bill at a church school, the words of his speech revealed the primary impetus behind the legislation. "We may be on the grounds of a Christian church but we all believe in standing up for the unborn," Perry preached.[53] "For too long, a blind eye has been turned to the rights of our most vulnerable human beings—that's the unborn in our society."[54]

Despite the transparent link between the pro-life movement and parental involvement mandates, many abortion rights supporters have been willing to bargain with pro-life proponents because the bypass option is available, carries the weight of law, and bears the constitutional imprimatur of the Supreme Court. Maybe as important, the bypass safety valve is placed in the hands of the judiciary, an institution thought to be capable of withstanding the muck of politics and the red tape of bureaucracies.

But the judiciary is not so capable. What, for instance, of the judge who classifies the bypass proceeding as "a capital case" since "[i]t involves the question whether [the minor's] unborn child should live or die,"[55] and who rules against the minor on the grounds that it is "not an act of maturity on her part to put the burden of the death of this child upon the conscience of the Court"?[56] And what of the telephone that rings and rings unanswered at the Tennessee Department of Children's Services? Many abortion rights supporters have not anticipated such possibilities and have instead fallen victim to "the myth of rights," an ideology that fosters a naïve faith in the impartiality and functionality of the judiciary.

The Myth of Rights

In *The Politics of Rights,* Stuart Scheingold appeals to law's "symbolic life."[57] To understand the political importance of American law, Scheingold insists,

> it is not enough to consider the concrete manifestations of legal institutions or to take into account the immediate reactions to or compliance with legal rulings. These are important matters, to be sure, but they must be understood in connection with the patterns of belief evoked by legal symbols. In its symbolic form, the law shapes the context in which American politics is conducted.[58]

Alerting us to law's symbolic life and power, Scheingold departs from the conventional view that law and politics are distinct realms.[59] Although neither the first nor the last to argue for a political analysis of law and rights, nor alone in focusing on the symbolic and ideological character of law,[60] Scheingold offers a unique and compelling depiction of the law's hold on the popular imagination in America:

> Like all fundamental social institutions [law] casts a shadow of popular belief that may ultimately be more significant, albeit more difficult to comprehend, than the authorities, rules, and penalties that we ordinarily associate with law. What we believe reflects our values; it also colors

our perceptions. What we believe about the law is directly related to the legitimacy of our political institutions.[61]

Scheingold dubs this popular belief about law "the myth of rights." The myth of rights is an ideology that "*rests on a faith in the political efficacy and ethical sufficiency of law as a principle of government.*"[62] In contrast with the distrusted political branches of government,[63] the courts and declarations of rights issued by the judiciary are perceived as both legitimate and effective for the task securing a just society. Those who subscribe to the myth of rights, Scheingold explains, believe that

> the political order in America actually functions in a manner consistent with the patterns of rights and obligations specified in the Constitution. The ethical connotations of this rule of law system are based on a willingness to identify constitutional values with social justice. It encourages us to break down social problems into the responsibilities and entitlements established under law in the same way that lawyers and judges deal with disputes among individuals. Once the problem is analyzed, the myth, moreover, suggests that it is well on its way to resolution, since these obligations and rights are not only legally enforceable but ethically persuasive, because they are rooted in constitutional values. Like all ideologies, then, the myth of rights "define[s] a particular program of social action as legitimate and worthy of support."[64]

Captivated by the myth of rights, people commonly believe that judicial declarations of rights will directly translate into social reform. With this faith in the legal paradigm, activists deploy litigation and turn to the courts with expectations of fair redress for perceived wrongs: "The assumption is that litigation can evoke a declaration of rights from courts; that it can, further, be used to assure the realization of these rights; and, finally, that realization is tantamount to meaningful change. The *myth of rights* is, in other words, premised on a direct linking of litigation, rights, and remedies with social change."[65]

The optimism and faith generated by the myth of rights has strong allure, for it bolsters our confidence that the rule of law prevails. But the allure, Scheingold warns, is problematic because, more often than not, law merely reinforces the status quo and maintains prevailing arrangements of power:[66]

A sober assessment of the status of rights in American politics raises serious doubts about the capabilities of legal and constitutional processes for neutralizing power relationships. The authoritative declaration of a right is perhaps best viewed as the beginning of a political process in which power relationships loom large and immediate.[67]

Furthermore, the seductive power of the myth of rights engenders complacency by creating false hope in the power and efficacy of the legal system. Once a right has received legal authorization, those who subscribe to the myth assume that the right has been actualized. Under the veil of the myth of rights, we are inclined to believe that gaps between rights articulated and rights effectuated do not exist or are anomalies that can easily be overcome.

The Myth of the Bypass

In the context of parental involvement laws, the myth of rights fosters an idealized view of the bypass process. With assuredness and without skepticism, those lured by the myth of rights presume that courts will be prepared to handle bypass requests, that minors will have access to those courts, and that, by and large, judges will treat requests neutrally.

The reality of the bypass process exposed in the preceding pages seeks to dismantle the idealization that surrounds and upholds parental involvement laws. But those who succumb to the myth of rights may hold fast to the ideology, saying that at most what has been shown is that the bypass needs fixing, not that involvement statutes should be discarded altogether. The protections afforded by statutory law and the Constitution, they may assert, provide the necessary shield against rights infringements and, even when the shield becomes permeable, obvious rights infringements will not long endure.

This line of argument goes as follows. Legal systems inevitably suffer instances of failed implementation, resulting from both innocent misapplication of and deliberate opposition to the law. While troubling, if we expect to maintain a legal system, we must tolerate some missteps. Were we to reverse policy in every instance of error, no policy would survive. The answer to implementation problems associated with the bypass process is, on this view, not the reversal of policy but, instead, the creation and implementation of additional measures to check and minimize these problems. Furthermore, the legal system affords the opportunity, by way of appellate review, to reverse errors that emerge when laws are misapplied. If the bypass route is defective, minors can sue to redress the defects, just as others have resorted to litigation to remedy rights violations, and the fact that we have not witnessed much in the way of legal challenges to the bypass option might be taken as evidence that the system functions reasonably well.

Plausible as this might sound, it is nothing more than an iteration of the myth of rights. As Kristin Bumiller explains in her analysis of the limits of antidiscrimination regulations, the argument rests on the assumption that the legal system affords the necessary tools to generate compliance with the law and that the victims of noncompliance can readily and with little sacrifice access these tools.[68] This assumption is false both in the case of antidiscrimination law, as Bumiller has shown, and in the case of pregnant teens.

The obstacles awaiting a pregnant minor who attempts to repair defects in the bypass make the prospect of a legal challenge decidedly unlikely. Take the minor who encounters ignorance or misconduct at the stage of attempting to gain access to a hearing. It is almost unimaginable that a minor, turned away from her county court, would have the capacity to not merely seek a bypass elsewhere but to sue the state. With the clock ticking on her pregnancy, and thus on her ability to secure an abortion, a minor is certain to focus on the immediacy of her situation. The prospect of taking on an arduous legal battle is outside her realm. In fact, such a minor is likely to have no idea that her rights are even being violated. What's more, a minor seeking a bypass typically does so to keep her parents from learning of her pregnancy.[69] In this context, it is the rare minor who is going to take on the increased risk of discovery to wage a legal campaign against the state.

Were a minor to have the wherewithal to sue the state, it is far from clear that such behavior would be in her best interest. Consider the minor who succeeds in getting her foot through the courthouse door, is assigned a lawyer, files a petition, and winds up before a trial judge who requires Sav-A-Life counseling or the presence of fetal representation. In this case, and despite having counsel (and hence wherewithal) at her side, the option of mounting a challenge in advance of the hearing must seem unfeasible and even ridiculous. As it is, a minor petitioning to waive parental involvement does so with considerable apprehension. Such a minor confronts not only the stress of an unwanted pregnancy

and the prospect of terminating that pregnancy but also a hearing before an authoritative stranger whose decision may dramatically alter her
life. "Generally, they're so frightened to be in there," one attorney said
of minors who appear before judges in waiver hearings.[70] To imagine
that such a minor would escalate this anxiety with a legal challenge
when she can instead yield to the court's procedures and thereby obtain
a hearing is to ignore the vulnerable position in which a minor finds
herself. Again, a minor who pursues such a challenge runs an increased
risk that her parents will discover her situation. Add to this the time
pressure of an advancing pregnancy, the additional stress associated
with protracted legal proceedings, and a less than certain appellate outcome, and we should hardly be surprised that when presented with the
option of initiating a lawsuit, a minor would decline. As one attorney
explained, the judges "want the girls to go to Sav-A-Life. I tell my girls
this, and I tell them you can go and listen to what they have to say at
Sav-A-Life, or we can appeal that. Most just go and get it over with. . . .
I haven't had a girl say, 'No, I won't go' and instead challenge it."[71]

Even when attorneys believe that judicial conduct during bypass
hearings violates a minor's rights, they are hard-pressed to encourage
the young women to file a legal challenge. According to some attorneys
who represent minors, serving the client in this type of case means securing a waiver rather than objecting to what might amount to impermissible hurdles placed in the minor's path. As one attorney explained:
"Whether I believe that this little girl should say she's prayed about it
and thinks it's a sin, whatever hoops she has to come through, she can
jump through and get her waiver, and as long as that happens, I'm
happy."[72] When asked whether objections to these hoops get raised at
hearings, this attorney added: "Do I object? No, because the waiver
would be denied. . . . And if I would have to take it up on appeal, I
don't know what the Court of Civil Appeals would do."[73] Emphasizing
the reality of pursuing a bypass in the "Bible Belt" and before conservative judges, this attorney defended her approach:

> This is the system that I work under. And the system is what those
> judges believe: as long as they follow the law, the ethereal constitutional
> right of being unduly burdened doesn't matter. . . . And if it were my
> choice, she would do a two-step and get her waiver. . . . Yes, these
> judges place more of a boulder in the pathway of abortion. . . . But it is

the system, and challenging them on the basis of that is not going to help these girls. . . . And if I do that, if I challenge all of these questions on religion and on whatever, I'm not going to be appointed to these cases. And I tell them that you have this choice [to terminate your pregnancy], this is not wrong, this is a constitutional right, and by God you have the right to do with your body what you want to do, but let me tell you how we're going to do this hearing.[74]

Another attorney also highlighted this reality in explaining how implementation of the bypass process goes unchallenged:

Who's going to stop it? And judges do what they want to do and when they want to do it. If you care about your next client and paying your bills, you have to get along with the judges. And what are you going to do, ask them to recuse themselves? They won't recuse themselves. And all you've done is ask them to recuse themselves, and then you have to deal with them. That can hurt your next client.[75]

While a prior or contemporaneous challenge to judicial procedures in bypass hearings is implausible, it may not seem so far-fetched to think that such a challenge could emerge once a bypass petition has been denied. With an expedited avenue of appeal available and legal counsel already appointed, minors have in fact appealed judicial denials of their petitions. But in these appeals the main order of business from the minor's perspective is getting the denial reversed, not challenging the process itself. These appeals typically concern whether the judge has properly applied the maturity and best-interest standards, with minors claiming, for example, that the judge failed to arrive at a finding on the best-interest prong[76] or failed to specify the grounds for denying the petition.[77] A minor might be understandably reluctant to complicate the appeal with a process-oriented challenge that questions the constitutionality of such things as the Sav-A-Life mandate or fetal representation. Such reluctance is especially understandable when the appellate courts have shown a lack of enthusiasm for taking up such challenges and when attorneys, like the one cited above, express doubts about the prospects of winning on such grounds.

Minors and their attorneys cannot be faulted for choosing pragmatism over principle. It might even be fair to say that the nature of the situation compels this sort of pragmatism. The situation here is not analogous to the state regulation of business or adult persons who are in a better position to challenge burdensome state regulations should they believe it to be necessary. Pregnant minors are in no such position.

Adopting this pragmatic approach, though, helps perpetuate the myth of rights. And therein lies the rub about the myth of rights. The myth is sustained by a tendency of the mind toward idealization, as if cases were adjudicated in Plato's courtroom. But in the world, it is sometimes necessary and often rational for those without resources or power to tough it out. There are worse things in this world than having one's rights violated. So unless we see through the façade of the bypass, ignorance and bureaucratic obstacles will continue to obstruct access to hearings; minors who gain access to hearings will continue to encounter judges who conduct those hearings in ways that fail to match up with our expectations; and minors will continue to tough it out in silence and out of sight, reinforcing the mistaken impression that the bypass option functions reasonably well.

The Myths of Separation

The actions of the recently emboldened religious right have made it easier to appreciate that judges, the supposed neutral and objective arbiters of our justice system, use the courts to advance their ideologies.[78] The behavior of Judges Anderson and Cappell in Montgomery, Alabama, as well as the numerous reports of judges who refuse to handle bypass petitions without taking steps to ensure a replacement judge, are instructive. And there is more evidence outside of bypass cases or even the abortion issue that demonstrates that courts have embraced rather than eschewed religious ideology.

Take the case of Roy Moore, former chief justice of the Alabama Supreme Court. Before his election to that position, he served as a circuit court judge and earned renown for displaying a hand-carved plaque of the Ten Commandments behind his bench and for inviting clergy to lead prayer at jury-organizing sessions.[79] During his run for the high court, his campaign committee christened him the "Ten Commandments Judge," using that moniker in his campaign publications and advertisements.[80] After his election to the state's high court, Chief Justice Moore made good on a campaign promise "to restore the moral foundation of law"[81] by designing and commissioning the production of a two-and-one-half-ton granite monument of the Ten Commandments for display at the courthouse.[82] On the evening of July 31, 2001, and on the orders of the chief justice, the monument was placed in the rotunda of the Alabama State Judicial Building. Though Moore did not notify his colleagues on the court of the installation, he did inform Coral Ridge Ministries—a Christian evangelical organization—and gave the group the exclusive privilege of filming the event.[83]

In a public ceremony the day after the Commandments' installation, Chief Justice Moore said,

> this monument will serve to remind the appellate courts and judges of the circuit and district courts of this state, the members of the bar who appear before them, as well as the people who visit the Alabama Judicial Building, of the truth stated in the preamble of the Alabama Constitution, that in order to establish justice, we must invoke "the favor and guidance of Almighty God."[84]

Further testimony of his purpose came later, during the lawsuit challenging, and subsequently overturning, the installation.[85] Specifically, Moore conceded that his goal was to acknowledge God's law, God's sovereignty, and God's overruling power over the affairs of men, and that the God to whom he referred was the Judeo-Christian God.[86] It is perhaps worth noting that during Moore's tenure as chief justice, the Alabama Supreme Court replaced the standard for reviewing bypass denials with one far more deferential to trial judges.[87]

Similar religious testimonials, though less publicized and less grand in scope, have emerged from the bench. In December 2004, a circuit judge in Covington County, Alabama, came to court sporting the latest in judicial fashion: a robe embroidered with the Ten Commandments. Explaining his new garb, Judge Ashley McKathan said the Ten Commandments represent the truth "and you can't divorce the law from the truth. . . . The Ten Commandments can help a judge know the difference between right and wrong."[88] He further explained his desire to acknowledge the scriptural foundation of modern law. Without the biblical "truth" he said, "there is no law."[89]

Enthusiasm for displaying the Ten Commandments is not peculiar to Alabama judges. In July 2000, Judge James DeWeese of the General

Division of the Court of Common Pleas in Richland County, Ohio, placed a framed poster of the Ten Commandments in his courtroom opposite a similarly framed poster of the Bill of Rights.[90] During the legal proceedings that ultimately led to a federal court order that the display be removed, DeWeese testified that he intended to use the documents for educational purposes, specifically to discuss the origins of law, legal philosophy, and the rule of law.[91] But as the Sixth Circuit Court of Appeals explains, he also testified

> that he chose the Ten Commandments because they were emblematic of moral absolutism and that he chose them to express the belief that law comes either from God or man, and to express his belief that the law of God is the "ultimate authority." He explained that in the course of his educational efforts he would point to the Ten Commandments as an example God as the ultimate authority in law.[92]

Other judges have revealed religious inspiration without putting the Ten Commandments on view. A district court judge in Kentucky includes a spiritual option when sentencing those convicted of misdemeanor drug or alcohol crimes. Judge Michael Caperton, a devout Christian, has offered some fifty substance abuse offenders the option of attending "worship services" in lieu of rehabilitation or serving time in jail.[93] For example, Scott Hays, convicted on a misdemeanor drug charge, faced a choice of "10 days in jail, a drug rehab program or 10 worship services."[94] Leaning toward the spiritual option, Hays said, "Services for 10 days rather than jail for 10 days, who wouldn't, you know?"[95] Judge Caperton asserts that his alternative sentence poses no Establishment Clause concern "because it's not mandatory and I say worship services instead of church."[96] But he also explains, according to an Associated Press report, that church attendance could help some of those convicted find spiritual guidance.[97]

In each of the above cases, as in the cases of Anderson and Cappel, judges have decided, whether literally or figuratively, to wear their religious views on their sleeves. Whether or not their actions are consistent with the Establishment Clause, these judges remind us that they are susceptible—like ordinary human beings—to the influence of religious ideology. These reminders should help us admit that separation between law and politics is folklore, a story we repeatedly try to convince ourselves is fact even while the world around us tells us that it is fiction.

These reminders should likewise help us admit that separation between religion and courts is a tall tale, a promise not fully realizable.

It might be countered that the preceding examples are anomalous—that, by and large, judges do their best to compartmentalize their religious and political ideologies while serving in their capacity as jurists. But there is at least as much reason to suspect that these examples just touch the tip of the iceberg and are emblematic of strong undercurrents that shape judicial decision-making.

To be sure, judges are socialized into the view that they must remain neutral, that they should "interpret law" rather than "make law"—in short, that they should not legislate from the bench. Jurists routinely profess this perspective on judicial decision-making, as did Chief Justice John Roberts during his confirmation hearings before the Senate Judiciary Committee:

> Judges and justices are servants of the law, not the other way around. Judges are like umpires. Umpires don't make the rules; they apply them. The role of an umpire and a judge is critical. They make sure everybody plays by the rules, but it is a limited role. Nobody ever went to a ballgame to see the umpire. . . . Judges are not politicians who can promise to do certain things in exchange for votes. I have no agenda, but I do have a commitment: If I am confirmed, I will confront every case with an open mind. I will fully and fairly analyze the legal arguments that are presented. I will be open to the considered views of my colleagues on the bench. And I will decide every case based on the record according to the rule of law without fear or favor to the best of my ability. And I will remember that it's my job to call balls and strikes and not to pitch or bat.[98]

This rhetoric of objectivity, however, is up against other competing forms of socialization. These forms—including political, moral, economic, and religious—join objectivity on the psychological ball field, and there is no telling in advance how the competition will play out.

As a final example, consider a county judge in Texas who received a warning from the state's Commission on Judicial Conduct for appearing in a theological seminary advertisement donning his judicial robe. Responding to this warning, Tarrant County Judge R. Brent Keis appealed to his sectarian duty. While the Texas Code of Judicial Conduct stipulates that "a judge shall not lend the prestige of the judicial office to advance the private interests of the judge or others," Judge Keis defended his decision to appear in the advertisement, saying, "I know my religious faith allowed only one answer to the seminary's request. . . . It is my sincere religious belief that for me to have said no to such a request would be equal to my denying Christ. This, I cannot do."[99] The seminary's spokesperson applauded Judge Keis and, in so doing, offered this apt characterization of the sectarian influence on the judge's actions:

> In our society today, many people want Christians to compartmentalize their faith. They want a politician to be a politician, not a Christian politician. They want a teacher to be a teacher, not a Christian teacher. In this case, they want a judge to be only a judge, and not a Christian judge. Judge Keis understands that faith in Christ is expressed in every part of his life. Faith in Christ is not checked baggage that he leaves at the office or courtroom door. I applaud his faith and willingness to endure sanction for Christ.[100]

Wherever a judge's faith resides and whether or not a judge tries to check her ideological baggage, there will always be at least some carry-on items that make their way into the courthouse. Chief Justice Roberts's romantic vision of the judge as neutral umpire pretends that it could be otherwise. But the analogy, as Peter Edelman of the Georgetown Law School pointed out during the Chief Justice's confirmation hearings, "is remarkably disingenuous":

> [Roberts] said the other day that judging's like being an umpire—just calling the balls and strikes. And I'm not one for adding to the pile of sports analogies here, but, you know, if the umpire stands two steps to the right behind the catcher, strikes are going to look like balls and many balls are going to look like strikes. . . . Constitutional interpretation is not like calling balls and strikes.[101]

It has not been my intention to suggest that judges who bring ideology to bear on their official activities are doing something wrong, as if the point here were to follow the observation of this commingling with the admonition "Don't do that." Rather, the point is to once and for all admit that there is really nothing else that judges can do. We ought to take account of this fact when we form our expectations about how proposed laws will operate, and, indeed, take account of these newly enlightened expectations when we decide whether a law is a good idea in the first place.

Conclusion

On November 30, 2005, the Supreme Court heard oral arguments in *Ayotte v. Planned Parenthood of Northern New England*,[102] a case addressing the constitutionality of New Hampshire's parental notification requirement. Under dispute was the statute's lack of an explicit exception allowing a physician to waive notice when a minor's health was at risk. The state argued that the judicial bypass option provided sufficient protection even in the context of a medical emergency. Responding to Planned Parenthood's contention that forcing a minor to obtain a judicial waiver in an emergency could lead to a dangerous delay in the receipt of medical care, Justice Scalia said: "Counsel, Surely not the delay for a quick phone call. Let's assume New Hampshire sets up a special office open 24 hours a day and this is the abortion judge, and he can be reached any time anywhere. It takes 30 seconds to place a phone call."[103] Scalia is perhaps a bit too optimistic.

The judicial bypass compromise is designed to balance competing rights and interests. It is sustained by the premise that courts function largely apolitically and without bureaucratic pitfalls. The preceding pages call this premise into question. Basing a policy that regulates the right to abortion on confidence that the law stands outside of politics and free of bureaucratic red tape is a mistake fraught with consequences for those whom the right ostensibly protects.

This is far from the first time evidence has shown sizable gaps in the implementation of law. Failure to comply with the Supreme Court's ruling in *Brown v. Board of Education*[104] is by now long established and familiar, providing what may be the most salient example of the disjuncture between idealized rights and actual practice.[105] Still, our illusions persist, and few people care to entertain whether the world actually accords with our imagination. The rhetoric of judicial competence and objectivity abounds, perpetuated by the dogma that the courts are situated in a realm replete with knowledge and safe from the political tug-of-war.

"Is this an unseemly discussion?" ask Suellyn Scarnecchia and Julie Kunce Field in highlighting acts of judicial discretion. "After all, we want to believe that judges will rise above differences between themselves and the litigants before them in order to make fair and equitable decisions."[106] This is, indeed, an unseemly discussion, at least when viewed through the rose-tinted lenses of the myth of rights. But sometimes it takes the unseemly—the admission of ignorance, inefficiency, incompetence, and defiance—to dislodge mythologies and to disabuse ourselves of the notion that we can be what we are not.

Notes

1. *Ohio v. Akron Center for Reproductive Health,* No. 88-805, 1989 U.S. S. Ct. Briefs LEXIS 946 (August 28, 1989) at Appendix A. Brief Amici Curiae of Focus on the Family and Family Research Council, Rachel Ely, Myoshi Callahan, Teresa Wibblesman Fangman, Holly Trimble, Linda Roselli, Ann Marie Lozinski, Robert C. Wibblesman, and American Victims of Abortion, in support of Appellants.

2. For a summary of research findings on the frequency of voluntary parental involvement in abortion decisions, *see* Nancy E. Adler, Emily J. Ozer, and Jeanne Tschann, "Abortion among Adolescents," *American Psychologist* 58 (2003): 214.

3. *See* Alan Guttmacher Institute, "Parental Involvement in Minors' Abortions," in *State Policies in Brief,* June 1, 2006, http://www.guttmacher.org/statecenter/spibs/spib_PIMA.pdf (accessed June 8, 2006). In addition, Maine encourages parental consent but allows minors to bypass that consent by receiving counseling. *See Me. Rev. Stat. Ann. tit.* 22, § 1597-A (2004).

4. *See* Alan Guttmacher Institute, "Parental Involvement in Minors' Abortions."

5. *Id.* For a breakdown of state-mandated involvement requirements, *see also* Chapter 2, Table 1, in this volume.

6. As Mary S. Griffin-Carlson and Paula J. Schwanenflugel say, "even pro-choice advocates are often uneasy when thinking about an adolescent having to face such a difficult experience without parental support." "Adolescent Abortion and Parental Notification: Evidence for the Importance of Family Functioning on the Perceived Quality of Parental Involvement in Families," *Journal of Child Psychology and Psychiatry* 39 (1998): 543 (citing R. Stone, *Adolescents and Abortion: Choice in Crisis* (Washington, D.C.: Center for Population Options, 1990)).

7. Satsie Veith, "The Judicial Bypass Procedure and Adolescents' Abortion Rights: The Fallacy of the 'Maturity' Standard," *Hofstra Law Review* 23 (1994): 458.

8. American Medical Association Council on Ethical and Judicial Affairs

(AMA), "Mandatory Parental Consent to Abortion," *Journal of the American Medical Association (JAMA)* 269 (1993): 82.

9. *See* Texas Department of Health, *Booklet on Induced Abortions,* http://www.tdh.state.tx.us/bvs/abortion/nowhat.htm#4 (accessed September 2004).

10. *See* Centers for Disease Control and Prevention, "Abortion Surveillance —United States, 1993 and 1994," *Morbidity and Mortality Weekly Report* 46(SS-4) (1997): 37–98 (cited in Adler, Ozer, and Tschann, "Abortion among Adolescents," 212).

11. *See* Centers for Disease Control and Prevention, "Pregnancy-Related Mortality Surveillance—United States, 1987–1990," *Morbidity and Mortality Weekly Report* 46(SS-4) (1997): 17–36 (cited in Adler, Ozer, and Tschann, "Abortion among Adolescents," 212).

12. American Academy of Pediatrics Committee on Adolescence (AAP), "The Adolescent's Right to Confidential Care When Considering Abortion," *Pediatrics* 97 (1996): 749.

13. The Parental Notification Act: Hearings on Tex. S.B. 30 before the House State Affairs Comm., 76th Leg., Reg. Sess. 23 (April 19, 1999) (statement by Leslie French) (quoted in Teresa Stanton Collett, "Seeking Solomon's Wisdom: Judicial Bypass of Parental Involvement in a Minor's Abortion Decision," *Baylor Law Review* 52 (2000): 546 n.139) (alterations in the original).

14. *Id.* (statement by Dr. Michael Love) (quoted in Collett, "Seeking Solomon's Wisdom," 546 n.139).

15. *Bellotti v. Baird (Bellotti II),* 443 U.S. 622 (1979) at 641 n.21 (plurality opinion).

16. Mandated parental notification, the Court has commented, serves a "significant state interest by providing an opportunity for parents to supply essential medical and other information to a physician. . . . Parents can provide medical and psychological data, refer the physician to other sources of medical history, such as family physicians, and authorize family physicians to give relevant data." *H. L. v. Matheson,* 450 U.S. 398 (1981) at 411.

17. Collett, "Seeking Solomon's Wisdom," 575 (citations omitted; internal quotation marks omitted).

18. *Id.* at 576.

19. Catherine Bernard, *The Long-Term Psychological Effects of Abortion* (Portsmouth, N.H.: Institute for Pregnancy Loss, 1990).

20. Westside Pregnancy Resource Center, *Mental Health Risks of Abortion: Scientific Studies Reveal Significant Risk, Major Psychological Sequelae of Abortion,* http://www.wprc.org/abortion/emotion.html (accessed October 1, 2005).

21. Jo Ann Rosenfeld, "Emotional Responses to Therapeutic Abortion," *American Family Physician* 45 (1992): 137.

22. *Id.*

23. Wanda Franz and David Reardon, "Differential Impact of Abortion on

Adolescents and Adults," *Adolescence* 27 (1992) (cited in Maggie O'Shaughnessy, "The Worst of Both Worlds? Parental Involvement Requirements and the Privacy Rights of Mature Minors," *Ohio State Law Journal* 57 (1996)).

24. Rosenfeld, "Emotional Responses to Therapeutic Abortion," 138 (citing J. S. Wallerstein, P. Kurtz, and M. Bar-Din, "Psychosocial Sequelae of Therapeutic Abortion in Young Unmarried Women," *Archives of General Psychiatry* 27 (1972)). *See also* O'Shaughnessy, "The Worst of Both Worlds?" 1757 (stating that "[r]esearchers have identified the most critical factor affecting the psyche of an adolescent during her pregnancy disposition decision: her perception of social support in making her decision. Perceived social support from her partner, parents, or peers has been reported as the single most important determinant of psychological reaction to abortion.").

25. Rosenfeld, "Emotional Responses to Therapeutic Abortion," 137.

26. Adler, Ozer, and Tschann, "Abortion among Adolescents," 212.

27. AAP, "Adolescent's Right to Confidential Care," 748.

28. AMA, "Mandatory Parental Consent to Abortion," 83.

29. *Matheson,* 450 U.S. at 411 n.20.

30. Florida Parental Notice of Abortion Act, 1999, ch. 99-322 (citing *Matheson,* 450 U.S. at 411). In 2003 and prior to a change to the Florida constitution that permits mandated parental involvement, the Florida Supreme Court declared this statute unconstitutional. *See North Florida Women's Health and Counseling Services v. Florida,* 866 So. 2d 612 (Fla. 2003).

31. *Ala. Code* § 26-21-1 (2004).

32. Katherine D. Katz, "The Pregnant Child's Right to Self-Determination," *Albany Law Review* 62 (1999): 1128.

33. *Parham v. J. R.,* 442 U.S. 584 (1979) at 602 (citations omitted; internal quotation marks omitted).

34. As of June 2006, Minnesota, Mississippi, and North Dakota required the involvement of both parents. *See* Alan Guttmacher Institute, "Parental Involvement in Minors' Abortions."

35. AAP, "Adolescent's Right to Confidential Care," 747.

36. AMA, "Mandatory Parental Consent to Abortion," 83.

37. Katz, "The Pregnant Child's Right to Self-Determination," 1142–43 (citing Margie Boule, "An American Tragedy," *Portland Oregonian,* August 27, 1989).

38. Quoted in Melissa Jacobs, "Are Courts Prepared to Handle Judicial Bypass Proceedings?" *Human Rights* 32 (Winter 2005): 4.

39. AMA, "Mandatory Parental Consent to Abortion," 83.

40. "Adolescents who are willing to involve parents in their abortion decisions will likely benefit from adult experience, wisdom, and support." AAP, "Adolescent's Right to Confidential Care," 748.

41. *Id.*

42. *Id.* at 749.

43. According to Mary S. Griffin-Carlson and K. J. Mackin, "In general, researchers believe that communication between adolescents and parents regarding sex is still quite limited." "Parental Consent: Factors Influencing Adolescent Disclosure Regarding Abortion," *Adolescence* 28 (1993): 8.

44. Quoted in Jacobs, "Are Courts Prepared to Handle Judicial Bypass Proceedings?" 4.

45. *Id.* According to another study of more than 1,500 unmarried minors having abortions, 73 percent of minors who did not tell their mothers about their pregnancies cited a desire not to disappoint. Stanley K. Henshaw and Kathryn Kost, "Parental Involvement in Minors' Abortion Decisions," *Family Planning Perspectives* 24 (1992): 203.

46. Henshaw and Kost, "Parental Involvement in Minors' Abortion Decisions," 203.

47. AMA, "Mandatory Parental Consent to Abortion," 83.

48. *Id.*

49. Jacobs, "Are Courts Prepared to Handle Judicial Bypass Proceedings?" 4.

50. An attorney who routinely represents minors seeking abortions in a large urban area said that some of the minors she has seen "have no idea where their parents are. Or their parents are in jail. Or their parents are deceased." Interview, June 24, 1996. An abortion provider who serves the same urban area reported the following: "We've had four instances now to date of daughters who were raised by a grandmother or aunt who have had to drag in their mothers who are drug addicts." Interview, June 24, 1996. In this and following chapters, I do not identify those interviewed except where the participants have consented to my inclusion of their names. For a complete discussion of interview methods, see Chapter 6.

51. *See, e.g., Bellotti II.*

52. Maryland is an exception. The Maryland statute authorizes physicians to waive mandated parental notification under some circumstances. *See* Md. *Code Ann., Health-Gen.* I § 20-103 (2006).

53. Quoted in Bradley C. Canon and Charles A. Johnson, *Judicial Policies: Implementation and Impact,* 2nd ed. (Washington, D.C.: CQ Press, 1999), 1.

54. Studies in various areas of law—so-called gap studies—have revealed substantial disparity between law as it appears on the books and law as it is experienced in the world. Consider, for example, Bradley C. Canon and Kenneth Kolson's classic gap study examining the extent to which rural courts in Kentucky complied with the Supreme Court *In re Gault* ruling, a decision that extended to juveniles the right to counsel. Finding considerable noncompliance, the authors argued that differences in caseload, the availability of lawyers, and the judges' approaches to juvenile justice helped explain the varying degrees of compliance. *See* Bradley C. Canon and Kenneth Kolson, "Compliance with

Gault in Rural America: Kentucky, A Case Study," *Journal of Family Law* 10 (1971): 300–326. In another paradigmatic study of the same era, Kenneth M. Dolbeare and Phillip E. Hammond found, in one Midwestern state, that widespread lack of conformity with the Supreme Court's school prayer rulings resulted from various forms of inertia—including, for example, conflict avoidance. *See* Kenneth M. Dolbeare and Phillip E. Hammond, *The School Prayer Decisions: From Court Policy to Local Practice* (Chicago: University of Chicago Press, 1971). For additional gap studies, *see, e.g.,* Stephen L. Wasby, *Small Town Police and the Supreme Court: Hearing the Word* (Lexington, Mass.: Lexington Books, 1976); Stephen L. Wasby, *The Impact of the United States Supreme Court* (Homewood, Ill.: Dorsey Press, 1970); Neal A. Milner, *The Court and Local Law Enforcement: The Impact of* Miranda (Beverly Hills, Calif.: Sage, 1971).

55. Stuart A. Scheingold, *The Politics of Rights: Lawyers, Public Policy, and Political Change* (New Haven, Conn.: Yale University Press, 1974).

NOTES TO CHAPTER 2

1. *Roe v. Wade,* 410 U.S. 113 (1973).

2. Barbara Hinkson Craig and David O'Brien, *Abortion and American Politics* (Chatham, N.J.: Chatham House, 1993), 79.

3. *Id.*

4. For a general discussion of state legislative responses to *Roe, see, e.g., id.* at 73–97.

5. *Id.* at 35. The power of the pro-life movement can be seen most recently in its ability to get South Dakota to pass legislation banning abortion throughout pregnancy except in cases where the mother's life is at stake. Unlike most other antiabortion legislation, this law, signed by the governor in March 2006, is not even seen by its backers to be consistent with *Roe* but rather aims to generate a legal challenge to *Roe. See, e.g.,* Monica Davey, "South Dakota Bans Abortion, Setting up a Battle," *New York Times,* March 7, 2006.

6. *See Planned Parenthood of Central Missouri v. Danforth,* 428 U.S. 52 (1976).

7. This statute was held unconstitutional in *Bellotti v. Baird (Bellotti I),* 428 U.S. 132 (1976).

8. In nine states (Alaska, California, Idaho, Illinois, Montana, Nevada, New Hampshire, New Jersey, and New Mexico), parental involvement measures have been passed but remain unenforced due to court challenges. *See* Table 1.

9. Craig and O'Brien, *Abortion and American Politics,* 89.

10. *See Danforth; Bellotti I; Bellotti v. Baird (Bellotti II),* 443 U.S. 622 (1979); *Akron v. Akron Ctr. for Reprod. Health, Inc. (Akron I),* 462 U.S. 416 (1983).

11. Though Justice Blackmun's opinion for the Court was joined by only two other justices, two additional justices, in a concurring opinion, agreed that the right to obtain an abortion extends to minors.

12. *Danforth*, 428 U.S. at 74 (plurality opinion) (citations omitted).

13. *Id.* at 75.

14. *Id.* at 74.

15. *Bellotti I*, 428 U.S. at 134–35 (1976).

16. The Supreme Court vacated the district court's decision that enjoined enforcement of the Massachusetts consent provision on the technical grounds that the meaning of the statute had not yet been authoritatively construed by a state court to determine whether the consent requirement constituted a parental veto of a young woman's decision to terminate her pregnancy. The Supreme Court remanded the case, holding that "the District Court should have certified to the Supreme Judicial Court of Massachusetts appropriate questions concerning the meaning of [the consent provision] and the procedure it imposes." *Id.* at 151.

17. *Id.* at 145.

18. *Bellotti II*, 443 U.S. 622 (1979) (plurality opinion).

19. *Id.* at 646–47.

20. *Id.* at 643.

21. *Id.* at 647. The Court notes that its requirement that minors be provided with the opportunity "to go directly to a court" is based on the specific provisions of the Massachusetts law and that the general opportunity to access a bypass process without prior parental involvement would extend to bypass procedures that do not involve courts. *Id.* at 643 n.22.

22. *Id.* at 643–44 (citations omitted). The plurality put forth these criteria as dictum. Four other justices concurred in finding the Massachusetts consent requirement unconstitutional but argued that the minor's abortion decision would be subject to an absolute third-party veto even with a judicial bypass option. *Id.* at 654–55 (Stevens, J., concurring).

23. *See, respectively, Planned Parenthood Ass'n v. Ashcroft*, 462 U.S. 476 (1983) and *Akron I*. In *Akron I*, the challenged regulation was a city ordinance that imposed a blanket parental consent provision for minors under fifteen years of age.

24. *Akron I*, 462 U.S. at 439. *See also Ashcroft*, 462 U.S. at 490.

25. *Planned Parenthood of Southeastern Pennsylvania v. Casey*, 505 U.S. 833 (1992).

26. *Id.* at 899 (plurality opinion).

27. *Bellotti II*, 443 U.S. at 633 (plurality opinion).

28. *Id.* at 642 (citations omitted).

29. *Akron I*, 462 U.S. at 427 n.10 (quoting *Danforth*, 428 U.S. at 75).

30. *Bellotti II*, 443 U.S. at 634 (plurality opinion) (citations omitted).

31. *Id.* at 635 (citations omitted).

32. *Id.*

33. *Id.* at 637–39 (citations omitted).

34. *Danforth,* 428 U.S. at 91 (Stewart, J., concurring).

35. *Hodgson v. Minnesota,* 497 U.S. 417 (1990). Four justices in *Hodgson* voted to reject Minnesota's two-parent notice law even though it included a bypass alternative modeled along the lines of *Bellotti II.* Another four justices voted to uphold the law, expressing the view that notification mandates would withstand constitutional scrutiny even in the absence of a bypass option. Splitting the difference, Justice Sandra Day O'Connor cast her deciding vote, holding that while a two-parent notice requirement imposes burdens on minors, the availability of a bypass option sufficiently mitigates those burdens.

36. *Ohio v. Akron Center for Reproductive Health (Akron II),* 497 U.S. 502 (1990).

37. *Id.* at 511.

38. *Id.* (citing *H. L. v. Matheson,* 450 U.S. 398 (1981) at 411 n.17).

39. *H. L. v. Matheson,* 450 U.S. 398 (1981).

40. *Id.* at 409.

41. *Bellotti II,* 443 U.S. at 647 (emphasis added).

42. *See* Alan Guttmacher Institute, "Parental Involvement in Minors' Abortions," in *State Policies in Brief,* June 1, 2006, http://www.guttmacher.org/state center/spibs/spib_PIMA.pdf (accessed June 8, 2006). In 2006, Utah changed its law to include a parental consent mandate that contains a bypass provision. But Utah still requires parental notification in certain cases (such as when a physician performs an emergency abortion), and this notification is not subject to a judicial bypass. *See Utah H.B.* 85 (2006). *See also* "Huntsman Signs Parental Consent Bill into Law," Associated Press State and Local Wire, March 17, 2006.

43. *Lambert v. Wicklund,* 520 U.S. 292 (1997).

44. *Mont. Code Ann.* § 50-20-212(5) (1995).

45. *Lambert,* 520 U.S. at 297 (emphasis in the original). The Montana parental notice law was later enjoined on the grounds that it violated state constitutional protection of abortion rights. *Wicklund v. Montana,* 1998 Mont. Dist. LEXIS 227 (1998).

46. *Bellotti II,* 443 U.S. at 642–43.

47. *Id.*

48. *Id.* at 643 n.23.

49. Scholarly examinations of parental involvement requirements frequently note the absence of Supreme Court guidance for determining when a judicial bypass should be granted. *See, e.g.,* Anita J. Pliner and Suzanne Yates, "Psychological and Legal Issues in Minors' Rights to Abortion," *Journal of Social Issues* 48 (1992); Wallace J. Mlyniec, "A Judge's Ethical Dilemma: Assessing a Child's Capacity to Choose," *Fordham Law Review* 64 (1996).

50. *Ind. Planned Parenthood Affiliates Ass'n v. Pearson*, 716 F.2d 1127 (7th Cir. 1983) at 1138.

51. *Id.*

52. *In re* T. W., 551 So. 2d 1186 (Fla. 1989) at 1196.

53. Delaware requires involvement for those under sixteen. *See* 24 *Del. C.* § 1782 (2004). South Carolina draws the line at seventeen. *See S.C. Code Ann.* § 44-41-10 (2004).

54. *See, e.g., S.C. Code Ann.* § 44-41-31 (2004).

55. Wisconsin, for example, requires the consent of a parent, legal guardian, or adult family member of the minor, defining "adult family member" as a grandparent, aunt, uncle, sister, or brother who is at least twenty-five years of age. *Wis. Stat.* §§ 48.375(2)(b), (4)(a) (2000).

56. *See, e.g., A.C.A.* § 20-16-801 (2005).

57. A handful of states do not specify a medical emergency exception. *See* Alan Guttmacher Institute, "Parental Involvement in Minors' Abortions."

58. *Minn. Stat.* § 144.343, Subd. 4 (2000). The Court's decision in *Ayotte v. Planned Parenthood of Northern New England*, 126 S. Ct. 961 (2006), calls into question the constitutionality of such a narrow emergency exception. There, in the context of a New Hampshire involvement statute, the Court said that a state must protect both the life and health of the mother when restricting access to abortion.

59. Colorado Parental Notification Act, *C.R.S.* § 12-37.5-103 (2005).

60. *See, e.g., id.,* § 12-37.5-105 (excepting parental notification if the minor declares that she is a victim of child abuse or neglect by the person who would be entitled to notice, and the attending physician has reported such child abuse or neglect).

61. Mississippi, for example, allows exceptions when parents are separated or where the minor claims sexual abuse on the part a parent. *See Miss. Code Ann.* § 41-41-53 (2006).

62. *See Md. Code Ann., Health-Gen.* I § 20-103 (2006).

63. Under the West Virginia code, parental notification may be waived on maturity or best-interest grounds by a physician other than the physician who is to perform the abortion, provided that "such other physician shall not be associated professionally or financially with the physician proposing to perform the abortion." *W. Va. Code* § 16-2F-3(c) (2004).

64. *See, e.g., A.R.S.* § 36-2152 (2004). The involvement statutes of Louisiana, North Dakota, and South Dakota do not explicitly provide for an attorney. *See, respectively, La. R.S.* 40:12999.35.5 (2004); *N.D. Cent. Code,* §§ 14-02.1–03.1 (2003); *S.D. Codified Laws* § 34-23A-7 (2004).

65. *See, e.g., Ala. Code* § 26-21-4(b) (2004).

66. *See, e.g., A.R.S.* § 36-2152 (2004).

67. *See, e.g., Miss. Code Ann.* § 41-41-55(7) (2006). A few states indicate

that fees will not apply if a minor declares her lack of ability to pay. *See, e.g., KRS § 311.732 (2004).* Some statutes are silent on court costs. *See, e.g., S.D. Codified Laws § 34-23A-7 (2004).*

68. *See, e.g., Miss. Code Ann. § 41-41-53 (2006).*

69. *See, e.g., N.D. Cent. Code §§ 14-02.1–03.1 (2003).*

70. *See, e.g., KRS § 311.732 (2004).*

71. *See, e.g., A.R.S. § 36-2152 (2004).*

72. *See, e.g., id.*

73. *See, e.g., id.* Holidays and weekends are excluded from this specified timeframe.

74. *See, e.g., Miss. Code Ann. § 41-41-55 (2006).*

75. *Ohio Rev. Code Ann. § 2151.85(C) (2006).*

76. *Akron II,* 497 U.S. at 516.

77. The legislature succeeded in placing on the November 2004 ballot a constitutional amendment that would empower the legislature to enact a parental notification statute, thereby effectively overturning a Florida Supreme Court decision finding that mandated parental involvement violated the Florida constitution. *See* Jennifer Liberto, "Abortion Bill for Minors Goes to Voters," *St. Petersburg Times,* sec. A, May 1, 2004. That ballot measure passed with 65 percent of the vote. *See* Jackie Hallifax, "High Court Knocks back Appeal over Abortion Measure," Associated Press State and Local Wire, January 13, 2005.

78. *See, e.g.,* Lisa Leff, "California Defeats Abortion Notification Proposition," Associated Press State and Local Wire, November 9, 2005; John Wildermuth, "Campaign 2006: November Initiatives; Abortion Notice Returns to Voters," *San Francisco Chronicle,* June 21, 2006.

79. The Texas legislature, for example, replaced its parental notification mandate with a parental consent requirement. *See* Jamie Stengle, "Governor Signs Abortion Bill at Church School," Associated Press, June 5, 2005. In Georgia, where a grandparent or other relative can act in lieu of a parent, a bill under consideration in the Senate would allow no such stand-in for a parent or legal guardian. *See* Carlos Campos, "Legislature 2005: Senate Panel OKs Bill to Restrict Abortions; Hearing Draws Foes, Supporters," *Atlanta Journal-Constitution,* February 3, 2005.

80. *See* Act No. 87-286, Acts of Alabama 1987.

81. *Ala. Code § 26-21-3(a) (2004).* The statute defines a medical emergency as one that "so compromises the health, safety, or well-being of the mother as to require an immediate abortion." *Id. § 26-21-5.*

82. *Id. § 26-21-3(e).*

83. *Id. § 26-21-4(a).*

84. *Id. § 26-21-4(f).*

85. *Id. § 26-21-4(i).*

86. *Id. § 26-21-4(a).*

87. *Id.* § 26-21-4(e).

88. *Id.* § 26-21-4(g).

89. *Id.* § 26-21-4(h).

90. *Id.* § 26-21-4(j).

91. *Id.* § 26-21-4(c). "Such assistance may be provided by court personnel including intake personnel of juvenile probation services." *Id.*

92. *Id.* § 26-21-4(b).

93. *See* 18 *Pa.C.S.* § 3206 (2005). Amended several times since 1982, the Pennsylvania Abortion Control Act includes for all women seeking an abortion an informed consent requirement and a twenty-four-hour waiting period. It also incorporates a reporting requirement on the facilities performing abortions. The spousal notification component of the act—directing a married woman seeking an abortion to sign a statement indicating that she has notified her husband— was deemed unconstitutional in *Casey*.

94. The two-year delay between the Court's ruling in *Casey* and the effective start date of the Abortion Control Act resulted from additional legal challenges.

95. 18 *Pa.C.S.* § 3206(a) (2005).

96. *Id.* § 3206(c).

97. *Id.* § 3206(d).

98. *Id.* § 3206(f).

99. *Id.*

100. *Id.*

101. *Id.* § 3206(h).

102. *Id.* § 3206(e).

103. *Id.*

104. *Id.* § 3206(f).

105. *See Tenn. Code Ann.* §§ 37-10-301–7 (2001). Legal challenges and court-imposed injunctions delayed the effective starting date of the consent mandate. In *Memphis Planned Parenthood v. Sundquist*, 2 F. Supp. 2d 997 (1997), U.S. District Court Judge John Nixon enjoined enforcement of the Tennessee statute. While the Court of Appeals reversed Nixon's ruling, *see Memphis Planned Parenthood v. Sundquist*, 175 F.3d 456 (1999), additional injunctions postponed enforcement of the law until 2000. *See* "Girls under 18 Must Get Consent for Abortion," Associated Press State and Local Wire, February 28, 2000.

106. *Tenn. Code Ann.* §§ 37-10-303, 37-10-305 (2001).

107. *Id.* § 37-10-304(e). A minor may petition a juvenile court judge for an order waiving that consent if "neither a parent nor a legal guardian is available to the person performing the abortion or such person's agent, or the party from whom consent must be obtained pursuant to this section refuses to consent to the performance of an abortion, or the minor elects not to seek consent of the parent or legal guardian whose consent is required." *Id.* § 37-10-303(b).

108. "No fees shall be required of any minor who makes use of the [bypass] procedures." *Id.* § 37-10-304(j).

109. *Id.* § 37-10-304(d).

110. *Id.* § 37-10-304(b).

111. *Id.* § 37-10-304(g).

112. *Id.* § 37-10-304(c).

113. *Id.* "Next friend" refers to a representative of a party who is not, by virtue of age or incapacity, able to represent him or herself in a legal proceeding.

114. *Id.*

115. *Id.* § 37-10-303(b).

116. See *In re* Anonymous, 720 So. 2d 497 (Ala. Civ. App. 1998); *Ex parte* Anonymous, 720 So. 2d 497 (Ala. 1998).

117. See, *e.g.*, "Court Rejects Appeal in Precedent-Setting Abortion Case," Associated Press State and Local Wire, July 22, 1998; Kendal Weaver, "Court Rejects Appeal by Attorney for Fetus of Pregnant Teen," Associated Press State and Local Wire, August 5, 1998. There has also been news coverage when minors have been denied their waiver requests and appealed those denials. See, *e.g.*, Bill Poovey, "Divided Court Upholds Denial of Abortion for Unemotional Teen," Associated Press State and Local Wire, August 17, 2001; Bill Poovey, "State Appeals Court Approves Teen-ager's Appeal of Abortion Denial," Associated Press State and Local Wire, May 30, 2000; "Ruling Restricts Teen Abortions," *Montgomery Advertiser*, May 25, 2001.

118. See Helena Silverstein, "Road Closed Ahead: Abortion Providers, Prochoice Advocates, and the Longevity of Pennsylvania's Parental Consent Requirement," unpublished paper presented at the annual meeting of the Western Political Science Association, San Jose, California, March 2000.

119. See "Girls under 18 Must Get Consent for Abortion."

120. Although most parental involvement statutes offer only the assistance of court-appointed counsel, a handful of states, like Tennessee, provide extra mechanisms to help minors. The parental consent provision adopted by Massachusetts, as modified by a standing order of the Superior Court, states that "one or more persons in the clerk's office should be at all times available to answer questions asked by a minor, either in person or by phone, and to assist the minor in expeditiously presenting her petition to the court. Each clerk shall designate one or more persons to receive and process [waiver] petitions and shall insure that one such person is available to insure prompt treatment." Massachusetts ALM Super. Ct. S.O. 5-81 (2002). Under the Delaware Code, "The Division of Child Mental Health Services, Department of Services for Children, Youth and Their Families, shall offer counseling and support to any minor who is pregnant and is considering filing or has filed an application [to waive parental notice], if the minor requests such services." 24 *Del. C.* § 1788 (2004). Statutes enacted by Nebraska and South Carolina include provisions for the

distribution of written material concerning mandated parental involvement and the judicial bypass option. *See, respectively, R.R.S. Nebraska* § 71-6909 (2002); *S.C. Code Ann.* § 44-41-37 (2004).

NOTES TO CHAPTER 3

1. *See* American Bar Association (ABA), "Building Momentum: The American Bar Association Call for a Moratorium on Executions Takes Hold," 2003, http://www.abanet.org/moratorium/reportsandlaw.html (accessed February 11, 2005). In January 2000, then Governor George Ryan of Illinois imposed a moratorium on the death penalty—the first of its kind in the country—citing a "shameful record of convicting innocent people and putting them on death row." Dirk Johnson, "Illinois, Citing Faulty Verdicts, Bars Executions," *New York Times,* sec. A, February 1, 2000. In May 2001, then Governor Parris Glendening of Maryland followed Ryan's lead by suspending executions, though that moratorium has since been lifted. *See* ABA, "Building Momentum."

2. There are sixty-seven counties in Alabama, sixty-seven in Pennsylvania, and ninety-five in Tennessee. In Pennsylvania, several counties have combined judicial districts. These are Elk/Cameron, Columbia/Montour, Forest/Warren, Franklin/Fulton, Juniata/Perry, Snyder/Union, and Wyoming/Sullivan. For the combined counties in Pennsylvania, we made only one inquiry. Our results, then, reflect the sixty-seven counties in Pennsylvania but are specified in terms of the state's sixty judicial districts.

3. At the time we conducted this research, the brochure published and distributed by DCS listed contact information for twenty-eight advocates designated to serve Tennessee's ninety-five counties. Some advocates are assigned to serve only one county. Others serve as many as eight counties.

4. My research assistants made virtually all the contacts. I was present during and transcribed all the conversations.

5. Many counties do not have a separate juvenile court facility.

6. Phone Contact, August 13, 1997. I reference the exchanges that emerged from surveys with court and DCS personnel as "phone contact." This is distinct from my reference to interviews with attorneys, judges, abortion providers, and so on, which I designate in notes as "interview." In recounting exchanges with court and DCS personnel, I do not use actual names of state employees or the counties and towns in which they work, and I remove identifying markers.

7. Phone Contact, July 29, 1997.

8. Phone Contact, September 26, 2001.

9. Phone Contact, April 17, 2002.

10. Phone Contact, April 24, 2002.

11. Phone Contact, May 6, 2002. This respondent offered the name and phone number of the advocate.

12. Phone Contact, July 30, 1997.

13. *Id.*

14. Phone Contact, May 20, 2002.

15. Phone Contact, May 1, 2002.

16. Phone Contact, April 17, 2002.

17. Phone Contact, September 21, 2001.

18. Phone Contact, October 17, 2001.

19. Phone Contact, June 14, 2002.

20. Phone Contact, October 14, 2002.

21. Phone Contact, June 18, 2002.

22. Phone Contact, June 13, 2002.

23. Phone Contact, June 13, 2002.

24. Phone Contact, June 14, 2002.

25. Phone Contact, June 13, 2002.

26. Phone Contact, June 13, 2002.

27. Phone Contact, June 14, 2002.

28. Phone Contact, June 20, 2002.

29. *Id.*

30. Phone Contact, June 18, 2002.

31. Debra J. Saunders, "Parents Should Be Notified," *San Francisco Chronicle*, November 3, 2005.

NOTES TO CHAPTER 4

1. Bradley C. Canon and Charles A. Johnson, *Judicial Policies: Implementation and Impact*, 2nd ed. (Washington, D.C.: CQ Press, 1999), 38.

2. When I count ignorant responses received from courts, I am referring to what is effectively the final response given by any court. For example, if an initial court contact proved unfamiliar with the bypass process but suggested that we speak to another court employee who turned out to be knowledgeable, those responses would not be included in the count of ignorant courts. If an initial respondent in a court lacked familiarity with the bypass process and recommended speaking with another court employee who said there was no such thing as a judicial bypass option, those responses taken together would count as one ignorant court.

3. Phone Contact, September 24, 2001.

4. Phone Contact, May 1, 2002.

5. Phone Contact, April 29, 2002.

6. Phone Contact, September 29, 1997.

7. Phone Contact, October 15, 2001.

8. Phone Contact, April 1, 2002.

9. Phone Contact, August 1, 1997.

10. Phone Contact, October 6, 1997.

11. Phone Contact, September 24, 2001.

12. Phone Contact, August 12, 1997.

13. Phone Contact, August 13, 1997.

14. *Id.*

15. Phone Contact, September 24, 2001.

16. Phone Contact, July 15, 2002.

17. Phone Contact, October 17, 2001.

18. Phone Contact, August 12, 1997.

19. Phone Contact, April 24, 2002.

20. Phone Contact, April 23, 2002.

21. Phone Contact, October 17, 2001.

22. I do not include in this discussion those courts in Tennessee that knowingly directed us to DCS. As noted in Chapter 3, such responses are perfectly appropriate.

23. Phone Contact, May 21, 2002.

24. Phone Contact, May 21, 2002.

25. Phone Contact, October 1, 2001.

26. Phone Contact, July 29, 1997.

27. Phone Contact, October 12, 2001.

28. Phone Contact, October 12, 2001.

29. Phone Contact, September 24, 2001.

30. Phone Contact, January 13, 1998.

31. In some counties, abortion providers, women's organizations, interested lawyers, and courts joined together to create a procedure whereby the abortion provider helps coordinate the petition process by arranging a court date and putting minors in touch with court-appointed counsel. I gathered this information in interviews I conducted between 1995 and 1998 with eleven people who work as directors or counselors at abortion clinics in Pennsylvania. I also interviewed a public defender who handles bypasses in her county, the executive director of a pro-choice advocacy group, and a staff attorney for a women's legal advocacy organization.

32. Phone Contact, April 12, 2001.

33. Phone Contact, April 3, 2002.

34. Phone Contact, April 5, 2002.

35. Phone Contact, April 5, 2002.

36. Phone Contact, October 1, 2001.

37. Phone Contact, October 15, 2001.

38. Phone Contact, August 13, 1997.

39. *Id.*

40. Phone Contact, September 24, 2001.

41. Phone Contact, April 16, 2002.

42. Phone Contact, May 6, 2002.

43. Phone Contact, April 15, 2002.

44. Phone Contact, October 10, 2001.

45. Phone Contact, May 8, 2002.

46. Phone Contact, April 16, 2002.

47. Phone Contact, October 1, 2001.

48. *Ind. Planned Parenthood Affiliates Ass'n v. Pearson,* 716 F.2d 1127 (7th Cir. 1983) at 1138.

49. Phone Contact, October 17, 2001.

50. Phone Contact, October 15, 2001.

51. Phone Contact, October 4, 2001.

52. Phone Contact, October 6, 1997.

53. *Id.*

54. Phone Contact, September 24, 2001.

55. Phone Contact, September 29, 1997.

56. Phone Contact, June 14, 2002.

57. *Id.*

58. For the purposes of tallying responses, I do not count these as a separate category. Responses described in this section overlap with those reported in the prior sections of this chapter. In Chapter 5, I consider separately court employees who presented accurate information about the bypass option but who expressed hostility toward that option or to abortion in general.

59. Phone Contact, April 17, 2002.

60. Phone Contact, May 1, 2002.

61. Phone Contact, October 11, 2001.

62. Phone Contact, October 19, 2001.

63. Phone Contact, August 13, 1997.

64. Phone Contact, April 24, 2002.

65. Phone Contact, June 14, 2002.

66. Phone Contact, May 6, 2002.

67. Phone Contact, May 8, 2002.

68. *Id.*

69. Phone Contact, August 13, 1997.

70. Phone Contact, August 14, 1997.

71. *Id.*

72. *Id.*

73. As discussed in Chapter 2, the Alabama law had been in effect for fourteen years, and the Pennsylvania law had been in effect for more than three.

74. Recall that the Tennessee consent provision took effect only after court officials received notice of the law and ninety-one counties acknowledged receipt of this notice. *See* "Girls under 18 Must Get Consent for Abortion," Associated Press State and Local Wire, February 28, 2000.

75. As discussed earlier, there are exceptions. For instance, the error committed when a respondent tells a minor she must file the waiver petition in another county is not mitigated by notice that a minor would receive court-appointed counsel in the other county.

76. Even the providers in Pennsylvania that have coordinated with courts and attorneys to establish a functioning bypass route do so only in the counties where the clinics are located.

77. This does not mean that government agencies cannot coordinate with private citizens or non-state institutions to generate a functioning system, as have several courts in Pennsylvania.

NOTES TO CHAPTER 5

1. *Tilton v. Richardson*, 403 U.S. 672 (1971) at 679.

2. American Academy of Pediatrics Committee on Adolescence (AAP), "The Adolescent's Right to Confidential Care When Considering Abortion," *Pediatrics* 97 (1996): 749.

3. While the physical risk associated with abortion is low (see Chapter 1), the "risk of complications increases by about 20% for each additional week past eight weeks." Stanley K. Henshaw, "The Impact of Requirements for Parental Consent on Minors' Abortions in Mississippi," *Family Planning Perspectives* 27 (1995): 122. "Later-trimester procedures (after 14 weeks) increase both the medical risks and financial costs to the patient, and a prolonged delay can eliminate abortion as an accessible option." AAP, "Adolescent's Right to Confidential Care," 749.

4. According to one study, more than 90 percent of abortion providers offer services at eight to ten weeks, but the proportion drops with each additional week of gestation after eight weeks since the woman's last menstrual period and "declines steeply after 12 weeks. At 20 weeks, for example, only 33% of all providers offer abortion services, and at 21 weeks, 24% still do so." Stanley K. Henshaw and Lawrence B. Finer, "The Accessibility of Abortion Services in the United States, 2001," *Perspectives on Sexual and Reproductive Health* 35 (2003): 18.

5. "As pregnancy advances into the second trimester, the abortion procedure becomes more complex, because it requires more time and more skill on the part of the clinician, and charges increase. At 16 weeks, the mean and median charges ($774 and $650 respectively) are more than half again the amounts at 10 weeks." *Id.* at 19.

6. *Bellotti v. Baird (Bellotti II)*, 443 U.S. 622 (1979) at 643 (plurality opinion).

7. *Ala. Code* § 26-21-4(e) (2004); 18 *Pa.C.S.* § 3206(f) (2005).

8. *Tenn. Code Ann.* § 37-10-304(d) (2001).

9. In fact, the statutes in Alabama and Tennessee use this exact language. *See, respectively, Ala. Code* § 26-21-4(e); *Tenn. Code Ann.* § 37-10-304(d). Pennsylvania's language requires that proceedings "be given such precedence over other pending matters as will ensure that the court may reach a decision promptly and without delay in order to serve the best interests of the pregnant woman." 18 *Pa.C.S.* § 3206(f).

10. Contacts with six courts, all in Tennessee, did not elicit sufficient information to assess the level of preparedness to implement the bypass process.

11. In recounting these exchanges, I have changed the names of state employees and the counties and towns in which they work.

12. Mr. Vinchur went on to provide the details of waiver proceedings, reading directly from the law and hitting all the main components of the process.

13. Phone Contact, October 15, 2001.

14. Phone Contact, June 14, 2002.

15. Phone Contact, June 17, 2002.

16. Phone Contact, June 13, 2002.

17. Bradley C. Canon and Charles A. Johnson, *Judicial Policies: Implementation and Impact,* 2nd ed. (Washington, D.C.: CQ Press, 1999).

18. *Id.* at 25.

19. *Id.*

20. Phone Contact, August 12, 1997.

21. Phone Contact, May 10, 2002.

22. Phone Contact, May 17, 2002.

23. Phone Contact, October 4, 2001.

24. Phone Contact, October 17, 2001.

25. Phone Contact, October 1, 2001.

26. Phone Contact, October 15, 2001.

27. Phone Contact, October 17, 2001.

28. Phone Contact, October 1, 2001.

29. Phone Contact, June 14, 2002.

30. Phone Contact, June 14, 2002.

31. Respondents who cautioned that judges would deny bypass petitions or recommended seeking petitions elsewhere would, in a sense, be doing a pregnant teen a favor by referring her to another county where she might find a more sympathetic judge. One might therefore argue that these respondents would facilitate the minor's chances of obtaining an abortion without parental consent. This does not change the fact that, upon hearing such responses, a minor may with good reason believe that an impartial hearing would be impossible in these counties.

32. Several legal scholars communicated their concern about blanket judicial

recusals in bypass cases to the Tennessee Supreme Court. *See* Paul D. Carrington et al., Letter to Chief Justice Frank F. Drowota III, August 12, 2005, http:// lib.law.washington.edu/tennesseejudges.pdf (accessed September 24, 2005). I am grateful to Professor Susan P. Koniak, Boston University School of Law, for bringing this letter to my attention.

33. Phone Contact, September 24, 2001.

34. Phone Contact, August 13, 1997.

35. Phone Contact, July 29, 1997.

36. Phone Contact, October 6, 1997.

37. Phone Contact, August 13, 1997.

38. *Hodgson v. Minnesota*, 497 U.S. 417 (1990) at 442.

39. Phone Contact, August 12, 1997.

40. Phone Contact, August 13, 1997.

41. Studies have shown that minors travel to neighboring states to avoid mandated parental involvement in their abortions. *See, e.g.,* Virginia G. Cartoof and Lorraine V. Klerman, "Parental Consent for Abortion: Impact of the Massachusetts Law," *American Journal of Public Health* 76 (1986): 399 (finding that, in the twenty months after the Massachusetts parental consent mandate took effect, more than 1,800 Massachusetts minors sought abortions in five neighboring states); Henshaw, "The Impact of Requirements for Parental Consent on Minors' Abortions in Mississippi," 121 (finding a large increase in the proportion of Mississippi minors traveling to other states for abortion upon enforcement of Mississippi's consent statute).

42. Such legislation has passed the House of Representatives on several occasions, as recently as September 26, 2006. Similar legislation passed the Senate on July 25, 2006. *See* Library of Congress, *Thomas Legislative Information on the Internet,* http://thomas.loc.gov/cgi-bin/query/z?c109:S.403: (accessed September 30, 2006).

43. Reconciliation of the House and Senate versions of the legislation did not occur before the fall 2006 congressional recess.

44. According to the American Medical Association, "Adolescents often underestimate the understanding of their parents and overestimate parental anger." American Medical Association Council on Ethical and Judicial Affairs (AMA), "Mandatory Parental Consent to Abortion," *Journal of the American Medical Association (JAMA)* 269 (1993): 83.

45. *See id. See also* Stanley K. Henshaw and Kathryn Kost, "Parental Involvement in Minors' Abortion Decisions," *Family Planning Perspectives* 24 (1992): 204 (studying 1,500 minors seeking abortions and finding that 3 percent reported at least one of the following results of parental knowledge of their pregnancy: "harm to the parents' health, physical violence in the home, being forced to leave home and being beaten.").

46. According to Henshaw and Kost, some minors choose to avoid parental

involvement in their abortion decisions for fear of being forced to continue their pregnancies. *See* Henshaw and Kost, "Parental Involvement in Minors' Abortion Decisions," 203. *See also* Aida Torres, Jacqueline Darroch Forrest, Susan Eisman, "Telling Parents: Clinic Policies and Adolescents' Use of Family Planning and Abortion Services," *Family Planning Perspectives* 12 (1980): 289 (finding that 9 percent of pregnant minors reported that they would proceed with their pregnancies if parental involvement was required).

47. AMA, "Mandatory Parental Consent to Abortion," 83.

48. Interview, July 12, 2001.

49. *Id.*

50. For example, while the Alabama consent law does not explicitly oblige minors to obtain a pregnancy test or to seek abortion counseling, it does require a petition made under oath, which includes a statement that the petitioner is pregnant. *See Ala. Code* § 26-21-4(d) (2004). In addition, to secure a waiver, minors typically seek to prove that they are sufficiently mature and well informed to intelligently decide whether to have an abortion without parental involvement. In effect, then, a minor must have a pregnancy test and abortion counseling in advance of the bypass hearing.

51. Because judges are not required to rule on bypass petitions on the same day as the hearing, arranging to have the abortion on the day of the hearing is not typically practical.

52. *Planned Parenthood of Central New Jersey v. Farmer*, 762 A.2d 620 (N.J. 2000) at 638.

53. *Memphis Planned Parenthood v. Sundquist*, 2 F. Supp. 2d 997 (1997) at 1002. This testimony was presented pursuant to a challenge to the Tennessee statute's appeal provision, which requires that a notice of appeal be filed within twenty-four hours of the juvenile court denial of a bypass petition. The challenge persuaded the district court judge for the Middle District of Tennessee to grant a preliminary injunction against the state's parental consent requirement. The Sixth Circuit Court of Appeals, however, reversed the district court finding, stating that, "[a]lthough we recognize that making phone calls may raise some difficulties for a minor attempting to act in secret, such a burden cannot be characterized as substantial." *Memphis Planned Parenthood v. Sundquist*, 175 F.3d 456 (1999) at 462.

54. *Farmer*, 762 A.2d at 636.

55. Several studies have suggested that parental involvement mandates lead minors to delay abortions, though not specifically owing to the challenges of making phone inquiries. According to one study, second-trimester abortions among Minnesota minors increased by 18 percent after the state's parental notification law took effect. *See* Patricia Donovan, *Our Daughters' Decisions: The Conflict in State Law on Abortion and Other Issues* (New York: Alan Guttmacher Institute, 1992), 21. A study of the repercussions of a Mississippi statute

arrived at a similar finding: "[M]inors who obtained an abortion under the parental consent law may have been about 10–20% more likely to do so after 12 weeks of gestation." *See* Henshaw, "The Impact of Requirements for Parental Consent on Minors' Abortions in Mississippi," 121. By contrast, another study concluded that the claim that Minnesota's parental notice statute caused later abortions is unsubstantiated. *See* James L. Rogers, Robert Boruch, George B. Stoms, and Dorothy DeMoya, "Impact of the Minnesota Parental Notification Law on Abortion and Birth," *American Journal of Public Health* 81 (1991): 297.

NOTES TO CHAPTER 6

1. *Bellotti v. Baird (Bellotti II)*, 443 U.S. 622 (1979) at 643–44.

2. *Id.* at 643 n.23.

3. For a classic discussion of the discretion lower court judges retain, *see* Walter F. Murphy, "Lower Court Checks on Supreme Court Power," *American Political Science Review* 53 (1959).

4. *See, e.g.,* Elizabeth Buchanan, "The Constitution and the Anomaly of the Pregnant Teenager," *Arizona Law Review* 24 (1982); Gene Lindsey, "The Viability of Parental Abortion Notification and Consent Statutes: Assessing Fact and Fiction," *American University Law Review* 38 (1989); Anita J. Pliner and Suzanne Yates, "Psychological and Legal Issues in Minors' Rights to Abortion," *Journal of Social Issues* 48 (1992); Wallace J. Mlyniec, "A Judge's Ethical Dilemma: Assessing a Child's Capacity to Choose," *Fordham Law Review* 64 (1996).

5. Suellyn Scarnecchia and Julie Kunce Field, "Judging Girls: Decision Making in Parental Consent to Abortion Cases," *Michigan Journal of Gender and Law* 3 (1995): 80.

6. *Id.* at 83.

7. *Id.* at 84.

8. *Bellotti II*, 443 U.S. at 655–56.

9. *Hodgson v. Minnesota*, 497 U.S. 417 (1990) at 474–75.

10. Quoted in John Milne, "Souter Note Helped Sink '81 N.H. Bill on Abortion," *Boston Globe*, July 26, 1990.

11. *Id.*

12. *Id.*

13. *Id.*

14. One of these counties is Montgomery, Alabama's fourth largest county.

15. The method I employed for surveying courts appears in Chapter 3, and references to these exchanges are designated "phone contact." In addition to surveys, between March and July 2001, I interviewed judges, intake officers, attorneys appointed to represent minors, and attorneys appointed to represent the unborn. I sought to gather a wide range of information about how bypass hear-

ings function, including information about the nature of the questions posed to the minors; the role played by judges, attorneys, and witnesses; the frequency of grants and denials; and the perceived fairness of the hearings. The interviews— designated as such in the notes that follow—lasted about forty-five minutes each. I do not include the names of those interviewed except where the participants have consented to identification.

16. In addition to these four judges, anecdotal reports suggest that judges in other states require Christian-based counseling as a condition for waiving parental consent. In Alabama, my survey of county courts shows that there may be others who require, or at least prefer, demonstration that a minor has received pro-life counseling. For example, a court intake officer in one Alabama county explained that pro-life counseling was a recommended component of the bypass process. He said:

> Part of the ruling that the judge makes, there's a couple of things he has to take into consideration: Is she mature enough to make an informed decision? The attorneys want to make sure that she can say she's informed. So they may send her to Sav-A-Life and talk with the folks at Sav-A-Life. Not that they want her to not choose an abortion. But so she could say to the judge, "Yes, I talked to this person and this is what they explained to me. And I understand my options." And then we'd have a hearing.

Phone Contact, September 24, 2001. Because this intake officer did not specify whether the absence of Sav-A-Life counseling would result in the denial of a bypass petition, I do not count this judge among those who require such counseling.

17. Phone Contact, October 10, 2001. This judge went on to provide the name and phone number of the local Sav-A-Life affiliate. The remarks of the director of the Sav-A-Life affiliate located in this county confirm that judges sometimes send minors for counseling: "We had a girl that came in for counseling and the judge required her to come to us before he would grant her a waiver." Interview, July 23, 2003.

18. Interview, June 1, 2001.

19. *Id.*

20. Interview, April 23, 2001.

21. Interview, June 1, 2001.

22. *Id.*

23. Interview, June 1, 2001. Some attorneys who participate in waiver hearings confirmed that minors face questions about whether they have visited a pro-life organization.

24. Interviews, May 23, 2001, and June 1, 2001.

25. Interview, June 1, 2001.

26. Interview, May 23, 2001.

27. *Id.*

28. As described in the appellate court's decision in this case:

The trial court characterized "the issue of [the minor's] maturity" as a "difficult call." It found that some of the evidence—such as the minor's academic record, extracurricular activities, employment history, and financial experience—tended to indicate maturity. The trial court concluded, however, that other evidence demonstrated immaturity. The court described the following evidence indicating immaturity: (1) her inexperience in making important decisions about her future, specifically her decision to engage in sexual relations without using birth control; (2) her failure to seek counseling from a facility that opposes abortion, from her parents, or from a mature relative or friend; (3) her statement that she did not wish to continue her pregnancy because she "didn't want to be fat for the prom"; and (4) her failure to consider what the trial court referred to as "the spiritual aspects of her decision to [have an abortion]."

In re Anonymous, 733 So. 2d 429 (Ala. Civ. App. 1999) at 431.

29. *Id.*

30. Interview, June 1, 2001.

31. *Id.*

32. I located ten crisis pregnancy centers in Alabama that are not affiliated with Sav-A-Life by performing a "Yahoo" yellow pages web-based search for "abortion alternatives," "crisis pregnancy," and "pregnancy counseling" in and beyond Tuscaloosa, Huntsville, Montgomery, Birmingham, Mobile, and Dothan. To the extent that crisis pregnancy centers are listed in Yahoo's yellow pages, this search covers virtually all of Alabama. In addition, I cross-checked these findings against the websites of the major crisis pregnancy center umbrella organizations, including Carenet (http://www.care-net.org/), Birthright International (http://www.birthright.org/), Heartbeat International (http://www.heartbeatinternational.org/), America's Crisis Pregnancy Helpline (http://www.thehelpline.org/), and Bethany Christian Services (http://www.bethany.org). I also cross-checked these findings against the list of crisis pregnancy centers available at OptionLine (http://www.pregnancycenters.org/) and Lifecall (http://www.lifecall.org/). While I cannot be certain that I located every non-Sav-A-Life crisis pregnancy center in Alabama, these searches likely identified most, if not all, of these organizations.

33. *See* Sav-A-Life Outreach Centers, *Crisis Pregnancy Centers Near You,* http://www.savalife.org/Default.aspx?tabid=44 (accessed October 1, 2005).

34. *Id.*

35. Sav-A-Life Outreach Centers, *Our Mission,* http://www.savalife.org/Default.aspx?tabid=45 (accessed February 1, 2005).

36. *See* Care Net, *About Care Net,* http://www.care-net.org/aboutus/ (accessed June 14, 2006).

37. *See* Sav-A-Life Outreach Centers, *Sav-A-Life Affiliates,* http://www.sava

life.org/Default.aspx?tabid=42 (accessed October 1, 2005); Sav-A-Life East, Inc., *About Us*, http://www.savalifeeast.org/about.htm (accessed January 18, 2005).

38. Sav-A-Life Outreach Centers, *Our Statement of Faith*, http://www.sava life.org/Default.aspx?tabid=47 (accessed October 1, 2005).

39. *Id.*

40. *Id.*

41. *Id.*

42. Sav-A-Life Outreach Centers, *Our Guiding Principles*, http://www.sava life.org/Default.aspx?tabid=48 (accessed October 1, 2005).

43. *Id.*

44. *Id.*

45. *Id.*

46. I received a copy Sav-A-Life's *Activism Policy* during an interview with the director of one affiliate.

47. Interview, July 21, 2003.

48. Interview, July 22, 2003.

49. Sav-A-Life Outreach Centers, *Our Guiding Principles*.

50. *Id.*

51. I received a copy of the *Volunteer Counselor Application* from the director of a Sav-A-Life affiliate.

52. *See* Care Net, *Southeastern-Based Pregnancy Center Ministry Merges with Care Net*, http://www.care-net.org/news/savalife.html (accessed June 14, 2006).

53. *See* Care Net, *The Care Net Team*, http://www.care-net.org/aboutus/ Staff%20Directory/PollyDuBose.html (accessed June 14, 2006).

54. *See* Care Net, *Southeastern-Based Pregnancy Center Ministry Merges with Care Net.*

55. *See* Care Net, *About Care Net.*

56. *See* Care Net, *Our Mission*, http://www.care-net.org/aboutus/mission .html (accessed June 14, 2006).

57. *See* Care Net, *About Care Net.*

58. According to Care Net's *Pregnancy Center Standards of Affiliation*, "Board members, staff, and volunteers of the center agree with the Care Net Statement of Faith and agree to fully comply with the Care Net Statement of Principle." *See* http://www.care-net.org/membership/standards.pdf (accessed June 14, 2006).

59. *See* Care Net *Statement of Faith*, http://www.care-net.org/membership/ faith.pdf (accessed June 14, 2006).

60. *See* Care Net *Statement of Principle*, http://www.care-net.org/membership/ principle.pdf (accessed June 14, 2006).

61. Sav-A-Life Outreach Centers, *Our History*, http://www.savalife.org/ Default.aspx?tabid=46 (accessed October 1, 2005).

62. In July 2003, I visited six Sav-A-Life affiliates in Alabama and interviewed their directors. Each interview lasted about an hour. I designed the interviews to elicit information on the nature of counseling offered to women who face unplanned pregnancies. I selected Sav-A-Life affiliates located in and around the counties where judges require pro-life counseling. I also interviewed the directors of three crisis pregnancy centers that are not associated with Sav-A-Life. As with my reports of other interviews, I withhold the names of participants except where they agreed to be identified.

63. Interview, July 22, 2003.

64. Interview, July 21, 2003.

65. Interview, July 21, 2003.

66. Interview, July 22, 2003.

67. Interview, July 22, 2003.

68. Interview, July 21, 2003.

69. Sav-A-Life Outreach Centers, *Our Mission.*

70. Interview, July 21, 2003.

71. Interview, July 21, 2003.

72. Interview, July 21, 2003.

73. Interview, July 21, 2003.

74. Interview, July 22, 2003.

75. Interview, July 21, 2003.

76. *Id.*

77. Interview, July 22, 2003.

78. Interview, July 21, 2003.

79. Interview, July 21, 2003.

80. Even if judges did not specifically direct minors to Sav-A-Life but, instead, merely required counseling from a crisis pregnancy center, minors would still face the prospect of receiving counseling from a religious organization. In fact, several of the ten crisis pregnancy centers in Alabama that were unaffiliated with Sav-A-Life at the time I conducted this research share the organization's evangelical mission. For example, the Real Life Crisis Pregnancy Center, with two locations in Alabama and working "[o]n behalf of countless unborn children," explains its mission in this way: "[W]e have presented each person that has come to us with the message of hope that is present in the life-changing gospel of Jesus Christ." Real Life Crisis Pregnancy Center, *Real Life Mission,* http://www.reallifecpc.org/mission.html (accessed October 3, 2005). The remaining crisis pregnancy centers, though not evangelical, serve a decidedly religious mission. These hold affiliations with Catholic churches or other Catholic organizations, or receive support from the Catholic Church. And while the crisis pregnancy centers associated with Catholic organizations do not adopt an evangelical approach, religion provides the foundation of their missions and thus the grounding for their counseling. As the director of one of these centers explained

in describing her organization's ecumenical approach, "Our spiritual dimension, we're not here to convert women. . . . We'll talk about God and the sanctity of life, and why life is precious." Interview, July 23, 2003.

NOTES TO CHAPTER 7

1. Carroll Dale Short, *The People's Lawyer: The Colorful Life and Times of Julian L. McPhillips, Jr.* (Montgomery, Ala.: NewSouth Books, 2000), 306.

2. The information I present about guardianship appointments derives from several sources, including the interviews drawn upon in Chapter 6. In this chapter I cite interviews only when they are the source of a direct quotation. I do not identify the names of those interviewed, except where the participants have consented to my inclusion of their names.

3. *See Ex parte* Anonymous, 720 So. 2d 497 (Ala. 1998) at 499. The ruling does not specify that the minor sought the waiver in Montgomery County.

4. Amy Bach, "No Choice for Teens," *Nation*, October 11, 1999, 7.

5. Interview, April 23, 2001.

6. Short, *The People's Lawyer*, 320, 306.

7. *Id.* at 307.

8. Quoted in *Ex parte* Anonymous, 720 So. 2d at 499 n.2.

9. Quoted in Bach, "No Choice for Teens," 7.

10. As noted in Chapter 2, some parental involvement laws incorporate provisions allowing for or mandating the appointment of a guardian ad litem to protect the interests of the minor. *See, e.g., KRS* § 311.732 (3)(c) (2004). While the Alabama parental consent statute does not mention such appointments, the Alabama Supreme Court has held "that the attorney to be appointed under the parental consent act is to be a guardian ad litem [for the minor], and that future appointments should be so designated and shall entail the responsibilities attendant to such appointments." *Ex parte* Anonymous, 531 So. 2d 901 (Ala. 1988) at 905.

11. *See* Bach, "No Choice for Teens," 7.

12. *Id.*

13. *Id.*

14. *Id.*

15. Interview, April 23, 2001.

16. Quoted in Bach, "No Choice for Teens," 7.

17. Interview, April 23, 2001.

18. *Id.*

19. *Id.*

20. *Id.*

21. *Id.*

22. *Ex parte* Anonymous, 720 So. 2d at 504.

23. Interview, April 23, 2001.

24. *Ala. Code* § 26-21-4(h) (2004).

25. *In re* Anonymous, 720 So. 2d 497 (Ala. Civ. App. 1998) at 497.

26. *Id.*

27. *Ex parte* Anonymous, 720 So. 2d 497 (Ala. 1998).

28. Justices Reneau Almon, Janie Shores, J. Gorman Houston, and Mark Kennedy joined the per curiam opinion. Justice Ralph Cook concurred, without opinion.

29. *Ex parte* Anonymous, 720 So. 2d at 499–500 (citations omitted).

30. The court's opinion addresses a separate issue raised by McPhillips—namely, whether the judicial waiver provision deprives parents of due process of law. The court notes the legislature's intention "to foster 'the family structure,' to preserve the family 'as a viable social unit,' and to protect 'the rights of parents to rear children who are members of their household.'" *Id.* at 500 (quoting *Ala. Code* § 26-21-1(a) (1975)). Nevertheless, the court concludes, and with little elaboration, that the statute does not unconstitutionally deny the due process rights of custodial parents. *Id.*

31. *See Ex parte* Martin, 565 So. 2d 1 (Ala. 1989).

32. *Ex parte* Anonymous, 720 So. 2d at 502 (Hooper, C. J., Maddox, J., See, J., and Lyons, J., concurring specially in part and dissenting in part).

33. *Id.*

34. *Id.* at 502–3.

35. Interview, April 23, 2001.

36. *See S.B.* 389, 1999 Ala. Reg. Sess. (1999). Sections 26-21-4 (i)–(j) of the proposed legislation would have provided for the following:

> (i) . . . [T]he Attorney General or his or her representative shall participate as an advocate for the state to examine the petitioner and any witnesses, and to present evidence for the purpose of providing the court with a sufficient record upon which to make an informed decision and to do substantial justice.

> (j) In the court's discretion, it may appoint a guardian ad litem for the interests of the unborn child of the petitioner who shall also have the same rights and obligations of participation in the proceeding as given to the Attorney General.

37. *See* Jay Reeves, "Bill Would Involve State Attorneys in Juvenile Abortion Cases," Associated Press State and Local Wire, February 23, 1999. That the bill died in committee was reported to me by the Legislative Reference Service of the State of Alabama.

38. Senate Democrats filibustered Pryor's nomination to the Eleventh Circuit Court of Appeals, prompting President Bush to install Pryor as a recess appointment. *See* Neil A. Lewis, "Bypassing Senate for Second Time, Bush Seats

Judge," *New York Times*, February 21, 2004. Pryor eventually earned Senate approval after a compromise that avoided a vote to eliminate filibusters of judicial nominees. Carl Hulse, "Bipartisan Group in Senate Averts Judge Showdown," *New York Times*, May 24, 2005.

39. Quoted in Reeves, "Bill Would Involve State Attorneys in Juvenile Abortion Cases."

40. *Id.*

41. Although there may be instances of such appointments that I have yet to discover, reports suggest that most judges who handle bypass petitions in Alabama typically do not assign a guardian to give a voice to the fetus. Outside of Alabama, there have been some reported cases of guardian appointments at bypass hearings in Florida, Indiana, and Louisiana. *See* Chapter 9 in this volume.

42. McPhillips was not called on in these cases to act as guardian ad litem. One attorney was appointed to handle two of these cases, a second attorney handled one case, and a third attorney has routinely served in this capacity. There was an additional instance in which a guardian was appointed to represent the fetus, but the minor, in the end, did not pursue the waiver option and the hearing was cancelled. There have likely been other instances in which guardians have served as fetal representatives. The seventeen I count since the McPhillips hearings are ones I have been able to document either by way of interviews or through appellate court rulings.

43. Interview, May 23, 2001.

44. Interview, April 26, 2001.

45. *Id.*

46. For example, the Alabama Supreme Court relayed the questioning of a minor by one guardian:

The lawyer appointed for the fetus, described in the record as a guardian ad litem, subjected [the minor] to a probing cross-examination concerning her knowledge of the negative consequences of undergoing an abortion and the possible consequences, including depression, sterility, and death. The appointed lawyer's cross-examination also explored at some length [the minor's] knowledge of the alternatives to abortion, including having her family help raise the baby or placing the baby for adoption.

Ex parte Anonymous, 810 So. 2d 786 (Ala. 2001) at 789.

47. Interview, May 16, 2001.

48. *Id.*

49. Interview, May 23, 2001.

50. *Id.*

51. *In re* Anonymous, 810 So. 2d 784 (Ala. Civ. App. 2001) at 785 (Yates, J., dissenting).

52. Among the witnesses called were the executive director of Sav-A-Life,

the director of COPE Crisis Pregnancy Center, and a woman who testified about her post-abortive experiences. *See In re* Anonymous, 733 So. 2d 429 (Ala. Civ. App. 1999).

53. Interview, April 26, 2001.

54. *Id.*

55. *Id.*

56. The U.S. Supreme Court has not faced the opportunity to address the constitutionality of these appointments. But the Florida Supreme Court did, finding in one case that "the appointment of a guardian ad litem for the fetus was clearly improper." *In re* T. W., 551 So. 2d 1186 (1989) at 1190.

57. *In re* Anonymous, 733 So. 2d 429 (Ala. Civ. App. 1999) at 431 n.1. The denial of the guardian's motion prompted a separate, one-paragraph concurrence written by Presiding Judge William Robertson and joined by Judge William Thompson. Agreeing that the trial court erred in failing to grant the bypass request, Robertson expressed his disagreement with the majority's decision to deny the guardian's motion to file a brief. Citing the Alabama Supreme Court's ruling on guardianship appointments, Robertson argued:

[I]t appears that Rule 17(c), Ala. R. Civ. P., would permit the appointment of a guardian ad litem to represent the interests of the fetus. It follows that when the trial court has made such an appointment, the guardian should be entitled to appear before an appellate court that is considering whether the trial court properly denied a waiver of parental consent to the minor . . . and should be allowed to submit a brief in support of the trial court's judgment, as the guardian sought to do here.

Id. at 433 (Robertson, J., concurring in the result).

58. *Ex parte* Anonymous, 810 So. 2d 786 (Ala. 2001).

59. *Id.* at 791.

60. *Id.* at 795.

61. *Ex parte* Anonymous, 889 So. 2d 525 (Ala. 2003) at 527 (Johnstone, J. dissenting).

62. *Id.*

63. *Id.*

64. Interview, May 17, 2001.

65. Interview, May 15, 2001.

66. Quoted in Short, *The People's Lawyer,* 320 (emphasis in the original).

67. Interview, May 16, 2001.

68. Interview, May 23, 2001.

69. Quoted in Short, *The People's Lawyer,* 320–21 (alteration in the original).

70. Interview, April 23, 2001.

71. Interview, June 1, 2001. Anderson explained that he arrived at his decision to appoint a guardian after serving on the bench for about a year and de-

claring that he would run for election against a Democratic opponent. About his decision to appoint McPhillips, Anderson said, "I believe it is Isaiah in the Bible who says, 'He who honors me I honor'; the day I did that my opponent dropped out of the race." *Id.*

72. *Wise v. Watson,* 236 So. 2d 681 (Ala. 1970) at 684 (citations omitted).

73. Interview, June 1, 2001.

74. Quoted in *In re* Anonymous, 810 So. 2d 784 (Ala. Civ. App. 2001) at 785 (Yates, J., dissenting).

75. Interview, June 1, 2001.

76. Bach, "No Choice for Teens," 7.

77. Interview, April 23, 2001.

NOTES TO CHAPTER 8

1. *Ex parte* Anonymous, 888 So. 2d 1275 (Ala. 2004) at 1275 (Johnstone, J., dissenting).

2. *See* Chapter 2 in this volume.

3. *See Planned Parenthood of Southeastern Pennsylvania v. Casey,* 505 U.S. 833 (1992).

4. *Id.*

5. *Roe v. Wade,* 410 U.S. 113 (1973).

6. According to *Roe,*

[F]rom and after this point, a State may regulate the abortion procedure to the extent that the regulation reasonably relates to the preservation and protection of maternal health. . . . [F]or the period of pregnancy prior to this "compelling" point, the attending physician, in consultation with his patient, is free to determine, without regulation by the State, that, in his medical judgment, the patient's pregnancy should be terminated. If that decision is reached, the judgment may be effectuated by an abortion free of interference by the State.

Id. at 163.

7. *Id.*

8. *Casey,* 505 U.S. at 869 (joint opinion).

9. *Id.* at 872–73 (citations omitted; internal quotation marks omitted).

10. *Id.* at 878.

11. *Id.* at 875.

12. *Id.* at 877 (citations omitted).

13. *See also Maher v. Roe,* 432 U.S. 464 (1977) (upholding Connecticut's prohibition of funding for non-therapeutic abortions); *Webster v. Reproductive Health Services,* 492 U.S. 490 (1989) at 511 ("The Constitution does not forbid a State or city, pursuant to democratic processes, from expressing a preference for normal childbirth.").

14. *Casey*, 505 U.S. at 877–78 (citations omitted) (joint opinion).

15. *See Akron v. Akron Ctr. for Reprod. Health, Inc. (Akron I)*, 462 U.S. 416 (1983) (applying *Roe* to overturn, among other provisions, an informed consent requirement and a twenty-four-hour waiting period).

16. *Casey*, 505 U.S. at 882 (joint opinion).

17. *Id.* at 882–83.

18. *Id.* at 886.

19. *Id.*

20. *Id.* at 873.

21. *Id.* at 873–74.

22. *Id.* at 887.

23. *Id.* at 893–94.

24. *Id.* at 936 n.7 (Blackmun, J., concurring in part, concurring in the judgment in part, and dissenting in part) (quoting *Casey* joint opinion, 505 U.S. at 883). Blackmun continues by saying,

> To this end, when the State requires the provision of certain information, the State may not alter the *manner* of presentation in order to inflict "psychological abuse," designed to shock or unnerve a woman seeking to exercise her liberty right. This, for example, would appear to preclude a State from requiring a woman to view graphic literature or films detailing the performance of an abortion operation.

Id. (quoting *Casey* joint opinion, 505 U.S. at 893).

25. *Id.* at 877 (joint opinion).

26. *Id.* at 986–87 (Scalia, J., concurring in judgment in part and dissenting in part) (quoting *Casey* joint opinion, 505 U.S. at 877, 877–79, 877 n.4) (alteration in the original).

27. *Planned Parenthood v. Miller*, 63 F.3d 1452 (1995). The appellate court used the standard to justify its holding that a parental notice requirement must be accompanied by a bypass option.

28. *See, e.g., Ohio v. Akron Center for Reproductive Health (Akron II)*, 497 U.S. 502 (1990) at 519–20.

29. *Hodgson v. Minnesota*, 497 U.S. 417 (1990) at 459 (O'Connor, J. concurring) (internal quotes and ellipses omitted).

30. *Casey*, 505 U.S. at 877 (joint opinion).

31. *Id.* at 873.

32. *Id.*

33. According to the accounts of those interviewed, in one case a minor was granted her bypass petition, but the trial judge ordered a "cooling-off" period between the time the petition was granted and the time the minor could obtain an abortion. Other delays have been incurred as well. In two cases, again according to reports of those interviewed, the guardian moved for a continuance

of the hearing so that the minor could seek counseling from a pro-life organization. In each of these instances, the judge granted the guardian's motion, and the minors in question sought counseling before returning to the court for a continuation of the judicial proceedings and the ultimate granting of their petitions.

34. *See In re* Anonymous, 720 So. 2d 497 (Ala. Civ. App. 1998) and *Ex parte* Anonymous, 720 So. 2d 497 (Ala. 1998).

35. The Alabama Supreme Court recently noted that the typical nonadversarial character of waiver hearings is altered by the presence of fetal representation. *See Ex parte* Anonymous, 810 So. 2d 786 (Ala. 2001). Describing a waiver hearing that included "a probing cross-examination," *id.* at 789, the court commented that "this was not a 'nonadversarial' proceeding." *Id.* at 791.

36. *Casey*, 505 U.S. at 872.

37. In addition to upholding a state-mandated twenty-four-hour waiting period for adult women seeking abortions, the Court in *Hodgson* upheld a Minnesota statute prohibiting the performance of an abortion on a minor until at least forty-eight hours after parental notification of the abortion. *See Hodgson*, 497 U.S. at 449.

38. The additional time is inconsequential only if guardians do not have the right to appeal grants of waiver petitions, as is currently the case in Alabama. Because the right to appeal a grant of a waiver forces the minor to further delay abortion, the minor's health is put at greater risk by allowing such appeals. However, guardianship appointments need not be accompanied by a right to appeal.

39. *Casey*, 505 U.S. at 894 (joint opinion).

40. Quoted in *In re* Anonymous, 810 So. 2d 784 (Ala. Civ. App. 2001) at 785 (Yates, J., dissenting).

41. *U.S. Const.* Amend. I

42. Though I will not here elaborate this argument in full, I will present its contours. For further discussion, *see* Helena Silverstein and Kathryn Lundwall Alessi, "Religious Establishment in Hearings to Waive Parental Consent for Abortion," *University of Pennsylvania Journal of Constitutional Law* 7 (2004).

43. *Lemon v. Kurtzman*, 403 U.S. 602 (1971).

44. *Id.* at 612–13 (citations omitted).

45. *Grand Rapids Sch. Dist. v. Ball*, 473 U.S. 373 (1985) at 385 (citations omitted). In *Ball*, the Court invalidated two public educational programs which financed and offered classes in sectarian schools to students of those schools. While the rules for assessing the likelihood of indoctrination have been relaxed since the Court's ruling in *Ball*, government-sponsored religious indoctrination remains absolutely forbidden under the Establishment Clause.

46. *Bowen v. Kendrick*, 487 U.S. 589 (1988).

47. Margo R. Drucker, "*Bowen v. Kendrick*: Establishing Chastity at the Expense of Constitutional Prophylactics," *New York University Law Review* 64 (1989): 1178.

48. *Bowen*, 487 U.S. at 610.

49. The *Bowen* Court held that "it is not enough to show that the recipient of a challenged grant is affiliated with a religious institution or that it is 'religiously inspired.'" *Id.* at 621. And according to standing precedent, the mere finding that an organization undertakes a religiously based mission does not make that organization pervasively sectarian. Consider, for example, cases that have upheld government funding of religiously affiliated institutions of higher education. In *Tilton v. Richardson*, 403 U.S. 672 (1971), the Court permitted government funding of church-related colleges and universities, including several schools governed by Catholic religious organizations (e.g., Sacred Heart University, Fairfield University, and Albertus Magnus College). In *Hunt v. McNair*, 413 U.S. 734 (1973), the Court upheld a funding program that permitted grant allocation to Baptist College at Charleston, an institution of higher learning governed in part by the South Carolina Baptist Convention. In *Roemer v. Bd. of Pub. Works of Md.*, 426 U.S. 736 (1976), the Court sanctioned sizable financial disbursements to four Roman Catholic–affiliated colleges located in Maryland: the College of Notre Dame, Mount Saint Mary's College, Saint Joseph College, and Loyola College. In none of these cases did the Court find these institutions to be pervasively sectarian. But, without doubt, these institutions have at their foundation a religious mission. For example, according to Sacred Heart University's mission statement, the University "is Catholic in tradition and spirit. As a Catholic university, it seeks to play its appropriate role in the modern world. It exemplifies in its life the Judeo-Christian values of the God-given freedom and dignity of every human person." Sacred Heart University, *Mission Statement*, http://www.sacredheart.edu/about/mission/index.html (accessed August 30, 2004).

50. The conclusion that Sav-A-Life is pervasively sectarian is not necessary to a finding that mandated Sav-A-Life counseling from the interviewed affiliates leads to efforts to indoctrinate minors. With respect to the interviewed affiliates, the evidence concerning the evangelical character of the counseling demonstrates that the risk of indoctrination is real. However, the conclusion that Sav-A-Life is pervasively sectarian does provide the grounds for generalizing about the risk of indoctrination at all Sav-A-Life affiliates, thereby supporting an organization-wide conclusion about the constitutional effect of the counseling mandate.

51. Sav-A-Life Outreach Centers, *Our Statement of Faith*, http://www.savalife.org/Default.aspx?tabid=47 (accessed October 1, 2005).

52. *Id.*

53. Interview, July 21, 2003.

54. *See, e.g., Hunt, Roemer,* and *Tilton.*

55. *Kendrick v. Bowen,* 657 F. Supp. 1547 (D.C. Cir. 1987) at 1568.

56. *Id.*

57. Justice Scalia is among the outspoken critics of *Lemon.* In one of his dissents he opined:

Our Religion Clause jurisprudence has become bedeviled (so to speak) by reliance on formulaic abstractions that are not derived from, but positively conflict with, our long-accepted constitutional traditions. Foremost among these has been the so-called *Lemon* test, which has received well-earned criticism from many Members of this Court. The Court today demonstrates the irrelevance of *Lemon* by essentially ignoring it, and the interment of that case may be the one happy byproduct of the Court's otherwise lamentable decision.

Lee v. Weisman, 505 U.S. 577 (1992) at 644 (citations omitted).

58. *Lee v. Weisman,* 505 U.S. 577 (1992).

59. *Id.* at 587 (citation omitted). Under this principle, coercion is sufficient but not necessary to show a breach of the Establishment Clause. *Id.* at 604 (Blackmun, J., concurring).

60. This owes, of course, to the explicit proscription of the coercion test, which forbids a government practice that compels "anyone to support or participate in religion or its exercise." *Lee,* 505 U.S. at 587. What counts as religion or its exercise remains unsettled, but the Court has classified religion as encompassing beliefs "based upon a power or being, or upon a faith, to which all else is subordinate or upon which all else is ultimately dependent." *United States v. Seeger,* 380 U.S. 163 (1965) at 176. The question as to whether an activity is a religion for constitutional purposes is fact-intensive. *Id.*

61. As *Lee* demonstrates, prayer constitutes religious activity. *See Lee,* 505 U.S. at 586–87. *See also Santa Fe Indep. Sch. Dist. v. Doe,* 530 U.S. 290 (2000) at 312 ("[T]he delivery of a pregame prayer [at a high school football game] has the improper effect of coercing those present to participate in an act of religious worship.").

62. Interview, July 21, 2003.

63. Interview, July 22, 2003.

64. Interview, July 22, 2003.

65. *Id.*

66. Interview, July 21, 2003.

67. The evidence also suggests, as explained above, that Sav-A-Life is pervasively sectarian, and we could arguably rely on this finding to settle the issue of whether mandated Sav-A-Life counseling fails the coercion test. As *Bowen* and other cases explain—albeit not in the context of analyzing the coercion test—pervasively sectarian institutions cannot separate the secular from the sectarian. *Bowen,* 487 U.S. at 589. If such is the context in which religious organizations

provide counseling, then we must assume that the facially neutral activity of offering adoption counseling, for example, does become a religious activity by virtue of being carried out by a pervasively sectarian organization. In short, since Sav-A-Life is pervasively sectarian, its education and counseling services constitute religious activity.

68. In *Edwards v. Aguillard*, 482 U.S. 578 (1987), the Court overturned a Louisiana statute that mandated treatment of both creationism and evolution in the state's public schools, saying:

> The Court has been particularly vigilant in monitoring compliance with the Establishment Clause in elementary and secondary schools. Families entrust public schools with the education of their children, but condition their trust on the understanding that the classroom will not purposely be used to advance religious views that may conflict with the private beliefs of the student and his or her family. Students in such institutions are impressionable and their attendance is involuntary.

Edwards, 482 U.S. at 583–84. *See also Lee*, 505 U.S. at 592. ("[T]here are heightened concerns with protecting freedom of conscience from subtle coercive pressure in the elementary and secondary public schools.").

69. *See, especially, Lynch v. Donnelly*, 465 U.S. 668 (1984) (upholding a public display of a nativity scene) and *Wallace v. Jaffree*, 472 U.S. 38 (1985) (rejecting a mandated moment of silence to begin each public school day).

70. *Wallace*, 472 U.S. at 69 (O'Connor, J., concurring).

71. *Id*. at 70 (O'Connor, J., concurring).

72. *Id*. (citations omitted; internal quotation marks omitted).

73. *Lynch*, 465 U.S. at 688.

74. *Griffin v. Coughlin*, 673 N.E.2d 98 (N.Y. 1996) at 106 (addressing compelled attendance of prisoners at Alcoholics Anonymous meetings) (citations omitted).

75. *Hodgson v. Minnesota*, 648 F. Supp. 756 (1986) at 765.

76. *Hodgson*, 497 U.S. at 449 (citations omitted).

77. *Hodgson*, 648 F. Supp. at 763.

78. As of June 2006, according to the Alan Guttmacher Institute, six of the thirty-two states that mandate informed consent for abortion require in-person delivery of state-directed counseling and information. In addition, these six states require that the counseling take place at least eighteen hours prior to the termination of a pregnancy. *See* Alan Guttmacher Institute, "Mandatory Counseling and Waiting Periods for Abortion," in *State Policies in Brief*, June 1, 2006, http://www.guttmacher.org/statecenter/spibs/spib_MWPA.pdf (accessed June 17, 2006).

79. *See* Catherine Candisky, "Abortion Provisions Begin Monday; Federal Appeals Court Lets Law Take Effect to Require Counseling, Parental Consent," *Columbus Dispatch*, October 4, 2005.

80. *See* "Granholm Signs Abortion Ultrasound Law," Associated Press State and Local Wire, March 24, 2006.

81. *See* Doug Gross, "Senate Approves Slate of Abortion-Related Bills," Associated Press State and Local Wire, March 2, 2006.

82. Such a measure could be incorporated into the informed consent provisions that states have adopted.

83. *Casey,* 505 U.S. at 873 (joint opinion).

84. *Casey,* 505 U.S. at 916 (Stevens, J., concurring in part and dissenting in part) (quoting *Casey* joint opinion, 505 U.S. at 878).

NOTES TO CHAPTER 9

1. Stuart A. Scheingold, *The Politics of Rights: Lawyers, Public Policy, and Political Change* (New Haven, Conn.: Yale University Press, 1974), 3.

2. Melissa Jacobs, "Are Courts Prepared to Handle Judicial Bypass Proceedings?" *Human Rights* 32 (Winter 2005): 5.

3. *Id.*

4. Quoted in Jane's Due Process, "Tales from the Front 2," distributed with Diana Philip, *Annual Report, Jane's Due Process,* January 22, 2002, to January 21, 2003.

5. Quoted in Jane's Due Process, "Tales from the Front," distributed with Diana Philip, *First Annual Report, Jane's Due Process,* January 22, 2001, to January 21, 2002.

6. *See* Laurence Hammack, "Notification Law: No Takers, Some Qualms 3 Days Later, No One in the Region Has Sought Judicial Permission for an Abortion," *Roanoke Times,* July 4, 1997.

7. Tamar Lewin, "Parental Consent to Abortion: How Enforcement Can Vary," *New York Times,* May 28, 1992.

8. Patricia Donovan, "Judging Teenagers: How Minors Fare When They Seek Court-Authorized Abortions," *Family Planning Perspectives* 15 (1983): 265.

9. Tamar Lewin, "The Anguish of Asking a Court for an Abortion," *New York Times,* May 28, 1992.

10. *Id.*

11. Donovan, "Judging Teenagers," 264.

12. *Hodgson v. Minnesota,* 648 F. Supp. 756 (1986) at 763.

13. *See* Child Custody Protection Act: Hearings on H.R. 1218 before the Subcomm. on the Constitution of the House Comm. on the Judiciary, 106th Cong. (May 27, 1999) (statement of Billie Lominick) at http://commdocs.house .gov/committees/judiciary/hju62490.000/hju62490_0.HTM (accessed September 29, 2006).

14. *Id.*

15. *Id.*

16. *Id.*

17. *Id.*

18. Attorney Jamie Subino, quoted in Donovan, "Judging Teenagers," 266.

19. *In re* T. W., 551 So. 2d 1186 (Fla. 1989) at 1190.

20. *In re:* Application of Jane Doe A Minor, 591 So. 2d 698 (La. 1991) at 698.

21. Amy Bach, "No Choice for Teens," *Nation,* October 11, 1999, 7.

22. *In re* T. W., 551 So. 2d at 1190.

23. *In re:* Application of Jane Doe A Minor, 591 So. 2d at 698.

24. Jacobs, "Are Courts Prepared to Handle Judicial Bypass Proceedings?" 5.

25. Diana Philip, *First Annual Report, Jane's Due Process,* January 22, 2001, to January 21, 2002.

26. Bach, "No Choice for Teens," 7.

27. *Id.*

28. Lynda Zielinski, "Jane Doe's Choice," *Ms.* (Winter 2006): 69.

29. David D. Kirkpatrick, "For New Judge, Self-Reliance in Life and Law," *New York Times,* May 26, 2005.

30. Elisabeth Bumiller, "Announcement of Supreme Court Nominee May Be Soon," *New York Times,* July 19, 2005.

31. *In re* Jane Doe, 19 S.W.3d 249 (Tex. 2005) at 264–65.

32. *Hodgson v. Minnesota,* 648 F. Supp. at 781.

33. Suzanne Yates and Anita J. Pliner, "Judging Maturity in the Courts: The Massachusetts Consent Statute," *American Journal of Public Health* 78 (1988): 647.

34. Phil Trexler, "Abortion Fiery Issue for Judges," *Akron Beacon Journal,* November 9, 2003.

35. *See also* Marie McCullough, "A 15-Year-Old Anguishes over Abortion Decision," *Philadelphia Inquirer,* May 29, 2001 (stating that "bypasses are almost automatic in some states, including Minnesota, Massachusetts and Pennsylvania").

36. Daniel Nguyen, "Few Bypass Abortion Rule," *Denver Post,* August 15, 2004.

37. Quoted in McCullough, "A 15-Year-Old Anguishes over Abortion Decision."

38. For example, the Yates and Pliner study of 477 minors petitioning in Massachusetts found the average age was 16.33 years. "Judging Maturity in the Courts," 647. *See also* Patricia Donovan, "Judging Teenagers," 261 (stating that "[d]ata from three states indicate that for the most part, it is 16- and 17-year-olds who decide to go before a judge; younger minors are more likely to consult with their parents").

39. According to an attorney in a Minnesota public defender's office who

represented hundreds of minors in the early 1980s, the bypass procedure "is one of jumping a number of hurdles to get into court and it seemed to me that the kids who were able to jump those hurdles almost by definition were going to be mature, were going to be intelligent, or whatever word you want to use to describe that." *Hodgson v. Minnesota,* Nos. 88-1125 and 88-1309, 1988 U.S. Briefs 1125 (September 1, 1989), Joint Appendix, trial testimony excerpts of David Knutson.

40. Quoted in *Hodgson v. Minnesota,* 648 F. Supp. at 767.

41. As Justice Thurgood Marshall said, writing separately and in opposition to Minnesota's two-parent involvement mandate, "even if judges authorized every abortion sought by petitioning minors, Minnesota's judicial bypass is far too burdensome to remedy an otherwise unconstitutional statute." *Hodgson v. Minnesota,* 497 U.S. 417 (1990) at 475 (concurring in part, concurring in judgment in part and dissenting in part).

42. Trexler, "Abortion Fiery Issue for Judges."

43. *Id.*

44. *Id.*

45. *Id.*

46. Interview, May 10, 2001.

47. *Id.*

48. Jamin B. Raskin, "The Paradox of Judicial Bypass Proceedings," *American University Journal of Gender, Social Policy and the Law* 10 (2002): 282.

49. Jamie Stengle, "Governor Signs Abortion Bill at Church School," Associated Press, June 5, 2005.

50. Ralph Blumenthal, "Governor Draws Criticism for a Bill-Signing Event at an Evangelical School," *New York Times,* June 6, 2005.

51. Matt Curry, "Perry Mobilizes Evangelicals as Governor's Race Heats Up," Associated Press, June 11, 2005.

52. Quoted in Stengle, "Governor Signs Abortion Bill at Church School."

53. Quoted in Blumenthal, "Governor Draws Criticism for a Bill-Signing Event."

54. Quoted in Stengle, "Governor Signs Abortion Bill at Church School."

55. Quoted in *In re* Anonymous, 905 So. 2d 845 (Ala. Civ. App. 2005) at 850.

56. *Id.* at 848. The trial judge arrived at this ruling in the context of a pregnant teen who would have reached the age of eighteen near the end of her first trimester or shortly after the onset of her second trimester.

57. Scheingold, *The Politics of Rights,* xi.

58. *Id.*

59. *Id.* at 14.

60. Scheingold cites the works of several scholars who have studied the political, symbolic, and ideological aspects of the law. *See, e.g.,* Judith N. Shklar,

Legalism: An Essay on Law, Morals, and Politics (Cambridge: Harvard University Press, 1964); Thurman Arnold, *The Symbols of Government* (New York: Harcourt, Brace, 1962); Murray Edelman, *Politics as Symbolic Action: Mass Arousal and Quiescence* (Chicago: Markham, 1971); Clifford Geertz, "Ideology as a Cultural System," in David E. Apter (ed.), *Ideology and Discontent* (New York: Free Press, 1964).

61. Scheingold, *The Politics of Rights*, 3.

62. *Id.* at 17 (emphasis in the original).

63. *Id.* at 14.

64. *Id.* at 17 (quoting Harry M. Johnson, "Ideology and the Social System," in *International Encyclopedia of Social Sciences* 7 (1968): 81).

65. *Id.* at 5.

66. *Id.* at 91.

67. *Id.* at 85.

68. Kristen Bumiller, "Victims in the Shadow of the Law," *Signs* 12 (1987).

69. This is not always the case. In some instances, parents know about the pregnancy but refuse to give consent. In other cases, the parents are not around.

70. Interview, May 16, 2001.

71. Interview, April 23, 2001.

72. Interview, June 1, 2001. Though "happy" with the outcome, this attorney expressed her frustration and anger at the manner in which judges implement the waiver process, saying, "I come home and slam my books around after these hearings." *Id.*

73. *Id.*

74. *Id.*

75. Interview, May 17, 2001.

76. *See, e.g., In re* Anonymous, 888 So. 2d 1265 (Ala. Civ. App. 2004).

77. *See, e.g., Ex parte* Anonymous, 889 So. 2d 518 (Ala. 2003).

78. This is ironic because the religious right lays claim to the rhetoric of the myth of rights, saying that judges should "judge" not "legislate" and that *Roe v. Wade* was the supreme example of activist and politically driven judicial legislation.

79. *Glassroth v. Moore*, 335 F.3d 1282 (2003) at 1284.

80. *Id.* at 1285.

81. *Glassroth v. Moore*, 242 F. Supp. 2d 1067 (M.D. Ala. 2002) at 1294.

82. *Moore v. Judicial Inquiry Commission of the State of Alabama*, 891 So. 2d 848 (2004) at 850.

83. Some of the funds raised by the sale of the film eventually went to help support the chief justice's legal defense. *Glassroth*, 335 F.3d at 1286.

84. *Id.*

85. Federal district and circuit courts both found that the chief justice violated the Establishment Clause and ordered Moore to remove the monument.

See, respectively, Glassroth v. Moore, 242 F. Supp. 2d and *Glassroth v. Moore,* 335 F.3d. Moore repeatedly failed to comply with the orders of the federal courts. In the end, the eight associate justices of the Alabama Supreme Court directed that the monument be removed. Moore faced a similar fate, ultimately being removed from the Alabama Supreme Court based on his refusal to comply with federal orders to remove the monument. *See Moore v. Judicial Inquiry Commission of the State of Alabama,* 891 So. 2d.

86. *Glassroth,* 335 F.3d at 1287.

87. *See, especially, Ex parte* Anonymous, 803 So. 2d 542 (Ala. 2001).

88. Quoted in Bob Johnson, "Alabama Judge Wears Ten Commandments on Robe," Associated Press State and Local Wire, December 15, 2004.

89. Quoted in "Judge's Robe Draws Big Attention," United Press International, December 16, 2004. McKathan had publicly backed Moore, speaking at a rally supporting Moore's efforts to keep the Ten Commandments display in the state Supreme Court building. Bob Johnson, "Quiet Judge Finds Controversy When He Dons Ten Commandments Robe," Associated Press State and Local Wire, January 9, 2005. In turn, McKathan's fashion statement earned praise from ousted Roy Moore, who said, "The recognition of the God who gave us the Ten Commandments is fundamental to an understanding of the First Amendment to the United States Constitution. I applaud Judge McKathan. It is time for our judiciary to recognize the moral basis of our law." Johnson, "Alabama Judge Wears Ten Commandments on Robe."

90. *American Civil Liberties Union of Ohio Foundation v. Ashbrook,* 375 F.3d 484 (2004).

91. *Id.* at 491.

92. *Id.* at 491–92. Based on this testimony, the appeals court affirmed the district court's ruling that the display violates the Establishment Clause and must be removed. The Supreme Court let this ruling stand after handing down its rulings on Ten Commandments displays in Kentucky (*McCreary County, Kentucky v. American Civil Liberties Union of Kentucky,* 125 S. Ct. 2722 (2005)) and Texas (*Van Orden v. Perry,* 125 S. Ct. 2854 (2005)). Hope Yen, "Appeals on Commandments Displays Rejected," Associated Press, June 28, 2005.

93. "Laurel Judge Gives Church Attendance Option to Some Offenders," Associated Press State and Local Wire, May 31, 2005.

94. Herryn Riendeau, "Kentucky Judge Offers Worship Services as an Alternative to Jail," June 2, 2005, http://www.WBIR.com (accessed August 3, 2005).

95. *Id.*

96. Quoted in "Laurel Judge Gives Church Attendance Option to Some Offenders."

97. *Id.*

98. Quoted in David G. Savage, "Roberts Sees Role as Judicial 'Umpire,'" *Los Angeles Times*, September 13, 2005.

99. Quoted in "Texas Judge Could Face Sanctions for Allowing Photo to Run in Newspaper Ad for Seminary," *BP News*, September 30, 2003, http://www.sbcbaptistpress.org/bpnews.asp?ID=16772 (accessed August 5, 2005).

100. *Id.*

101. "Panel V of the Hearing of the Senate Judiciary Committee," *Federal News Service*, September 15, 2005.

102. *Ayotte v. Planned Parenthood of Northern New England*, 126 S. Ct. 961 (2006).

103. *See Ayotte v. Planned Parenthood of Northern New England*, Oral Arguments Transcript, at http://www.supremecourtus.gov/oral_arguments/argument _transcripts/04-1144.pdf.

104. *Brown v. Board of Education*, 347 U.S 483 (1954).

105. *See, e.g.*, Gerald N. Rosenberg, *The Hollow Hope: Can the Courts Bring about Social Change?* (Chicago: University of Chicago Press, 1991).

106. Suellyn Scarnecchia and Julie Kunce Field, "Judging Girls: Decision Making in Parental Consent to Abortion Cases," *Michigan Journal of Gender and Law* 3 (1995): 87–88.

Bibliography

BOOKS, ARTICLES, AND ONLINE MATERIAL

Adler, Nancy E., Emily J. Ozer, and Jeanne Tschann. "Abortion among Adolescents." *American Psychologist* 58 (2003).

Alan Guttmacher Institute. "Mandatory Counseling and Waiting Periods for Abortion." In *State Policies in Brief*, June 1, 2006. http://www.guttmacher.org/statecenter/spibs/spib_MWPA.pdf (accessed June 17, 2006).

———. "Parental Involvement in Minors' Abortions." In *State Policies in Brief*, June 1, 2006. http://www.guttmacher.org/statecenter/spibs/spib_PIMA.pdf (accessed June 8, 2006).

American Academy of Pediatrics Committee on Adolescence (AAP). "The Adolescent's Right to Confidential Care When Considering Abortion." *Pediatrics* 97 (1996).

American Bar Association (ABA). "Building Momentum: The American Bar Association Call for a Moratorium on Executions Takes Hold." 2003. http://www.abanet.org/moratorium/reportsandlaw.html (accessed February 11, 2005).

American Medical Association Council on Ethical and Judicial Affairs (AMA). "Mandatory Parental Consent to Abortion." *Journal of the American Medical Association (JAMA)* 269 (1993).

Arnold, Thurman. *The Symbols of Government*. New York: Harcourt, Brace, 1962.

Bach, Amy. "No Choice for Teens." *Nation*, October 11, 1999.

Bernard, Catherine. *The Long-Term Psychological Effects of Abortion*. Portsmouth, N.H.: Institute for Pregnancy Loss, 1990.

Blumenthal, Ralph. "Governor Draws Criticism for a Bill-Signing Event at an Evangelical School." *New York Times*, June 6, 2005.

Boule, Margie. "An American Tragedy." *Portland Oregonian*, August 27, 1989.

Buchanan, Elizabeth. "The Constitution and the Anomaly of the Pregnant Teenager." *Arizona Law Review* 24 (1982).

Bumiller, Elisabeth. "Announcement of Supreme Court Nominee May Be Soon." *New York Times*, July 19, 2005.

Bumiller, Kristen. "Victims in the Shadow of the Law." *Signs* 12 (1987).

Campos, Carlos. "Legislature 2005: Senate Panel OKs Bill to Restrict Abortions; Hearing Draws Foes, Supporters." *Atlanta Journal-Constitution*, February 3, 2005.

Candisky, Catherine. "Abortion Provisions Begin Monday; Federal Appeals Court Lets Law Take Effect to Require Counseling, Parental Consent." *Columbus Dispatch*, October 4, 2005.

Canon, Bradley C., and Charles A. Johnson. *Judicial Policies: Implementation and Impact*, 2nd ed. Washington, D.C.: CQ Press, 1999.

Canon, Bradley C., and Kenneth Kolson. "Compliance with *Gault* in Rural America: Kentucky, A Case Study." *Journal of Family Law* 10 (1971).

Care Net. *About Care Net*. http://www.care-net.org/aboutus/ (accessed June 14, 2006).

———. *The Care Net Team*. http://www.care-net.org/aboutus/Staff%20Directory/PollyDuBose.html (accessed June 14, 2006).

———. *Our Mission*. http://www.care-net.org/aboutus/mission.html (accessed June 14, 2006).

———. *Pregnancy Center Standards of Affiliation*. http://www.care-net.org/membership/standards.pdf (accessed June 14, 2006).

———. *Southeastern-Based Pregnancy Center Ministry Merges with Care Net*. http://www.care-net.org/news/savalife.html (accessed June 14, 2006).

———. *Statement of Faith*. http://www.care-net.org/membership/faith.pdf (accessed June 14, 2006).

———. *Statement of Principle*. http://www.care-net.org/membership/principle.pdf (accessed June 14, 2006).

Carrington, Paul D. et al. Letter to Chief Justice Frank F. Drowota III. August 12, 2005. http://lib.law.washington.edu/tennesseejudges.pdf (accessed September 24, 2005).

Cartoof, Virginia G., and Lorraine V. Klerman. "Parental Consent for Abortion: Impact of the Massachusetts Law." *American Journal of Public Health* 76 (1986).

Centers for Disease Control and Prevention. "Abortion Surveillance—United States, 1993 and 1994." *Morbidity and Mortality Weekly Report* 46(SS-4) (1997).

———. "Pregnancy-Related Mortality Surveillance—United States, 1987–1990." *Morbidity and Mortality Weekly Report* 46(SS-4) (1997).

Child Custody Protection Act: Hearings on H.R. 1218 before the Subcomm. on the Constitution of the House Comm. on the Judiciary, 106th Cong. May 27, 1999 (statement of Billie Lominick). http://commdocs.house.gov/committees/judiciary/hju62490.000/hju62490_0.HTM (accessed September 29, 2006).

Collett, Teresa Stanton. "Seeking Solomon's Wisdom: Judicial Bypass of Parental Involvement in a Minor's Abortion Decision." *Baylor Law Review* 52 (2000).

Craig, Barbara Hinkson, and David O'Brien. *Abortion and American Politics.* Chatham, N.J.: Chatham House, 1993.

"Court Rejects Appeal in Precedent-Setting Abortion Case." Associated Press State and Local Wire, July 22, 1998.

Curry, Matt. "Perry Mobilizes Evangelicals as Governor's Race Heats Up." Associated Press, June 11, 2005.

Davey, Monica. "South Dakota Bans Abortion, Setting up a Battle." *New York Times*, March 7, 2006.

Dolbeare, Kenneth M., and Phillip E. Hammond. *The School Prayer Decisions: From Court Policy to Local Practice.* Chicago: University of Chicago Press, 1971.

Donovan, Patricia. "Judging Teenagers: How Minors Fare When They Seek Court-Authorized Abortions." *Family Planning Perspectives* 15 (1983).

———. *Our Daughters' Decisions: The Conflict in State Law on Abortion and Other Issues.* New York: Alan Guttmacher Institute, 1992.

Drucker, Margo R. "*Bowen v. Kendrick*: Establishing Chastity at the Expense of Constitutional Prophylactics." *New York University Law Review* 64 (1989).

Edelman, Murray. *Politics as Symbolic Action: Mass Arousal and Quiescence.* Chicago: Markham, 1971.

Franz, Wanda, and David Reardon. "Differential Impact of Abortion on Adolescents and Adults." *Adolescence* 27 (1992).

Geertz, Clifford. "Ideology as a Cultural System." In David E. Apter, ed., *Ideology and Discontent*. New York: Free Press, 1964.

"Girls under 18 Must Get Consent for Abortion." Associated Press State and Local Wire, February 28, 2000.

"Granholm Signs Abortion Ultrasound Law." Associated Press State and Local Wire, March 24, 2006.

Griffin-Carlson, Mary S., and K. J. Mackin. "Parental Consent: Factors Influencing Adolescent Disclosure Regarding Abortion." *Adolescence* 28 (1993).

Griffin-Carlson, Mary S., and Paula J. Schwanenflugel. "Adolescent Abortion and Parental Notification: Evidence for the Importance of Family Functioning on the Perceived Quality of Parental Involvement in Families." *Journal of Child Psychology and Psychiatry* 39 (1998).

Gross, Doug. "Senate Approves Slate of Abortion-Related Bills." Associated Press State and Local Wire, March 2, 2006.

Hallifax, Jackie. "High Court Knocks back Appeal over Abortion Measure." Associated Press State and Local Wire, January 13, 2005.

Hammack, Laurence. "Notification Law: No Takers, Some Qualms 3 Days

Later, No One in the Region Has Sought Judicial Permission for an Abortion." *Roanoke Times,* July 4, 1997.

Henshaw, Stanley K. "The Impact of Requirements for Parental Consent on Minors' Abortions in Mississippi." *Family Planning Perspectives* 27 (1995).

Henshaw, Stanley K., and Lawrence B. Finer. "The Accessibility of Abortion Services in the United States, 2001." *Perspectives on Sexual and Reproductive Health* 35 (2003).

Henshaw, Stanley K., and Kathryn Kost. "Parental Involvement in Minors' Abortion Decisions." *Family Planning Perspectives* 24 (1992).

Hulse, Carl. "Bipartisan Group in Senate Averts Judge Showdown." *New York Times,* May 24, 2005.

"Huntsman Signs Parental Consent Bill into Law." Associated Press State and Local Wire, March 17, 2006.

Jacobs, Melissa. "Are Courts Prepared to Handle Judicial Bypass Proceedings?" *Human Rights* 32 (Winter 2005).

Jane's Due Process. "Tales from the Front," distributed with Diana Philip, *First Annual Report, Jane's Due Process,* January 22, 2001, to January 21, 2002.

———. "Tales from the Front 2," distributed with Diana Philip, *Annual Report, Jane's Due Process,* January 22, 2002, to January 21, 2003.

Johnson, Bob. "Alabama Judge Wears Ten Commandments on Robe." Associated Press State and Local Wire, December 15, 2004.

———. "Quiet Judge Finds Controversy When He Dons Ten Commandments Robe." Associated Press State and Local Wire, January 9, 2005.

Johnson, Dirk. "Illinois, Citing Faulty Verdicts, Bars Executions." *New York Times,* sec. A, February 1, 2000.

Johnson, Harry M. "Ideology and the Social System." In *International Encyclopedia of Social Sciences* 7 (1968).

"Judge's Robe Draws Big Attention." United Press International, December 16, 2004.

Katz, Katherine D. "The Pregnant Child's Right to Self-Determination." *Albany Law Review* 62 (1999).

Kirkpatrick, David D. "For New Judge, Self-Reliance in Life and Law." *New York Times,* May 26, 2005.

"Laurel Judge Gives Church Attendance Option to Some Offenders." Associated Press State and Local Wire, May 31, 2005.

Leff, Lisa. "California Defeats Abortion Notification Proposition." Associated Press State and Local Wire, November 9, 2005.

Lewin, Tamar. "The Anguish of Asking a Court for an Abortion." *New York Times,* May 28, 1992.

———. "Parental Consent to Abortion: How Enforcement Can Vary." *New York Times,* May 28, 1992.

Lewis, Neil A. "Bypassing Senate for Second Time, Bush Seats Judge." *New York Times,* February 21, 2004.

Liberto, Jennifer. "Abortion Bill for Minors Goes to Voters." *St. Petersburg Times,* sec. A, May 1, 2004.

Library of Congress. *Thomas Legislative Information on the Internet.* http://thomas.loc.gov/cgi-bin/query/z?c109:S.403: (accessed September 30, 2006).

Lindsey, Gene. "The Viability of Parental Abortion Notification and Consent Statutes: Assessing Fact and Fiction." *American University Law Review* 38 (1989).

McCullough, Marie. "A 15-Year-Old Anguishes over Abortion Decision." *Philadelphia Inquirer,* May, 29, 2001.

Milne, John. "Souter Note Helped Sink '81 N.H. Bill on Abortion." *Boston Globe,* July 26, 1990.

Milner, Neal A. *The Court and Local Law Enforcement: The Impact of Miranda.* Beverly Hills, Calif.: Sage, 1971.

Mlyniec, Wallace J. "A Judge's Ethical Dilemma: Assessing a Child's Capacity to Choose." *Fordham Law Review* 64 (1996).

Murphy, Walter F. "Lower Court Checks on Supreme Court Power." *American Political Science Review* 53 (1959).

Nguyen, Daniel. "Few Bypass Abortion Rule." *Denver Post,* August 15, 2004.

O'Shaughnessy, Maggie. "The Worst of Both Worlds? Parental Involvement Requirements and the Privacy Rights of Mature Minors." *Ohio State Law Journal* 57 (1996).

"Panel V of the Hearing of the Senate Judiciary Committee." *Federal News Service,* September 15, 2005.

Parental Notification Act: Hearings on Tex. S.B. 30 before the House State Affairs Comm., 76th Leg., Reg. Sess. 23, April 19, 1999.

Philip, Diana. *First Annual Report, Jane's Due Process,* January 22, 2001, to January 21, 2002.

Pliner, Anita J., and Suzanne Yates. "Psychological and Legal Issues in Minors' Rights to Abortion." *Journal of Social Issues* 48 (1992).

Poovey, Bill. "Divided Court Upholds Denial of Abortion for Unemotional Teen." Associated Press State and Local Wire, August 17, 2001.

———. "State Appeals Court Approves Teen-ager's Appeal of Abortion Denial." Associated Press State and Local Wire, May 30, 2000.

Raskin, Jamin B. "The Paradox of Judicial Bypass Proceedings." *American University Journal of Gender, Social Policy and the Law* 10 (2002).

Real Life Crisis Pregnancy Center. *Real Life Mission.* http://www.reallifecpc.org/mission.html (accessed October 3, 2005).

Reeves, Jay. "Bill Would Involve State Attorneys in Juvenile Abortion Cases." Associated Press State and Local Wire, February 23, 1999.

Riendeau, Herryn. "Kentucky Judge Offers Worship Services as an Alternative to Jail." June 2, 2005. http://www.WBIR.com (accessed August 3, 2005).

Rogers, James L., Robert Boruch, George B. Stoms, and Dorothy DeMoya. "Impact of the Minnesota Parental Notification Law on Abortion and Birth." *American Journal of Public Health* 81 (1991).

Rosenberg, Gerald N. *The Hollow Hope: Can the Courts Bring about Social Change?* Chicago: University of Chicago Press, 1991.

Rosenfeld, Jo Ann. "Emotional Responses to Therapeutic Abortion." *American Family Physician* 45 (1992).

"Ruling Restricts Teen Abortions." *Montgomery Advertiser,* May 25, 2001.

Sacred Heart University. *Mission Statement.* http://www.sacredheart.edu/about/mission/index.html (accessed August 30, 2004).

Saunders, Debra J. "Parents Should Be Notified." *San Francisco Chronicle,* November 3, 2005.

Savage, David G. "Roberts Sees Role as Judicial 'Umpire.'" *Los Angeles Times,* September 13, 2005.

Sav-A-Life East, Inc. *About Us.* http://www.savalifeeast.org/about.htm (accessed January 18, 2005).

Sav-A-Life Outreach Centers. *Crisis Pregnancy Centers Near You.* http://www.savalife.org/Default.aspx?tabid=44 (accessed October 1, 2005).

———. *Our Guiding Principles.* http://www.savalife.org/Default.aspx?tabid=48 (accessed October 1, 2005).

———. *Our History.* http://www.savalife.org/Default.aspx?tabid=46 (accessed October 1, 2005).

———. *Our Mission.* http://www.savalife.org/Default.aspx?tabid=45 (accessed October 1, 2005).

———. *Our Statement of Faith.* http://www.savalife.org/Default.aspx?tabid=47 (accessed October 1, 2005).

———. *Sav-A-Life Affiliates.* http://www.savalife.org/Default.aspx?tabid=42 (accessed October 1, 2005).

Scarnecchia, Suellyn, and Julie Kunce Field. "Judging Girls: Decision Making in Parental Consent to Abortion Cases." *Michigan Journal of Gender and Law* 3 (1995).

Scheingold, Stuart A. *The Politics of Rights: Lawyers, Public Policy, and Political Change.* New Haven, Conn.: Yale University Press, 1974.

Shklar, Judith N. *Legalism: An Essay on Law, Morals, and Politics.* Cambridge: Harvard University Press, 1964.

Short, Carroll Dale. *The People's Lawyer: The Colorful Life and Times of Julian L. McPhillips, Jr.* Montgomery, Ala.: NewSouth Books, 2000.

Silverstein, Helena. "Road Closed Ahead: Abortion Providers, Pro-choice Advocates, and the Longevity of Pennsylvania's Parental Consent Requirement."

Unpublished paper presented at the annual meeting of the Western Political Science Association, San Jose, California, March 2000.

Silverstein, Helena, and Kathryn Lundwall Alessi. "Religious Establishment in Hearings to Waive Parental Consent for Abortion." *University of Pennsylvania Journal of Constitutional Law* 7 (2004).

Stengle, Jamie. "Governor Signs Abortion Bill at Church School." Associated Press, June 5, 2005.

Stone, R. *Adolescents and Abortion: Choice in Crisis.* Washington, D.C.: Center for Population Options, 1990.

Texas Department of Health. *Booklet on Induced Abortions.* http://www.tdh.state.tx.us/bvs/abortion/nowhat.htm#4 (accessed September 2004).

"Texas Judge Could Face Sanctions for Allowing Photo to Run in Newspaper Ad for Seminary." *BP News,* September 30, 2003. http://www.sbcbaptistpress.org/bpnews.asp?ID=16772 (accessed August 5, 2005).

Torres, Aida, Jacqueline Darroch Forrest, and Susan Eisman. "Telling Parents: Clinic Policies and Adolescents' Use of Family Planning and Abortion Services." *Family Planning Perspectives* 12 (1980).

Trexler, Phil. "Abortion Fiery Issue for Judges." *Akron Beacon Journal,* November 9, 2003.

Veith, Satsie. "The Judicial Bypass Procedure and Adolescents' Abortion Rights: The Fallacy of the 'Maturity' Standard." *Hofstra Law Review* 23 (1994).

Wallerstein, J. S., P. Kurtz, and M. Bar-Din. "Psychosocial Sequelae of Therapeutic Abortion in Young Unmarried Women." *Archives of General Psychiatry* 27 (1972).

Wasby, Stephen L. *The Impact of the United States Supreme Court.* Homewood, Ill.: Dorsey Press, 1970.

———. *Small Town Police and the Supreme Court: Hearing the Word.* Lexington, Mass.: Lexington Books, 1976.

Weaver, Kendal. "Court Rejects Appeal by Attorney for Fetus of Pregnant Teen." Associated Press State and Local Wire, August 5, 1998.

Westside Pregnancy Resource Center. *Mental Health Risks of Abortion: Scientific Studies Reveal Significant Risk, Major Psychological Sequelae of Abortion.* http://www.wprc.org/abortion/emotion.html (accessed October 1, 2005).

Wildermuth, John. "Campaign 2006: November Initiatives; Abortion Notice Returns to Voters." *San Francisco Chronicle,* June 21, 2006.

Yates, Suzanne, and Anita J. Pliner. "Judging Maturity in the Courts: The Massachusetts Consent Statute." *American Journal of Public Health* 78 (1988).

Yen, Hope. "Appeals on Commandments Displays Rejected." Associated Press, June 28, 2005.

Zielinski, Lynda. "Jane Doe's Choice." *Ms.* (Winter 2006).

CASES

Akron v. Akron Ctr. for Reprod. Health, Inc. (Akron I), 462 U.S. 416 (1983).
American Civil Liberties Union of Ohio Foundation v. Ashbrook, 375 F.3d 484 (2004).
Ayotte v. Planned Parenthood of Northern New England, 126 S. Ct. 961 (2006).
Ayotte v. Planned Parenthood of Northern New England, Oral Arguments Transcript, http://www.supremecourtus.gov/oral_arguments/argument_transcripts/04-1144.pdf.
Bellotti v. Baird (Bellotti I), 428 U.S. 132 (1976).
Bellotti v. Baird (Bellotti II), 443 U.S. 622 (1979).
Bowen v. Kendrick, 487 U.S. 589 (1988).
Brown v. Board of Education, 347 U.S 483 (1954).
Edwards v. Aguillard, 482 U.S. 578 (1987).
Ex parte Anonymous, 531 So. 2d 901 (Ala. 1988).
Ex parte Anonymous, 720 So. 2d 497 (Ala. 1998).
Ex parte Anonymous, 803 So. 2d 542 (Ala. 2001).
Ex parte Anonymous, 810 So. 2d 786 (Ala. 2001).
Ex parte Anonymous, 889 So. 2d 518 (Ala. 2003).
Ex parte Anonymous, 889 So. 2d 525 (Ala. 2003).
Ex parte Anonymous, 888 So. 2d 1275 (Ala. 2004).
Ex parte Martin, 565 So. 2d 1 (Ala. 1989).
Glassroth v. Moore, 242 F. Supp. 2d 1067 (M.D. Ala. 2002).
Glassroth v. Moore, 335 F.3d 1282 (2003).
Grand Rapids Sch. Dist. v. Ball, 473 U.S. 373 (1985).
Griffin v. Coughlin, 673 N.E.2d 98 (N.Y. 1996).
H. L. v. Matheson, 450 U.S. 398 (1981).
Hodgson v. Minnesota, 648 F. Supp. 756 (1986).
Hodgson v. Minnesota, Nos. 88-1125 and 88-1309, 1988 U.S. Briefs 1125 (September 1, 1989), Joint Appendix.
Hodgson v. Minnesota, 497 U.S. 417 (1990).
Hunt v. McNair, 413 U.S. 734 (1973).
Ind. Planned Parenthood Affiliates Ass'n v. Pearson, 716 F.2d 1127 (7th Cir. 1983).
In re Anonymous, 720 So. 2d 497 (Ala. Civ. App. 1998).
In re Anonymous, 733 So. 2d 429 (Ala. Civ. App. 1999).
In re Anonymous, 810 So. 2d 784 (Ala. Civ. App. 2001).
In re Anonymous, 888 So. 2d 1265 (Ala. Civ. App. 2004).
In re Anonymous, 905 So. 2d 845 (Ala. Civ. App. 2005).
In re: Application of Jane Doe A Minor, 591 So. 2d 698 (La. 1991).
In re Jane Doe, 19 S.W.3d 249 (Tex. 2005).
In re T. W., 551 So. 2d 1186 (Fla. 1989).

Kendrick v. Bowen, 657 F. Supp. 1547 (D.C. Cir. 1987).

Lambert v. Wicklund, 520 U.S. 292 (1997).

Lee v. Weisman, 505 U.S. 577 (1992).

Lemon v. Kurtzman, 403 U.S. 602 (1971).

Lynch v. Donnelly, 465 U.S. 668 (1984).

Maher v. Roe, 432 U.S. 464 (1977).

McCreary County, Kentucky v. American Civil Liberties Union of Kentucky, 125 S. Ct. 2722 (2005).

Memphis Planned Parenthood v. Sundquist, 2 F. Supp. 2d 997 (1997).

Memphis Planned Parenthood v. Sundquist, 175 F.3d 456 (1999).

Moore v. Judicial Inquiry Commission of the State of Alabama, 891 So. 2d 848 (2004).

North Florida Women's Health and Counseling Services v. Florida, 866 So. 2d 612 (Fla. 2003).

Ohio v. Akron Center for Reproductive Health, No. 88-805, 1989 U.S. S. Ct. Briefs LEXIS 946 (1989).

Ohio v. Akron Center for Reproductive Health (Akron II), 497 U.S. 502 (1990).

Parham v. J. R., 442 U.S. 584 (1979).

Planned Parenthood Ass'n v. Ashcroft, 462 U.S. 476 (1983).

Planned Parenthood of Central Missouri v. Danforth, 428 U.S. 52 (1976).

Planned Parenthood of Central New Jersey v. Farmer, 762 A.2d 620 (N.J. 2000).

Planned Parenthood of Southeastern Pennsylvania v. Casey, 505 U.S. 833 (1992).

Planned Parenthood v. Miller, 63 F.3d 1452 (1995).

Roe v. Wade, 410 U.S. 113 (1973).

Roemer v. Bd. of Pub. Works of Md., 426 U.S. 736 (1976).

Santa Fe Indep. Sch. Dist. v. Doe, 530 U.S. 290 (2000).

Tilton v. Richardson, 403 U.S. 672 (1971).

United States v. Seeger, 380 U.S. 163 (1965).

Van Orden v. Perry, 125 S. Ct. 2854 (2005).

Wallace v. Jaffree, 472 U.S. 38 (1985).

Webster v. Reproductive Health Services, 492 U.S. 490 (1989).

Wicklund v. Montana, 1998 Mont. Dist. LEXIS 227 (1998).

Wise v. Watson, 236 So. 2d 681 (Ala. 1970).

STATUTES AND BILLS

24 *Del. C.* §§ 1782 and 1788 (2004).

A.C.A. § 20-16-801 (2005).

A.R.S. § 36-2152 (2004).

Alabama Parental Consent Act, Act No. 87-286, Acts of Alabama 1987.

Alabama Parental Consent Statute, *Ala. Code* § 26-21 (2004).

Colorado Parental Notification Act, C.R.S. § 12-37.5 (2005).

Florida Parental Notice of Abortion Act, 1999, ch. 99-322.

KRS § 311.732 (2004).

La. R.S. 40:12999.35 (2004).

Massachusetts ALM Super. Ct. S.O. 5-81 (2002).

Md. Code Ann., Health-Gen. I § 20-103 (2006).

Me. Rev. Stat. Ann. tit. 22, § 1597 (2004).

Minn. Stat. § 144.343 (2000).

Miss. Code Ann. § 41-41 (2006).

Mont. Code Ann. § 50-20-212 (1995).

N.D. Cent. Code §§ 14-02.1–03.1 (2003).

Ohio Rev. Code Ann. § 2151.85 (2006).

Pennsylvania Abortion Control Act, 18 *Pa.C.S.* § 3206 (2005).

R.R.S. Nebraska § 71-6909 (2002).

Rule 17(c) of the Alabama Rules of Civil Procedure.

S.B. 389, 1999 Ala. Reg. Sess. (1999).

S.C. Code Ann. § 44-41 (2004).

S.D. Codified Laws § 34-23A-7 (2004).

Tennessee Parental Consent for Abortion by Minors Act, *Tenn. Code Ann.* § 37-10 (2001).

Utah H.B. 85 (2006).

W. Va. Code § 16-2F-3 (2004).

Wis. Stat. § 48.375 (2000).

Index

About the Author

Helena Silverstein is Professor of Government and Law at Lafayette College. She is author of *Unleashing Rights: Law, Meaning, and the Animal Rights Movement.*

Printed in the United States
146029LV00001B/4/P